LOOM OF MANY THREADS

"In Him the whole fabric is bound together, as it grows into a temple, dedicated to the Lord. . . ."

(Ephesians 2:21)

By
Sister Rose Maria Laverty, S.C.

Mount Saint Vincent-on-Hudson
New York

Maria Laverty

Sister Rose

SISTERS OF CHARITY
New York

Contents

Introduction

THE LIFE STORY OF MOTHER ELIZABETH SETON, Foundress of the American Sisters of Charity, seems well known, and perhaps in a general way, we are justified in thinking it so. But the textural design of her life was not a simple one, nor were all the threads from a single strand. If we look closely at the pattern, we shall observe two strong tones dominating the whole and intricately interwoven into a background motif of the English rose and the French lily. To disregard these underlying traceries is to rob the tapestry of much of its meaning and much of its wealth. It is to ignore in Elizabeth Seton the very things that made her what she was.

Elizabeth will be known to posterity by her marriage name, but the qualities for which she will be remembered did not derive from the Setons. Rather it was the Le Contes and the Bayleys—names that bow to none in their proud tradition—that gave her their family traits and lent her their distinguishing features for the molding of her beautiful personality. It was the Le Contes and the Bayleys who produced Elizabeth Bayley Seton.

Though we have learned to think of this intrepid woman as a New Yorker, there were other atmospheres no less familiar to her which affected her history strikingly. One such locality was New Rochelle in Westchester County, New York, whose air was indigenous to her. Here the achievements of her family had woven a richly historical fabric. It would seem that some attention might well be paid to the ancestral influences of these New Rochelle forebears on the development of Elizabeth's character. Whence her temperament, her idealism, her training? Even her physical appearance?

Really to understand Elizabeth Seton, therefore, one must study her in her natural setting; see her among her relatives whose names have become a vital part of the New Rochelle town records; watch develop within her as she grows, the fiery independence of a great-great-grandfather who preferred rather to flee his native land than submit to Papal authority; absorb with her the sturdiness of her English forefathers, their staunch adherence to the Church of England, their British tenacity to national traditions. All these we must try to understand before we can grasp with proper appreciation the horrifying shock to her relatives upon her "desertion" to the Church of Rome. It will help to explain her sister Mary's lamentation: "She has gone over to the Church that persecuted her ancestors!" It is only by a study of these backgrounds that we can fully realize what a heart-breaking struggle Elizabeth endured in her decision to cut herself off from all that she must have loved with every fibre of her being.

It was one thing to be deserted by the Setons; they were merely her husband's people. It was quite something else to be disowned by the Le Contes and the Bayleys. They were her own people!

Foreword

INSPIRED BY THE CORRESPONDENCE between Mother Seton and Archbishop Carroll, His Eminence James Cardinal Gibbons, Archbishop of Baltimore, espoused the Cause of Elizabeth Seton's holiness and possible canonization as early as 1880, barely sixty years after her death. But the Cause was not formally introduced at Rome until the pronouncement of the Sacred Congregation of Rites on February 28, 1940. In this first decree we read how "God Himself prepared her for a life of grace and she, on her part, doing what in her lay, and simply yielding her whole heart to divine grace ... recognized the Faith, embraced it with a generous mind, set forth courageously on the road of perfection and in a wondrous way became the mother of many daughters."

On October 11, 1958, his Holiness Pope John XXIII, in a beautiful tribute delivered at a plenary session of the Sacred College of Cardinals, spoke of Mother Seton as the "flower of American piety" and proclaimed his enthusiasm for, and interest in, her Cause. It was not too surprising, therefore, that on December 18, 1958, he declared her virtues to be "heroic" and added the title Venerable to her name, the second official step in the process of canonization. This second decree emphasizes her three-fold vocation as wife, mother, and foundress: "Just as she had shown herself to be an admirable daughter, wife, and mother, so she likewise showed herself a distinguished administrator.... The seed which the servant of God sowed increased to such a size that this Family of God now number almost nine thousand, in seven Congregations and seven hundred houses."

Catholic America's longed-for day arrived on February 19, 1963, when Pope John XXIII made solemn proclamation of the beatification of Venerable Elizabeth Ann, to take place

in St. Peter's in Rome, on March 17, the patronal feast of
the Archdiocese of New York. This was a dual honor for the
City. It gave priority to Manhattan as the birthplace of the
"beata"; it gave to the Archdiocese of New York, principally
in the person of His Eminence Francis Cardinal Spellman,
a zealous promoter of Mother Seton's Cause, and to the Sisters of Charity of New York, the unspeakable joy and distinction of being the first to publicly honor this great citizen
of the United States, the first of our country to be raised to
the ranks of the "Blessed."

We may well be proud of the pioneering spirit of this
courageous woman! Mother Seton is considered the foundress of Catholic elementary education in the United States.
The parochial school system may justly be said to have been
organized by her, since she established the first free school
on American soil. Her foundation of the first native sisterhood was typically American: outgoing, active, democratic
in its social aspects. Her welfare work needs no apology
today—the era of welfare achievements. Through the seven
branches of her religious family—spread across the length
and breadth of this land—the orphan, the sick, the young,
and the old are cared for.

In all these undertakings Elizabeth Ann Seton was a
pioneer, a breaker of ground in the virgin fields of Catholic
education and Catholic Charities. She has been assigned a
unique place in the history of the Catholic Church in America as the "sole prop of Archbishop Carroll in the work of
education." No account of the struggles of the Catholic
Church in our country will ever be complete without a more
than cursory mention of this little woman of dauntless courage who dared to chart the unknown. By the prudent and
practical management of her affairs, the charm of her personality, her loyal devotion to her friends, her contacts with
almost all great Churchmen of her day, her letters to and
relationships with so many of the famous families of her
times—by all these human assets her life holds an attraction
all its own.

But that is not all. Mother Seton was but forty-seven years old when she died. She was thirty-one at the time of her conversion. Into those sixteen intervening years she compressed the sanctity and heroism, the suffering and accomplishments which brought about her beatification. She can, like St. Paul, be said to be many things to many souls: a loving mother, a courageous and resourceful widow, a true religious. She was a natural teacher whose pedagogical methods are sound practice today. She might be the patron of American converts, or of the dying—having assisted at so many deathbeds with utmost tenderness and prayerful encouragement. Bishops, former students, distant friends sought a written word from her and treasured as relics her letters, so filled with the unction of Christian love.

It is the purpose of this book to make Mother Seton better known and loved that, in the fullness of time, Holy Mother Church may add the final jewel to her crown of sanctity by proclaiming Blessed Elizabeth Ann the first American Saint.

Acknowledgements

There are many to whom I am deeply indebted for their assistance in the preparation of this book.

First and foremost, Reverend Mother Mary without whose interest and encouragement there would have been no book.

I am grateful to the several members of my Community who gave so generously of their time and skill to the work of editing and reviewing the manuscript.

Sincere appreciation for assistance in various ways must be made to:

Mr. Edward Stitt, Westchester County Historian, for his invaluable service in tracing the history of the property at No. 41 Washington Avenue, New Rochelle.

Mr. Frank Madden, Assistant Title Officer, Title Guarantee and Trust Company, White Plains, New York, for procuring the deeds to, and drawing maps of Richard Bayley's property in New Rochelle.

Mr. Richard Kemble, for his gracious courtesy in permitting me to examine the Bayley house, and to photograph it.

Mrs. Belle Egan, Parish Clerk, Trinity Episcopal Church, New Rochelle, for her research in the Church records and obtaining for me a copy of William Bayley's baptismal record.

Mrs. Jean Ross, Mrs. Ann Clark, Mr. George Krzyzac, reference librarians of the New Rochelle Public Library, for their enthusiastic and intelligent assistance in my many problems.

To the Sister typists, and to those who helped in any way to bring this work to completion.

I

First Threads on the Loom
1685-1710

I

The Romance
of a Road

1

A NARROW RIBBON OF ROAD ran in a northeasterly direction along the gray-blue waters of Long Island Sound and
stretched its dusty length into the towns of Pelham and New
Rochelle. Dark acres of virgin forests drew back from the
water line, opening now and again to disclose the traditional
red farmhouse or rolling pasture land watered by upland
creeks. Salt meadows bordered the shore's edge where a view
across the Sound showed the low-flung outline of Long Island
seven miles away. Merchant packets and pleasure boats gave
life and sound to the peaceful scene.

The history of the Shore Road, as it has been known
for these three hundred years, was not always peaceful, but
it was always interesting. Originally not much more than a
cow path or wagon rut winding from one farm to the next,
it absorbed into its tenuous substance the smiles and tears,
the fears and hopes of all those who had chosen to dwell
beside it, and seemed in its wandering way to offer them
safety and a future remote from the sorrows they had left
behind them over the seas.

As the settlements grew, the route was broadened and
extended until at the time of our story, in 1774, one could
travel on it from Davenport Neck in New Rochelle west into
Pelham and south to the Bronx in New York City. Leisurely
riders, wishing to avoid the cumbersome Conestoga wagons

or the bustle of stage coaches hurtling along the Post Road, chose the Shore Road where, in their stately gilded carriages or in light sulkies, they might enjoy equally the beauties of the countryside and the refreshing breezes blowing in from the water. Others came up the Sound in sailboats and anchored at privately owned wharves. Most of these gentleman farmers could point out to visitors their own sloops in the inlet off Pelham. Rum runners, sugar-cane boats, timber rafts, pleasure craft jostled one another in these busy tidewaters, while up in the sturdy houses overlooking the Sound, their owners discussed the latest news from the Mother Country or laid plans for a village get-together.

The settlement at New Rochelle and Pelham (originally there was no boundary line between the towns which functioned as a unit) was predominantly French with a scattering of English and Dutch families. In 1710, New Rochelle records listed 49 families, all French except seven. In 1771, there were 67 families, all French except half, 27 of these being British. The other six were presumably Dutch. By far the greater number, as indicated by their names, were aristocrats who struggled to maintain in their primitive surroundings some scant reflection of their former social manners and elegance. Before the outbreak of the War in 1775, the settlers in these towns had built up a landed gentry who engaged in mercantile activities in New York City while continuing to farm vast estates in Westchester. Such were the Philipses, the Van Cortlandts, the Pells, the Harrisons, and others after whom whole areas have been named. Such, in a lesser degree, were the Le Contes and the Bayleys.

*   *   *

We have mentioned the date 1774 because on August 28 of that year was born a child to whom the Shore Road would be very dear; its environs would be cherished among her fondest memories; its lands and history would be her birthright. Very early in her life, Elizabeth Ann Bayley must have been taken by her father, Dr. Richard Bayley, to visit his relatives in New Rochelle. This would have been a most likely trip particularly after the death of his first wife when Elizabeth was not quite three years of age. Although by that time the Doctor's mother had moved to Yonkers, and it appears probable that his brother William still lived in New York City near his several stores, there were yet other relatives—numerous Le Contes, Merciers, Coutants, and Pells—to all of whom Richard Bayley would feel sufficiently close to warrant at least an occasional visit. As a destination for a weekend trip, New Rochelle was ideal, situated within a few hours' ride from the city and offering in its natural resources the pleasures of seaside and rural relaxation. The first stage coach between New York and Boston had been started on June 24, 1772. Its fortnightly trips followed the Boston Post Road through the Westchester towns into Connecticut by way of Hartford. Under these circumstances, occasional visits at least may have been made by the Bayleys while Elizabeth was still a very small child. Later, she herself was to spend intervals in New Rochelle, in a house on the Shore Road whence, she tells us, she loved to look out at the Sound. But however and whenever Elizabeth made her first trip along this historic highway, it was to be a familiar route to her for more than twenty years.

In this regard she would be but carrying out a long tradition on both sides of her family. Her Huguenot great-great-great-grandfather Jacques Lasty (also spelled Laty) had come from the West Indies in the middle of the seventeenth century and had settled in New Rochelle. Having purchased a large tract of land and an off-shore island, he became a pioneer settler and one of the earliest landowners of the town. He left this property as a legacy to his eldest daughter who had married another Huguenot refugee, Guillaume Le Conte. The latter, in partnership with Jacob Leisler, friend of the Huguenot settlers and representative for them with the Dutch government, owned all of what is now Davenport Neck and Fort Slocum Island, besides several parcels of land in nearby areas. Thus for two generations Elizabeth's French ancestors were to command the lion's share of the original 6,000 acres now known as New Rochelle. A monument erected there in Hudson Park to the memory of the Huguenot Founding Fathers, bears upon its bronze plaque the names of two very distinguished pioneers,—Jacques Lasty and Guillaume Le Conte. Of the one hundred and fifty others so mentioned, eleven had varying degrees of relationship to Elizabeth's ancestors.

By such sturdy threads was the first tracing of the French pattern made upon the loom.

2

Elizabeth, daughter of revolutions that she was, had had her baby ears attuned to the tread of marching feet. Three days before her second birthday, the Americans had evacuated New York City. From then until her ninth year she lived under the surveillance of the British. Their drums beat for muster on the Commons; their cannon boomed from warships in the harbor; their red coats were the only military garb she remembered. Her own father, a British sympathizer, held a medical appointment on Lord Howe's staff. There was certainly no lack of Tory influence in those first days of Elizabeth's childhood. Traditionally, her kin were royalists, as most of the upper class were. Their scorn for the "Yankee ragamuffins" who had had the temerity to withstand the power of the Mother Country was evident in well-seasoned jibes at the rebel army, and in heated discussions on the progress of the War. It may well be that these remarks had the ironic effect of arousing the little girl's sympathy for the unfortunate patriots. She who later would espouse the cause of the poor, and who could not bear to see even a little bird suffer, may have felt her child's heart moved in defense of the ragged, starving handful of men who formed the Continental Army. Was she not a child of the times? The spirit of those days was in her blood, as it was in the very air she breathed and in all she saw during her formative years. Her subsequent rebellion against the coldness and inadequacy of her Protestant upbringing would not seem so strange when she recalled the price her fellowmen had been willing to pay for political peace and personal freedom. When, therefore, in 1783, the British left the city to the rebels, it is not hard to imagine this ardent little American among the enthusiastic New Yorkers who gathered on the green to jeer at the retreating British and wildly welcome their conquering countrymen.

Cornwallis had surrendered to Washington two years before, in 1781. And two years prior to that, the British had burned Fairfield, Connecticut, where her father had been born. This town, a few hours' sail up the Sound from New Rochelle, had strong sentimental memories for the British Pelhamites, for it was a sort of liaison town between the Old World and the New. Many of the English in Westchester, including the Bayleys, had made their first homes in this country at Fairfield. Excitement and resentment, therefore, ran high and served to drive all wavering residents to the rebel cause. White Plains, Eastchester, Throgg's Neck, Pell's Point—all these and many other places in Westchester, had been scenes of skirmishes between English and English: between those who had come from England long before to seek their personal liberties, and those who came now with bared bayonets to snatch those liberties away from them, if they could.

Elizabeth, who passed her entire eighth year in New Rochelle, was in a veritable hot-bed of Yankee support. Pelham men bound for frontline duty swung along the Shore Road whistling "Yankee Doodle" and waving deceptively cheerful farewells to relatives and friends. Often during that year Elizabeth, her sister Mary, and their cousins would hear discussed the advances or setbacks of General Washington's forces. Over and over again the children would beg to be told the story of the Battle of Pelham lasting for seven days in October 1776, during which skirmish the British had captured a "churchful of salt." "Yes," Uncle William would answer to their amazed gasps, "all the salt for the rebel troops had been stored in the old French church as the safest place. Later, the Redcoats used the church as a jail for their prisoners of war." Just a few yards beyond his property, to the west, he would show them Old Split Rock Road along which the Continental Army had retreated to City Island.

Another tale that the children never tired of hearing was that of Israel Bissel. One Sunday in April 1775, just as the people of Westchester were preparing to go to church, hard down the Post Road galloped Bissell, startling good squires and their wives by his reckless speed, but more by his news, "War! War has begun! Battle near Boston; Liberty Boys licked the Redcoats!" On and on he sped, into Haarlem, and down the Bouwerie Road to the Commons. There, sliding from his sweating horse, he gave the details of his message to those hastily gathered at the Liberty Pole. He bore two dispatches. One, telling of the clash at Lexington, announced that the "bearer, Israel Bissel, is charged to alarm the country, and all Persons are desired to furnish him with fresh horses as they may be needed...." The other was a similar dispatch from Concord.

The shot that was to be heard round the world had been fired.

*   *   *

During one of Elizabeth's visits to New Rochelle, Uncle William had taken her and her sister Mary out to Bonnefoy

Point, now Davenport Neck. "I want you to see the cradle
of the Huguenot settlement here in New Rochelle," he had
said, as he pointed out to them a historic cave still revered
as the lowly shelter of the first refugees to come to Westchester from New York City. "Right over there," he continued, "our ancestor Guillaume Le Conte built his house.
My grandfather, your great-grandfather, was born on this
neck of land."

Bonnefoy Point saw a more imposing but less friendly
landing than that of the Huguenots not quite a hundred
years later when, on October 19, 1776, the seventy-two
vessels carrying German mercenaries had anchored here.
These hated Hessians, after encamping in New Rochelle
and plundering the property of its citizens, marched up the
Post Road to Larchmont Manor and joined the forces of
Lord Howe in the Battle of White Plains on October 28.

The Bayleys and the Le Contes had a personal memento
of this landing. Katherine Coutant, maternal great-grandaunt to Uncle William and his brother Richard, Elizabeth's
father, died at the advanced age of eighty-eight, on October
18, 1776, the very day that the British forces under Lord
Howe disembarked on Pell's Point and set up camp on the
heights around Pelham. Owing to military regulations pro-
scribing public funerals, Katherine's son, Isaac Coutant, Jr.,
buried his mother in a secluded part of his farm where he
had the added sorrow of laying his daughter two years later.
These two burials were the beginning of a family burying
plot known as the Coutant Cemetery. It is now in the
very heart of New Rochelle at the intersection of Webster
Avenue and Eastchester Road. Elizabeth Bayley was two
years old when Mme. Coutant, her great-great-grandaunt,
made her untimely departure out of life, and no doubt, the
child heard the story often during her visits to New Rochelle.

Returning home from Bonnefoy Point, Uncle William
drove out North Street to show the children the Pugsley
house, a Quaker home commandeered by Lord Howe as
his headquarters from October 18-28, the ten days that

elapsed between his landing on Pell Point and the Battle of White Plains. It was the barn, however, that aroused their real interest, for high in one of the gables might be seen for many years after, the peep hole made by the four Americans fleeing British capture. The children were saddened to learn that only three escaped.

Their route back to the Shore Road took them past the old Besley tavern where they were fortunate in seeing a stagecoach drawn up awaiting fresh horses, while making also an exchange of mail and passengers. Here, their uncle told them, local offenders were tried by Captain Besley,[a] himself a Justice of the Peace. And here a man named Thomas Paine, hated by the citizenry of this place, had once tried to vote and had been prohibited by this same Justice Besley.

As they drove south on the Post Road, Bayley stopped the horse before an old stone building typical of the very early architecture in the Huguenot settlement. This was once the tavern owned and operated by their great-grandfather William Le Conte, Jr., and often the scene of political as well as socially prominent gatherings. As late as 1771, three years before Elizabeth's birth, the place was still known as Le Conte's Tavern, although William, Jr., had died in 1758. Whether the business was continued by his daughter Ann, or whether it simply was carried on after sale under the original name, is not clear from the records.

Little Elizabeth Ann often visited the homes of her Huguenot relatives to whom, because of her French beauty and vivacity of manner, she easily endeared herself. Patriotic devotion to the rebel cause had good reason for flourishing among these people who had already suffered too much in their own country to be willing to sacrifice their new-found liberty without a heroic struggle. How proudly they spoke

---

[a] It is this Captain Besley, one of the original Huguenot settlers in New Rochelle, whom the records have frequently confused with Capt. Wm. Bayley, an Englishman. The Le Contes, the Besleys and Bayleys were, however, related by marriage.

of the help being given to General Washington by the young
Marquis de Lafayette. What rejoicing over the arrival of
the French fleet of twenty-nine vessels under Rochambeau
and de Grasse! Many other French names became household words during those days: the Duke St. Simon, General
Mathieu Dumas, Admiral Barras, Count Guillaume des
Deux-Ponts, the Duke de Choisy were among those generous
leaders who contributed so effectively to the success of the
American struggle.

Everywhere Elizabeth went with her New Rochelle
cousins, their French and English ancestry rose up to meet
them in tales of daring and trail-blazing. Both strains thereby
laid early siege to her pride and loyalty. Where the French
skein appeared on the pattern, there it was met by the English thread, no less distinguished, no less honored. There is
no monument in a public park bearing the names of Elizabeth's British forebears, but in a New Rochelle cemetery,
Daughters of the American Revolution yearly decorate the
grave of her uncle, Captain William Bayley. (See illustra-
tion p. 128.)

At noon of December 4, 1783, the flag of the new nation
with its thirteen stripes and thirteen stars was flapping
proudly over the bastion of Fort George. In late November
George Washington, at the head of a handful of ragged
veterans, had returned in triumph to this city from which he
had departed in defeat in 1776. Today this intrepid soldier
and war leader was taking a formal leave of his subordinate
officers whom he had invited to meet him at Fraunces Tavern.
Through the narrow streets of old New York now rode these
heroic companions to a last rendezvous with their Commander-in-chief. There was stiff and proper Baron von
Steuben; vast Henry Knox, a former bookseller of Boston;
James Clinton, rough and able soldier; young Benjamin Tal-
madge, erect and handsome, and many others, solemn and
tense with the emotion of the hour.

Down Bouwerie Lane came a body of tried and veteran
troops. They halted at the Bull's Head, while an advance

guard marched down to Queen Street, through which they passed to Wall Street and to Broad Way, following the retiring British. There was a little delay while the British flag was being hauled down from the greased flag-pole at the Battery and the American flag was being put in its place; then the guard was formed at Fraunces Tavern and

> Beat of drum and thrill of fife
>   Down the Bowery lane;
> Tramp of troops, in exile long,
>   Marching home again.
> Battle-seasoned these,
>   In their buff and blue:
> Victors in a wasteful war,
>   Tried, triumphant, true.

The actual leave-taking was brief and sincerely sorrowful. Washington, probably for the first time in his life, found himself unable to control his feelings, and wept openly. After embracing each of these men who had served him so loyally, and uttering a few choked words, he went out on the balcony to give and receive for the last time the soldier's salute. Then he turned, and with his hand lifted high in a final gesture of farewell, he hurried down the flight of steps to the street where a carriage awaited to take him to the barge at the foot of Whitehall Street.

But the progress was to be a slow ride of triumph between solid walls of wildly cheering New Yorkers. Mothers held their little ones high to catch a brief glimpse of this loved Father of his country. All the way from the Tavern to the docks, the streets echoed to the huzzas of his fellowmen. But the sound he could not hear was their tears of gratitude and affection. New York City has, since that time, witnessed many an ovation for heroes, both our own and those who have visited our shores, but never have the love, respect, and loyalty of the entire nation been represented so completely as in this tribute to the humble man who told the Congress at the time of his appointment: "I feel myself wholly incapable of fulfilling the great task you have laid upon me."

Nine-year-old Elizabeth stood with her father and the other members of her family to honor the retiring General. As she looked about at the soldiers standing at attention, she may well have felt a deeper claim on all that those threadbare heroes had fought for and saved than did many of the others around her. For the loom of many threads that were to be woven into the Le Conte-Bayley tapestry had been set up on American soil by her forefathers exactly one hundred years before the young Republic of America was born!

II

From La Rochelle
to New Rochelle

1

ON A CERTAIN BLUSTERY NOVEMBER DAY IN 1686, the lookout at James Fort peered intently through his spy glasses at a two-masted vessel inching her way through the choppy waters of New York Bay. At that distance she looked for all the world like a huge sea gull riding the waves and flapping her wings in the strong gale. Slowly she took more definite shape as she came, bucking with obvious difficulty the wind that tore through the channel between the headlands of Staten Island and New York like an angry howling spirit, snatching at everything in its way with destructive fingers, not sparing the light ship that nevertheless came doggedly on with symbolic persistence. For she bore upon her sea-weathered decks forty or fifty of the stoutest hearts ever to approach the shores of America.

The watch stopped looking long enough to shout a brief message to a lad lolling at the foot of the sea wall and then resumed his eager study of the oncoming vessel. The boy scurried through a small gateway, his coattails flapping against him, the red of his cheeks almost one with that of the worsted scarf tied snugly around his neck. Bringing himself up short at the door of the custom-house, he doffed his cap, calling in to the two men sitting on high stools at their counters, "Ship sighted, sir! A brig . . . coming up the Bay now, sir." His duty done, he lost no time in retracing his steps to the wall of the Fort, this time mounting beside the watch for a better view of the harbor. Shortly, the Fort seemed to come alive. Men, women, and children came streaming from their houses as the news passed from door to door, for this was no ordinary occurrence. Boats had not been putting in at New York so regularly since the more northerly Boston had become the first port of call for European traders. Nor had New Yorkers fared any better with vessels from the West Indies, since most of the shipmasters preferred not to hazard the wintry blasts of the northern Atlantic, but contented themselves with setting up their markets in the southern towns of the Carolinas and Virginia. There was, moreover, a group of people in New York for whom the arrival of this ship might put an end to a long period of anxiety about relatives and friends. These were the French, many of whom had themselves come to this city but a year or two before as fugitives from the long, persecuting arm of France.

All jostled one another now in friendly excitement; the jovial, sturdy Dutch and the impetuous, gay French stood side by side with the staid, reserved British—lords and masters of this town for the past twenty years. All eyes were strained to get a better view of the oncoming ship, and many were the conjectures made by the wise ones among them as to her port of sail, her master, and her purpose in putting in here. Suddenly the watch shouted to those around him that the white banner streaming proudly out behind the mast like a plume, bore the fleur-de-lis. At once this news was passed along and the cry was taken up: "The fleur-de-lis! A French boat . . . the Huguenots have come!"

Among those to whom this was the most welcome sort of news was a young French couple, Bartholomew Mercier and his wife Katherine Lasty. Several months before, they had received word that the year-old persecution of the Huguenots was daily mounting in fury through the several islands of the West Indies, whence they themselves had come, by way of Boston, two years earlier. The fate of

Bartholomew's brother Isaac, of Katherine's father Jacques Lasty and her sister, Anne Martha, along with the well-being of many other relatives and friends would be decided for them by the arrival of this boat upon which all eyes were fastened in curious wonder. Now that she was within halloing distance, the more keen-eyed on shore could pick out individual forms, and even features. In the prow, close-huddled for protection against the wind, stood a silent group of men, women, and several children, their faces tense and unsmiling as they strained through the hazy light of a late November afternoon for whatever signs of encouragement might be theirs on this unknown coastline. Frail women and even sturdy men shivered in the unaccustomed cold that nipped hands and noses, for the air was already damp with the smell of the first snow. This change from the sunny, almost tropical shores of the West Indies, to the bleakness of a late northern fall was one for which few of those on board were prepared.

Standing in the lee of the Fort wall for protection, Katherine pulled her shawl more closely about her and tucked the loose end of it around the head of the infant she was holding in her arms. Suddenly she gripped her husband. "Look, there, in front of the others,—that is my father, isn't it?" How she wished she could snatch the spy-glass from the watch for just one quick look! Yet she knew it was her father; she would know him in any crowd, head and shoulders over those around him. He would be the natural leader of this group, if they were from the West Indies. He had already traded with the people of New York, he was the eldest in the West Indian colony of friends and relatives, and he was the wealthiest.

Slowly the brigantine tacked and veered as the captain steered her into the little inlet near the Fort, and sought anchorage. As she turned her side to the shore, several by-standers called out the half-obliterated name inscribed along her prow—"La Pointe de Sable," Katherine Mercier's heart gave a bound. Then it was he—that was her father's brig which he owned in partnership with his young overseer, Guillaume Le Conte. Suddenly there rose before her mind the West Indian plantation, its vast fields of tobacco, cotton, and sugarcane, green and fragrant in the soft breeze; the low melancholy chant of the Negro workers as they toiled their way up and down the rows of waving crops; the warm tints of the southern sky. Looking about her now, she shuddered as much from her nostalgic emotion as from the biting cold and the gray darkness of her present surroundings.

All aboard was now commotion while the crew and sea-stiffened passengers made ready their simple luggage; some lowered the dinghies and the first few travelers started their precarious climb down the rope ladders; others lined the gunwales and scanned the faces of those on shore, or laughed merrily at the staggering efforts of their fellow passengers to settle themselves in the swaying boats for the short run to land. In the confusion, Katherine lost sight of her father for some time, but suddenly she saw him step out of one of the boats and turn to assist a young woman. Swift as air, Mme. Mercier was beside her father, and with a cry of relief she threw herself into his arms. Tears of sorrow mingled with those of joy in this meeting, in a strange land, so far from home, and under such tragic circumstances. After a short time, Katherine turned to greet her sister. With surprise she saw that Anne Martha, smiling proudly, was clinging to the arm of a tall, handsome aristocrat whom Katherine had known on St. Kitt's as her father's business partner. Drawing the couple forward, laughing the while at his daughter's confusion, Lasty said to Katherine, "And now, greet your sister, Mme. Le Conte! Of course, you know Guillaume."

Bartholomew Mercier had, in the meanwhile, located his brother Isaac and had greeted other friends among the new arrivals. There were Alexandre Allaire, Pierre Flandreau, Pierre Le Conte, Etienne Valleau and his daughter Marguerite, Elie de Bonrepos—Huguenot minister, Etienne Mahault with his family, and others whom he was happy to see

and welcome. With Isaac he now rejoined his wife and her
family who were at the moment expressing delighted admiration of Katherine's baby, Henry.

The next few hours were busy ones for the men. All
must register with the customs officials for themselves and
their families, after which they were warmly welcomed to
New York by Mayor Nicholas Bayard, nephew to Peter
Stuyvesant, and himself the grandson of a Huguenot theolo-
gian who had fled from Paris to Holland. He well understood
the plight of these people seeking asylum in his city. Lasty
and Le Conte, as owners of the brigantine that had brought
the group from St. Christopher's, must attend to its unload-
ing, pay the master and crew, and arrange for permanent
docking space for the boat. By evening, however, all newcomers had been hospitably housed with relatives and
friends, or with the kindly citizens, many of whom had
themselves been exiles from home and kin.

Late into the night the Merciers and the Le Contes re-
hearsed the sorry saga of their odyssey from picturesque
Normandy to this wild unbroken country. It was the second
time in less than ten years that they had been forced to flee
before persecution. The present was doubtful and insecure;
a guess at the future could not be hazarded, and indeed, it
would have been scant comfort to them on that first night in
New York to know that in this same city, a daughter of
their house would one day revert to that very Church whose
influence they had so violently rejected. One hundred and
twenty-five years later, Elizabeth Bayley Seton, to whom
many of those who had arrived that afternoon would be
related by ties of marriage, would be forced to leave this
same city, also for religious reasons. The pattern had indeed
begun to take shape.

2

The forty or so Huguenots who had arrived in New
York on the afternoon just described had left behind them

a trail of sorrow and bloodshed. Only with the deepest
heartaches could they recall those far-off days when France,
their dearly loved mother, had cast them out like strangers,
even like enemies.

The bitter struggle between French Catholics and Protestants resulting from the Reformation had finally reached
at least a semblance of peace with the issuance of the Edict
of Nantes by Henry IV, in 1598. This decree allowed the
Huguenots (French term for Protestants)[a] political but not
religious freedom. They were given several large walled
cities within which to hold their services. La Rochelle was
the most strongly fortified of these and served both as a
rallying point and a symbol of endurance for all the sect.

In 1685, however, the Edict was revoked. Huguenot
worship was banned, yet it became unlawful for these
people, most of whom were wealthy and influential citizens,
to leave France. Although roads and ports were heavily
guarded against their escape, many ran the blockade by
night to boats lying off the coasts. The methods of escape
were various. Some persuaded captains of passing boats to
take them on, together with their entire households; others,
fortunate in owning their own sloops, smuggled their families aboard and sailed for a foreign port. The greater number
made their way to some Protestant country of Europe, such
as England or Holland, and thence to America. British sympathy for the Huguenot cause had led her to station warships
off the island of Rhé, opposite La Rochelle, to receive fleeing
Frenchmen and convey them to England. A coffee house
in Soho Square, London, kept by a refugee, was the resort
of these exiles. The founding of New Amsterdam in
America—attributed to the Dutch—was in reality a Huguenot sanctuary established under Dutch auspices. The first
ship load of emigrants sent from Holland to the New World
for colonization consisted entirely of Huguenots under Peter

---

[a] The name "Huguenot" is thought to have derived from the
German "Eidgenossen"—bound together by oath.

Minuit, himself a French-speaking Walloon.[b] Some sailed up
the Hudson River as early as 1660 and settled Fort Orange,
later Albany; others stopped off lower down at a spot to
which they gave the name New Paltz. In 1877, Hackensack,
New Jersey, was colonized by the Huguenots, but in all these
places mentioned the French were very soon outnumbered by
their overlords, the Dutch. New Rochelle in Westchester
County and Huguenot Park on Staten Island alone retained
their French characteristics far into the second generation.

In 1626, a French trading company was formed, with
Richelieu's support, to settle the West Indies with five
hundred families, many of them Huguenots who either vol-
unteered or were enforced into exile in those remote islands.
The Crown hoped thereby to enrich its royal treasuries by
the revenues from the plantations commissioned out there.
St. Christopher Island, frequently referred to as St. Kitts,
Martinique and Guadalupe Islands were colonized in this
manner. But the company officials were tyrants empowered
by Richelieu to exact 50 pounds of cotton, or 100 weight
of tobacco from each inhabitant from fifteen to sixty years
of age. This situation made life almost unbearable for the
settlers. When the Dutch heard of these conditions, they
came offering more agreeable terms for provisions and merchandise. Thereby was laid the foundations for extensive
coastwise trading between the West Indies and the New York
colonies, which however, had to be carried on surreptitiously
for fear of reprisals from the French government. In this
insecure fashion the Huguenots had enjoyed a safe retreat
during the fifty years preceding the Revocation of the Edict
of Nantes.

Into this milieu came Jacques Lasty, from Caen, France.
He seems to have been in the West Indies as early as 1672,
probably having arrived with one of the first waves of
Huguenot immigration. Almost at once he received his
allotted plantation on St. Kitts and began successful trading

---

[b] "Walloon"—one of the Huguenot colonists who came to America
from Artois, France.

with the Dutch in tobacco and sugar, by which he amassed a small fortune. However, after the Revocation in 1685, the West Indies were used by France as penal colonies for the offending Huguenots. Among those who arrived for one reason or another at this time were the Le Contes from the province of Normandy: Guillaume from Rouen, Pierre from Diep, and Francois from Pont l'Eveque. That they were related has been generally surmised but never completely proved, which uncertainty, especially regarding Guillaume and Francois, has given rise to many mistaken conclusions regarding their individual histories. All three left long lines of distinguished heirs. Guillaume, who perhaps had been fortunate enough to have smuggled out with him a sizable sum of money, entered into partnership with Lasty on his plantation, where, according to his own words, he worked for three years, also allowing Lasty the use of his Negroes. Together they bought the brigantine "La Pointe de Sable" which Lasty as the senior, and also the more experienced trader used as his own, paying Le Conte 200 pounds of sugar a day for this right. Both men appear to have profited handsomely from this arrangement. It was about this time that Le Conte married Anne Martha Lasty, his partner's elder daughter.

But the French government was determined to wipe out the Huguenots. When, therefore, the local officials in the West Indies were ordered to subjugate these people or to launch a dragonade [c] against them, the news was followed by a wholesale stampede of Huguenots to whatever ports on the mainland of North America they could reach with an offer of help. The greater number preferred the more southern settlements of South Carolina and Florida, as being already established by their exiled countrymen besides offering a temperature similar to that of France. Lasty and Le Conte, however, had mercantile interests with their Dutch associates in the North. Another determining factor in their

---

[c] "Dragonade"—quartering of troops on the French Protestants to harass them and force them to abjure their religion.

case may have been the news that New York's Catholic
Government, Thomas Dongan, had recently granted religious
freedom to all Christians in his province. They decided,
therefore, to throw in their lot with the general exodus of
200 families that left St. Kitts for New York in November
1686. By 1687 the nucleus of a French colony had taken
shape on a narrow point of land bordering Long Island
Sound in Westchester County, New York. The settlement
would eventually be known as New Rochelle in loving
tribute to La Rochelle, the famous fortress city of the
Huguenots in France.

3

One of the first to become a property owner in the new
area was Jacques Lasty who purchased 180 acres in several
parcels, and a small island. Le Conte followed him from New
York City a year later. Both are listed as among the Founding Fathers of New Rochelle. It was Lasty's evident intention to try to reproduce the type of life he had led in St.
Christopher's. Le Conte declares in an inventory submitted
to the Provincial government after Lasty's death that there
were "extensive farming operations." He stocked up with
seven oxen, eight cows, twelve pigs, besides flocks of hens
and geese. The numbers sound ludicrous in these days of
seven and eight figures, but at the time—and for a Huguenot refugee—they represented considerable wealth. He
owned also four "great" Negroes with their wives and children. These probably were employed on his plantation—this
term being used by the early Huguenot settlers to designate
their farms.

Although Lasty apparently entered upon his life in the
New World with enthusiasm, yet there is no record of his
ever having applied for citizenship as did all the other members of his family. We are not, then, too greatly surprised

to find that in 1689 he left New York and returned to St. Kitts. It is not clear why he did so, but there could have been several reasons. One might have been the sale of his former plantation—if it had not been already confiscated by the French government. Another reason could have been the difficulty of adjusting himself to a harsh climate in a strange land that was predominantly English or Dutch. We may also draw the conclusion that he did not expect to return to the North from the fact that on March 19, 1688, Lasty had made a deed of his property in New Rochelle to his daughter Anne Martha and had appointed his son-in-law Guillaume to act as the administrator of his wife's estate.

Whatever the reason that prompted this rugged pioneer to give up so promising a future, he adhered to his decision. It was a sad little group that gathered once more on the dock at James Fort. Katherine had again brought her son Henry, now a healthy three-year-old, who domineered over his grandfather with all the tryanny of babyhood. Anne Martha and Guillaume had no children as yet, but they were young, notably prosperous, and the future would fulfill their dreams. Relinquishing the hope of seeing around him his children's children was not the least in the older man's pangs of separation.

Slowly the boat turned her prow to the open seas. A last waving of hands to those on shore; then as the anchor was drawn up, the wind snatched at the sails that bellied out and carried the vessel far into the wide bay. The brigantine gathered power and Lasty turned for a final look at those dear ones still waving to him from the Fort. Soon "La Pointe de Sable" was but a receding speck on the horizon.

Jacques Lasty's children never saw him again. In 1691, two years after his departure, word was received in New York that he had died. This founder of two lines had done his work. He had brought to American shores the unbroken strain of French influence that would live on in his descendants whose melding would produce in time one of the fairest flowers of the New World, his great-great-great-granddaughter, Elizabeth Ann Bayley.

III

A Huguenot Becomes
An American

1

ANNE MARTHA TURNED RELUCTANT EYES from the all-but-invisible ship, and looking up at Guillaume, tried to smile through her tears. This was her first separation from her father and her heart smote her with forebodings. Mme. Le Conte—already twice an exile—certainly did not lack courage in facing her future in a strange land, but she had a woman's intuition and a woman's heart. She had, in addition, the ardent and affectionate nature of her people, so quickly and so keenly responsive to love and pain. Of all the nations, the French have ever been the least inclined to move around. Contrary to the English idea that a young man was not educated until he had travelled, the French were rooted in their loyalty to and contentment in their own provinces. What a wrench, then, to their every tradition was this upheaval and flight, this uncertain and nomadic existence they had so recently experienced.

The young woman squared her shoulders and slipped her arm confidingly through that of her tall, handsome husband. After all, she thought to herself, they were young, and strong—and together. Guillaume, sensing her inner struggle, gave her hand a little squeeze of encouragement, and thus reassured, each by the other, they passed through the low gate at James Fort onto the Broad Way. Though perhaps neither was aware of the significance of that act, it was,

nevertheless, symbolic of the irrevocable decision just made
—the closing of a door on the Old World and a stepping
over the threshold into the New.

That evening in their little brick house on Bouwerie
Lane, the Le Contes discussed the future. Up to this time
Guillaume had considered himself more of a merchant than
a farmer, though he was already one of the largest landowners in New Rochelle. It now seemed feasible to him to
take over the prosperous farm of Jacques Lasty whose departure had left his son-in-law the acknowledged head of the
family at the age of thirty-three. This hardy progenitor of
an equally hardy line of French Americans had already paid
a high price for his personal liberties. Rebellion, persecution,
flight and exile were the materials of the strands that would
fashion the new pattern of things in a New World.

But Guillaume had the courage and daring required of
those who would succeed in the work of pioneering. For the
second time he began his life on a strange soil, among
strange people, and his first official act was significant of his
attitude. He applied for citizenship. On January 21, 1690,
he was admitted to the privileges of residence in New York
City which gave him the right to practice a trade or to do
mercantile business with other ports. On November 9, 1691,
Lieutenant-Governor Richard Ingoldsby would sanction this
citizenship in confirming Lasty's deed to Anne Martha by
appointing Guillaume administrator of her estate.

With the settlement of the Le Contes in New Rochelle
there is opened one of the most interesting chapters in the
history of this remarkable family. Native shrewdness and
the natural gifts of leadership enabled Guillaume to rise to
prominence and financial security in a very brief space of
time. As early as 1690, probably the very year of his taking
residence in Westchester, his name appears on public records
and in private deeds of sale. This rapid success can also be
partly accounted for by calling to mind that many of the
Huguenots in New Rochelle were already close friends and

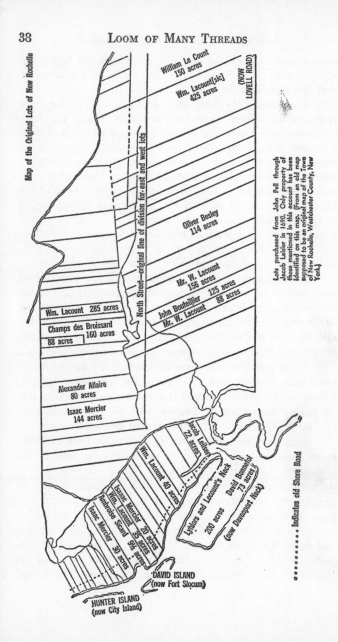

Map of the Original Lots of New Rochelle

William Le Count
150 acres

Wm. Lacount[sic]
425 acres

(NOW LOVELL ROAD)

North Street—original line of division for east and west lots

Oliver Besley
114 acres

Mr. W. Lacount
156 acres

John Bonteillier 125 acres
Mr. W. Lacount 88 acres

Wm. Lacount 285 acres

Champs des Broissard
88 acres | 160 acres

Alexander Allaire
80 acres

Isaac Mercier
144 acres

Lots purchased from John Pell through Jacob Leisler in 1690. Only property of those mentioned in this account has been identified on this map. (From an old map supposed to be an original map of the Town of New Rochelle, Westchester County, New York.)

Jacob Leisler
22 acres

Wm. Lacount 40 acres

Isaac Mercier 20 acres
Wm. Lacount 35 acres
Ambroise Sicard 9¼ acres
Isaac Mercier 30 acres

Lybtors and Lacount's Neck
200 acres

David Bonnefot
73 acres

Lacount's Neck

David Bonnefot (now Davenport Neck)

·········· Indicates old Shore Road

DAVID ISLAND
(now Fort Slocum)

HUNTER ISLAND
(now City Island)

countrymen of Guillaume and knew his ability while respecting his character.

It was a happy move for both husband and wife, for they were among their own people once more. French was spoken everywhere. Their natural gayety and love of the social amenities might here be practised without fear of offending the susceptibilities of other foreign elements. For Anne Martha it also meant proximity to her sister and the latter's family. Katherine and Bartholomew had set up their homestead in New Rochelle nearly four years earlier, probably on land given by Jacques Lasty to his younger daughter as a belated dowry.

It may be said without exaggeration that Le Conte himself sank deep roots into the soil of New Rochelle, for on an old map showing the location and extent of grants to the original settlers, the name "Wm. LeCount" [sic] covers 1,179 acres in parcels varying from 35 to 425 acres. This was the largest holding possessed by any New Rochelle inhabitant of that period. Included in this total were also the 180 acres belonging to Anne Martha's estate. It is evident from the descriptions of the properties given in deeds of sale that Le Conte did not buy all this land at the time of the original purchase from Pell, but by keeping his business eye open, was quick to pick up offers of sale from other settlers, who, for one reason or another, could not retain their land. Thus we read in one of the earliest transactions on record in the city clerk's office of a deed made by Le Conte to Ambroise Sicard and his son of property "of the hundred and fifty acres which the seller has acquired of Monsieur Brossard des Champs." The deed is dated 1692. Another such sale to Daniel Bonnet was made "from those lands he bought from Jacob Leisler." These details show the alertness of the young land dealer in acquiring valuable pieces of property.

2

The personality of Elizabeth Bayley's great-great-grandfather emerges from the records with certain decisive characteristics. He was an astute business man who did not
hesitate to drive a cute bargain. The aforementioned transactions are among the most detailed documents in the
records. Nothing is left to chance. Le Conte sells the land,
but takes a mortgage on it to enable his purchaser to meet
the sale. He establishes the species to be received . . . which,
however, "is payable in all kinds of good grain and market-
able at the current price it would be worth in cash money
. . . deducting the boat transport." Furthermore, if the
buyers are not able to meet the payments within the six
years allotted, they shall pay the interest on the sum owed
"at the rate of six per cent." Another deed dated January
22, 1702, was made between "M. Guilluame Le Conte, merchant residing in New York, on the one part, and Pierre
Simon, ploughman, residing in New Rochelle, on the other."
This sale, providing for the payment of a thousand Reiles,
interest on the sum during the year allowed for its payment,
was drawn up at New Rochelle, giving evidence that Le
Conte moved back and forth between New York and New
Rochelle according to the demands of his dual role of farmer
and merchant.[a] The deed was witnessed by Francois Le Conte,
living in Westchester since 1699 and listed as a victualler
and a baker. It bears out the close relationship that persisted
between these two men whose kinship no one has satisfac-
torily explained.

After Lasty's death Guillaume made a determined claim

---

[a] These transactions may be viewed in their original French. The
New Rochelle records extend from 1692 to 1775. The earliest entries
were in French, but since English townsmen frequently alternated with
the Huguenots in the position of town clerk, the resulting variations in
spellings of proper names and other important items have led to
serious difficulties in correctly interpreting some of the deeds recorded.

for refunds of loans made to his father-in-law during their
partnership on the island of St. Christopher. In a "memorandum" of what was due to him "by the late James Latys"
there were listed some curious items: "1,300£ of money lent;
16,000 lbs. of sugar, in goods and merchandize." "For his
half of the Brigantine named 'La Pointe de Sable,' 18,000
pounds of sugar." To this he adds salary claims for "three
years of my service upon his Plantation with the use of my
negroes. . . ." It should be noted that these claims were
"acknowledged and certified" to by his sister-in-law "Katherine Laty wife of Bartelemy Mercier . . . as due to him."

Though Le Conte may have driven a hard bargain, it
appears also that his claims were just and honorable. Besides the testimony of his sister-in-law just cited, there is the
curious affair of the miller. For some reason not disclosed
in the records, Guillaume had been deprived of his right to
use the mill of one Laysclav. At a town meeting held in 1708,
at which presumably Le Conte had represented his case, the
verdict arrived at "with the consent of all the inhabitants
of the town of New Rochelle" was that "Monsieur Guillaume
Le Conte will have the right to mill like all the other inhabitants. . . ." In that same meeting he was elected supervisor of highways, certainly a nice gesture of confidence.

Le Conte was an educated man according to the standards of his day. Besides his ability to keep his own records,
he signed his full name to every document while the other
parties frequently were able only to make a mark. His intelligent mind and sound judgment were no doubt the com-
pelling factors in his success as a public-spirited citizen.
"With the consent of the Assembly of 1702" he was one of a
five-man committee set up to map out a road for the "con-
venience of the inhabitants to convey their hay to the
wharf," probably for shipping to New York City. He must
have been an energetic person, for beyond these varied business matters requiring much of his time and interest, he
found occasion also for being a good country squire and an
active, civic-minded resident. He served in various capaci-

ties: as elder of the French Church, as assessor, as surveyor
of highways, as townsman, as justice of the peace. And there
is no doubt that he was one of the earliest real estate dealers
that the Westchester records immortalized!

In 1691 many of the Huguenots were shocked and
grieved when their friend and adviser, Jacob Leisler, was
hanged for political connivance. No one was more disturbed
by this tragic event than Guillaume Le Conte, Leisler's partner in several large land transactions in New Rochelle. As
late as 1710 the promontory now known as Davenport Neck
was referred to as Leisler's and Le Conte's Neck, their joint
ownership of this and David's Island (now Fort Slocum)
giving them the status of land magnates.

Guillaume and Anne Martha experienced a great joy in
1693 with the birth of their first child, a daughter whom
they named Hester. In the following year a son was born
and called Guillaume. The pattern in the loom takes on a
richer hue with these new strands—the first American-born
Le Contes. In probably the same year died Anne Martha's
brother-in-law, Bartholomew Mercier, leaving her sister
Katherine, at an early age, a widow with a small boy. So
the lights and shadows were intermingled in the lives of
these first settlers as they must ever be in the lives of all
humankind.

Although the Le Contes had moved to New Rochelle,
they did not cease to remain in close contact with their former way of life; there is ample evidence for the belief that
they retained their city home, and often visited back and
forth, enjoying the society of numerous well-born friends
and business associates, as became their own rank. Nothing
definite can be claimed for Mme. Le Conte in the matter of
ancestry, but according to several reliable sources, Le Conte
belonged to the nobility of France, being descended on his
mother's side from the barons of Nonant. He and his wife
were the social peers of the de Peysters, the Jays, the Pin-
tards, and the De Lanceys, their countrymen; and of the
Roosevelts, the Schuylers, and the Bayeux, their neighbors.

Before three generations have passed Le Conte's great-grand-children will be marrying into all the families mentioned.

Each of these newcomers was struggling, and growing into the ways of the new land. The only immigrant possessing substantial wealth at the time of his arrival was Etienne De Lancey whose aged mother had pressed the family jewels upon him at the time of his flight. All these families, however, lived in the comparative comfort of brick houses, probably in Bouwerie Lane, the focal point for the Huguenots in New York. Merchants among them, like Lasty and Le Conte, traded with Canada, New England, the Carolinas, and the West Indies. Negro and Indian slaves performed the heaviest labor and the general housework. At the early date of 1688 there was a Huguenot church "butting North-ward on Pettycoat Lane," at one time the name for Market-field Street, at present the section of Battery Place between Broadway and the Bay.

Le Conte was now at the height of his career, a much respected resident, an influential citizen, a successful and happy father. Evidence of his legal and social standing may best be gleaned from a testimonial presented to Lord Corn-bury, the Lieutenant-Governor, by the "chieftest inhabitants and freeholders of the City of New York on October 2, 1702." Among those who signed the original address was William Le Cont, [sic] one of the 153 signees for New York City. Others listed were Augustus Jay, William Norris, Johannes V. Cortlandt, Louis Carré. Following this, on November 1, 1705, Le Conte, still described as a farmer, became a Freedman of New York City, a most cherished honor. None but the possessor could exercise the right of suffrage, or be eligible to hold office.

However much he might need to be in New York to attend to his mercantile affairs and to perform various civic duties, Le Conte seems to have considered New Rochelle his real home. Here he had his farm on Bonnefoy Point, ap-proximately on the area now covered by Hudson Park.

3

In 1698, eight years after its foundation, the village of New Rochelle claimed 232 men, women, and children: 188 whites, 44 slaves. There were 44 families, all of whom were French but five. Slave trade had been introduced into the colonies by the Dutch West India Company and was flourishing, but, to the credit of the Huguenots it may be said that, although they engaged in the buying and selling of these Negroes, they treated them humanely, saw that they were instructed in religious beliefs, baptized, and admitted to the Church as members of good standing. In many instances they even taught them to read and write.

The Huguenots, who had suffered so much in France for their beliefs, were themselves faithful and zealous worshipers in their new surroundings. Benefiting by the enactment of the First Legislative Assembly under the Catholic Governor Thomas Dongan, which enactment granted religious toleration "for all professing faith in God by Jesus Christ," they made great sacrifices to attend the only Huguenot church then built, in New York City. This structure on Pine Street, which succeeded the former one on Pettycoat Lane, had been made possible through the generosity of the wealthiest of the Huguenots, Etienne De Lancey.[b] There the Huguenots from Westchester and Staten Island attended Sunday worship as often as they could make the difficult journey thither, during mild weather—many coming on foot because they were poor. One of these pilgrimages describes "a delegation from New Rochelle, Mamaroneck, Scarsdale, and other places meeting at a prearranged spot at midnight between Saturday and Sunday and singing hymns to hearten them as they trudged on, a long line of bobbing lanterns in the darkness, down to the

[b] Etienne De Lancey married Ann Van Cortlandt in 1700. He it was who built the house on Broad Street that later became the famous Fraunces Tavern.

Haarlem River, where they ferried across by daybreak or
before. Here they paused at a large rock to rest and to have
a lunch. Then pressed on—arriving at Bouwerie Village in
time for breakfast. . . ." Thirty miles or more! Upon reading of these fervent and intrepid people, one understands
very readily the intensely religious nature that will carry
Elizabeth Bayley through similar difficulties with equal
courage. If not of their faith, she was decidedly of their
breed!

However, the residents of New Rochelle could not long
continue their observance of Sunday under these hardships,
and resolved to have their own church. The first structure
was a crude frame building built on a 100-acre plot deeded
to them by John Pell for this purpose. They were so eager,
nevertheless, to have a stone edifice that even the women
assisted in its erection, carrying the mortar in their aprons
to their husbands. Consequently, in 1692, only two years
after their arrival, the stone church was opened for divine
worship, the services being conducted according to the Reformed Church of France, the only one tolerated. The following year, Governor Fletcher enacted a law by which the
Church of England was fastened upon the counties of New
York, Richmond, Queens, and Westchester as the State
church, to be supported by public charge. In 1706 all de-
nominations except the Church of England were defran-
chised. The Huguenots were bribed into submission by
government support of their Church and by having the
liturgy translated into French. Vestrymen and other important members named in the records include: Lispenard,
Guion, Bertain, Le Conte, Nicolle, Angevine . . . names that
would be carried on New Rochelle registers for the next 250
years.

Like all the Huguenots, Guillaume Le Conte and his
friends were ideal colonists: cheerful, resourceful, and tol-
erant. They brought with them the knowledge of gardening, husbandry, and skills in the manufacture of glass and

jewelry. In the earliest days practically every man was a farmer.

> As the people are all farmers, they are dispersed up and
> down the country: and even in towns every one has a plot
> of at least ten acres, which distances his neighbor from
> him. . . .

There were no food stores—each one raised his own supplies while depending on New York City for articles of luxury from abroad. Every farmer had another specialty such as butchering, saddle-making, tanning, or, as in the case of Le Conte and similarly prosperous individuals, a mercantile trade with other areas. Carpenters were in great demand for their skill in fine woodwork and cabinet making.

The Le Contes set up the typical home of a well-to-do Huguenot settler, still surprisingly primitive according to later standards. When Guillaume had acquired the materials for his house, which was first of wood, later of stone, he invited his friends to help in building it. House-raising was a community affair in those days, many a debt being "worked off" in this way. The dwelling would be one and a half stories high with a chimney in the center. Windows on the first floor were constructed with 24 panes of glass, 12 in each sash. The stairs were placed in front of the entrance alongside the chimney, which was capped with brick. The exterior was generally shingled.

While the construction of the house was going on, Anne Martha had not been idle. With the assistance of friends and relatives, she had been spinning the yarn to be woven into curtains and bedspreads. Then it was dyed into favorite shades, the Huguenots preferring light blue, dusky green, or soft gold. Deft fingers tossed lace shuttles back and forth in the making of beautiful doilies and samplers. It is said that the Huguenots were the first to utilize old garments to cover the floors against the dreadful winter drafts. These coverings were the famous rag rugs. A Frenchwoman would leave nothing undone to add color and grace to her surroundings.

4

Although deeply religious, these people were very different in spirit from the Puritans who repelled by their morose views and their stern manners. The Huguenots were truly French. Celebrated for their industry and frugality, they were yet happy and gay, much given to laughter and song, possessing a fine culture. The vast majority of this first group of settlers were literate, as their ability to read, write, and sign their names to documents well testifies. It is in the second and third generations that recourse to symbols in place of signatures becomes a commonplace, owing, no doubt, to the utter lack of schooling while these groups were growing up. Their parents, harried by the pressing necessities of making a living in this wild, primitive country, could spare little time for the formal education of their families.

Huguenots in New York City may have fared somewhat better than their country relatives, although the reports of attempts by various schoolmasters to support themselves entirely by their profession are lamentable. One Adam Roelentsen, appointed in 1637 and supposedly the first Dutch schoolmaster on Manhattan Island, had to eke out his scanty salary by taking in washing! The first Latin school in New York was established by three Jesuits in 1685-1687 under the aegis of Governor Dongan. But Jacob Leisler, so bitterly anti-Catholic, complained to Dongan's successor in a letter of August 12, 1689:

I have formerly urged to inform your honr. that Coll:
(colleague) Dongan, in his time did erect a Jesuite College
upon Cullour to learn Latine to the judges West,—Mr.
Graham Judge Palmer and John Tudor did contribute their

sones for some time, but no boddy imitating them, the collidge vanished.[c]

A spirit of "Anti-Popery" was rampant at this time, the arrival of the Huguenots adding fuel to the feeling of bigotry already sweeping over the Dutch and British colonies. The burning of the Pope in effigy on Guy Fawkes Day was continued by the English colonists down to 1774 when General Washington issued an order that it be forbidden as "senseless and insulting to our French allies." Among the Huguenots, abjurations by those who had been "enforced Catholics" in France were solemn and public occasions. Francois Le Conte made his abjuration in the Huguenot Church in New York City on May 7, 1693, in the presence of the entire congregation, the earliest abjuration on record.

Notwithstanding the crude manner of life and the lack of all but the barest means of livelihood, the Huguenot children were carefully trained in politeness; they were taught graceful gestures through little games. How typically French it is to hear Elizabeth Bayley Seton, a hundred years later, in a note of thanks to her friend Julia Scott for a gift of $100, declare that ". . . on the head of it Anna will attend an excellent dancing master at Mrs. Farquhar's . . . not for the steps but to obtain a little polish. . . ." So speaks a true daughter of the Le Contes, and that at a time when she was experiencing the direst need!

The Huguenots were also very careful about the religious training of their children. In the regular sitting-room of most Huguenot houses, the mantelpiece was finished off with Dutch tiles representing chiefly the parables and stories of the New Testament. On Sunday afternoon the children were instructed on the meanings of these religious pictures.

---

[c] Because of this and other complaints of a similar nature, Governor Dongan, a staunch Catholic, was forced to retire in 1688. He went for some time to Staten Island. Upon his return to Ireland, he was created Earl of Limerick. Dongan Hills in Staten Island is named after his family who had extensive lands there. (For a more complete account of the Dongans, see Appendix No. 12)

About 1701, in the midst of their prosperity and new-found happiness, Anne Martha died. Guillaume had not only his personal grief to bear but his concern for the future of his seven and eight-year-old son and daughter. Accordingly, on May 3, 1703, he married Margaret Mahault, daughter of Etienne Mahault, one of those who had come with Lasty from St. Christopher's. Guillaume was forty-five; Margaret, about thirty-five. That strange pattern of deceased wives and second marriages that will accompany the Le Conte and Bayley line down through the years had its precedent right here.

In the New Rochelle census taken on December 9, 1710, the first citizen named was William Le Conte, aged 52. Then follow the names of his wife Margaret, 42; William Le Conte, Jr., 16; Hester, 17, and Jean Pierre, 8. Just what led to the Le Contes' being named first on this town list is, of course, not known, but it is interesting to conjecture. If families were expected to "go to the polls" somewhat in the manner of today's registering for voting, it would appear that Monsieur Guillaume saw to it that his family was prompt! Nor is the record in alphabetical order, which rules out that suggestion. The only other one that offers itself plausibly is the importance of the Le Conte name in New Rochelle life. We may put beside this instance another exactly like it. In the records kept by the Huguenot minister, Daniel Bondet, for the Church of New Rochelle, the first entry in the book is for the marriage of Guillaume Le Conte to Margaret Mahault.

But Guillaume's fortunes took a sudden turn. On June 15, 1710, he had made his will "being at this point very sick in body, in the city of New York. . . ." This will was not probated, however, until March 2, 1711. There is a tradition that Guillaume and Margaret died on the same day in New York of yellow fever. That fearful scourge of those early days when sanitation and medical skill alike were at their lowest in the colonies, would reach out for another victim, Guillaume's great-grandson, Dr. Richard Bayley, who would give his life to assist the plague-ridden of a later era.

The foresight and intelligence of this remarkable Founding Father shines forth in a final testament to his descendants. Unlike the vast majority of his contemporaries, Le Conte put no hampering clauses to his wife's enjoyment of his estate in case of a second marriage. But he did enjoin upon her the obligation of using the income of all his estate for the education of his children "until his son Guillaume or his daughter Esther should come of age or be married."

In the tradition thus set by her great-great-grandfather, Elizabeth Bayley will herself become a pioneer educator in America. To her may be rightfully attributed the development of the parochial school system in this country.

In his eagerness for his children's education Guillaume Le Conte was only conscious of handing on the traditional culture of the French people. He could not know, of course, that the torch thus kept burning by his bequest would brand whole generations of Le Contes and their families with an unquenchable love of learning. As one commentator has put it:

> The Le Conte family affords a striking example of the intellectual virility of the Huguenot character, as they have furnished a very large number of distinguished names, especially in the field of science.

In New Rochelle, Guillaume lived out the last years of his life, in the enjoyment of peace after strife, honor after disgrace, stability in the place of exile and flight. As a well-to-do country squire, he spent a full and active life, lending his prestige and experience to both civil and church affairs.

At his death he was listed as a "Farmer"; in his will he called himself a "Gentleman." It was fitting that this intrepid defender of his convictions, this rugged pioneer and admirable forefather, should epitomize his own character for future generations. In every sense of the word, he was a—gentleman.

IV

Intricate Traceries

1

ELIZABETH BAYLEY'S GREAT-GREAT-GRANDAUNT, Katherine Lasty, is a lady likely to be passed over in the midst of other historically more important personages of this story, but indeed she was the pivotal character in bringing together many of the leading families of early New Rochelle. By her two marriages she united in ties of blood relationship several French households in a strong line of continuity extending from the earliest days of Huguenot life in America down to Elizabeth herself.

Her story begins on the island of St. Christopher when she married Bartholomew Mercier, whose family her father had known in Caen, Normandy. The young couple left shortly afterwards, in 1681, to join a relative, Andre Mercier, distinguished preacher of Boston. After a stay of uncertain duration, they arrived in New York City where, on October 29, 1684, Bartholomew petitioned for exemption from the payment of duties. This privilege had been granted by the Dutch to the first Huguenots, who later sought to maintain the favor under British rule. In the following year Mercier obtained citizenship papers for his wife Katherine, his son Henri, and himself. Elizabeth Bayley's hold on American backgrounds had an early start.

About this same time, another Huguenot named Jean Bouteillier, obtained permission for a refugee settlement on a neck of land off Long Island Sound, just northeast of Pelham Manor. In 1687 a dozen or so Huguenot families, numbering in all 32 persons, came up from New York by boat. Landing on the promontory, they built a fire in a cave where they also took shelter until a communal dwelling could be hastily erected. Adjacent lands were under cultivation by the Siwanoy Indians with whom the Huguenots established peaceable relations. The new settlement was called Bonnefoy's Neck, after David Bonnefoy, a member of the party, and evidently a leader. Bouteillier also bought David's Island (Fort Slocum) which he later sold to Guillaume Le Conte and Jacob Leisler, Jr. Within a few months Bonnefoy's Neck proved inadequate for the rapidly increasing number of refugee arrivals so that when the large group comprising Lasty and Le Conte's party reached New York from St. Kitts, negotiations were opened with John Pell for the 6,000 acres on the mainland that subsequently became New Rochelle. It has been suggested by one historian that Bouteillier, or others in the original group, represented the interests of Jacques Lasty for whom they bought shares on Bonnefoy Neck, probably the 180 acres that became Anne Martha's estate. Whether this is so or not, we know that Bouteillier and Lasty returned together to the island of St. Christopher.

Among the 32 persons to settle on the Neck were Bartholomew and Katherine Mercier and their small son Henri. If Bouteillier was her father's representative, it is understandable that Katherine and her husband would benefit by joining the project. At any rate, their names occur in New Rochelle records at about this time. The rigors of the northern climate, in addition to the strain and anxiety of providing for his family proved too much for Bartholomew. At the age of 31 he died. Pioneer life provided no nooks for widows, and Katherine, still young, attractive and well-to-do, had no reason for long remaining one. Her second husband was none other than David Bonnefoy. There were two children by this marriage, Katherine and David, Jr.

Mme. Bonnefoy outlived her second husband; her will dated
October 25, 1714, one month before her death, states that
she was a widow. Her probable age was fifty-two. Neither
she nor her sister Anne Martha enjoyed for long the hard-
won blessings of peace and a happy family life.

Of Jacques Lasty's two daughters, Katherine seems to
have possessed her father's rugged spirit to a greater degree
than her older sister. Perhaps circumstances cast her life in
a bolder mold for she has left a more definite imprint on the
history of those early days than did Anne Martha. As the
younger daughter, Katherine did not receive the rich land
dowry of her sister, but she was fortunate in procuring in
both her marriages, husbands whose family prominence
gave her social prestige equal to that of Mme. Le Conte.
Katherine stands out as a pioneer and an individualist, able
and very willing to make her own decisions, courageous in
attempting the new and the unknown. Her will is one of
the few early documents of this area drawn up by a woman.
She stands at the head of her family, the proud strong matri-
arch of widespread and distinguished descendants.

One of her more famous grandsons was William Mercier, an extremely interesting personality of the Revolutionary War. This collateral relative of Elizabeth Bayley had
entered the American Navy where, like his forebears, bravery
marked him as outstanding. In 1747, at the age of thirty,
he was made captain of the "Porpoise." His grandmother
would have been proud of him during the War when, in
1775, he commanded the "York," in 1776, the U. S. ship
"Congress," and again in 1777, the frigate "Montgomery."
He married Maria Bradford, granddaughter of the famous
printer of the *Bradford Gazette*, and direct descendant from
Governor Bradford of Puritan fame. Captain Mercier's
exploits must have been treasured family tales to which
Elizabeth would listen with pride. Indeed she may have
known the renowned Captain well since he lived to the age
of eighty-two. Elizabeth was in her twenty-third year when
he died in 1797.

2

On a certain wintry day in 1711, Mme. Bonnefoy tied on her bonnet, and wrapped in her husband's greatcoat, which she still kept because it came in so handy for making short trips around the Neck, she struck out for her brother-in-law's house some distance up the road. A stiff gale from the Sound pushed roughly against her and gulls screamed overhead, their raucous cries jarring on her thoughts which were sombre indeed. For Katherine was the bearer of very bad news. Often in her lifetime she had faced disagreeable situations, but never one that would match the double sorrow of today's message. Mme. Bonnefoy was on her way to tell her niece and nephews that both their parents were dead. Little six-year-old Pierre she did not worry about. She could comfort him and probably fill his lonely little heart with her affection, but what could she do for Hester, Anne Martha's lovely seventeen-year-old daughter, and young Guillaume, already approaching manhood and measuring his sixteen years against the stature of his father?

Several days before, Monsieur Le Conte and Madame, his wife, had gone to New York City, as they frequently did, to enjoy the company of old friends. Stricken with yellow fever almost upon their arrival, they were at this moment already buried, as the courier who brought the news late last night had told her—buried hastily for fear of spreading the contagion. Even their graves would not be known! Katherine drew a shuddering sigh. It was such an ignoble way to die, she thought, when one had lived as vibrant and vigorous a life as Guillaume Le Conte.

A shout of welcome reached her and Pierre dashed down the path to meet her. Tenderly she kissed the small boy, and taking his hand firmly in hers, as if for strength, she strode resolutely into the house.

*　　*　　*　　*　　*　　*

Some days later, Hester and her brother William, as he preferred to be called, sat before the fire in their Aunt Katherine's kitchen. Their young faces wan, and serious, showed the strain of the past week when, it seemed, their world had suddenly fallen apart. Both remembered the death of their mother when they were six and seven years old, and although they had come to love their stepmother, and were fondly proud of their baby half-brother, they never quite forgot the beautiful and gentle French woman whom they always referred to as "Maman."

Today they had closed the house that had been their home, for from now on, they would live with Mme. Bonnefoy. Katherine, her teen-age daughter, was delighted to have another girl of her own age to discuss furbelows with, and little David Bonnefoy had already taken over the younger Pierre. William would miss the companionship of Henri, who, eight years his senior, had already married Christiana Hendricks and was living over in New Rochelle village.

Of their household possessions, Hester had made selection of a few inherited treasures which she would add to her half-filled hope chest. A small silken shawl belonging to her own mother, some linen sheets, and a hand-woven table cloth, its edges heavy with embroidery, and which had come with her parents from the island of St. Christopher—these things she would lovingly store away against the day of her own marriage, which she had reason to believe would not be too far off.

William ran his finger over the shining blade of his father's great sword, turning it this way and that to let the firelight play on the jeweled hilt and the gold braid of the scabbard. On a chair beside him lay the elder Le Conte's gun, a blunderbuss, which William himself had frequently used under his father's watchful eye. The boy's heart contracted with sudden sorrow as he remembered the fellowship his father had shared with him on these hunting trips. Looking now at the sword, William seemed to see it as a symbol of his father's life—the undaunted spirit of a Norman nobleman, cutting his way through obstacles, cleaving through opposition, achieving at last.

His spirits lifted with these thoughts of pride and admiration, and buoyed up by a sudden determination to carry on the tradition of his forebears, William knew that only death could part him from this gun—and this sword.

Life was resumed in this new pattern—perhaps not too sadly—for the Le Contes were young, and the wounds borne in youth heal more readily. The smooth tenor of rural life on the Neck might have flowed on indefinitely for them had not Sorrow once again cast her unwelcome shadow. In November, 1714, three years after Hester, William, and Pierre had become part of her household, Mme. Katherine Bonnefoy died.

In her death the Le Contes lost the last direct tie with their parents' national backgrounds. From this point, a new generation, born and reared in a New World, would replace Old World memories and a way of life with those of a young America.

V

William Le Conte

1

WITH THEIR AUNT KATHERINE'S DEATH, Hester and William were faced with the grim necessity of making several far-reaching decisions. A few months earlier, Hester had announced her engagement to Ezekiel Bonyot, a mariner. William, now titular head of the family, urged her to proceed with her plans for a wedding after the turn of the new year. Hinging upon this arrangement was the future of nine-year-old Pierre. It would be unfair to Hester and her husband to make them responsible for the boy, and though reluctant to separate from their little brother, both young people realized that neither of them would henceforth be in a position to train and rear Pierre as their father would have wished. They decided, therefore, to accept the offer of the Mahaults, their step-mother's people, to take the child to Staten Island where he would grow up among his mother's relatives.

This decision must have cost the older brother and sister great distress, for the three children had grown closer than ever with each new sorrow. That these ties were retained through the years, despite distance and circumstances, may be deduced from the fact that Pierre was godfather for William's second child, while Pierre's oldest daughter was named Hester.

The third decision concerned the disposal of the large estate left by their father. The Le Conte children were land-rich, but Hester must have a dowry. Pierre must receive his share of the patrimony, probably in monetary form since he would not be using the land, and William, still but nineteen years old, could scarcely assume such a burden alone. It was decided, therefore, to sell their father's share of Bonnefoy Neck, but to retain his holdings on the mainland.

With the sale of the land to Antoine Lispenard, their last bonds with the original settlement were severed, for the old home was included, the house which their father had built, the house in which they had been born, and in which they had grown up. What wonderful times they had had as children, romping over the high back of the hillock that forms the promontory, or jumping from rock to rock along the craggy shore while the stiff Long Island breeze blew salt spray in their faces.

Hester Le Conte and Katherine Bonnefoy, William, his cousin Henri, young Isaac Mercier—a younger cousin on Aunt Katherine's side—and later, the two little boys, David Bonnefoy and Pierre Le Conte, roamed the length and breadth of this point. They knew every cave, creek, and berry bush within walking distance of their homes. The boys had their greatest lark while visiting the remains of the nearby Indian village where they poked around for arrows and spear heads, knives and grooved axes. Each boy had a sizeable collection of these objects left by the Siwanoys when they had abandoned their village to the encroachments of the white man. With the deeds to the property went also the first, and perhaps the happiest, chapter of their lives.

2

Inheritor of a vast tradition of courage, industry, and leadership, young Le Conte lived up to the example set by his father and followed pretty closely in his sire's footsteps. He assumed the care of the extensive properties in New

Rochelle and the mercantile business in New York City, of
which he and his sister were now the proprietors. New
Rochelle records contain this quaint recording of a deed:

> I william Lecote of the cyty of New York Sendeth Greeting
> in Our Lord God everlasting Now know yea that I the said
> William LeConte for and in consideration of the sum of two
> hunert and fifteen pounds of good silver money . . .

This transaction bears the double signature, "Gme LeConte
and Ester LeConte." In looking at the spelling of this document, one is reminded of a playful remark made by Elizabeth Bayley to her friend Mrs. Sadler:

> It is two months since I have written to you, and they have
> been passed amid scenes familiar to you. I cannot *spell* the
> place, that is past my art.
>
>   April 11, 1796

In those days boys learned to take on responsibility at a
very early age; it is quite possible, therefore, that William
was already acquainted with much of his father's business
interests even before the latter's death. His time would be
fairly well divided between New York and New Rochelle
until 1720, when, it appears, he gave up the mercantile trade
and retired to New Rochelle as a permanent resident.

As a citizen, William Le Conte played an important part
in the civic life of the community. The records list him
through the years in successive positions of supervisor, assessor, purveyor,[a] overseer of fences and highways, constable,
and townsman. As late as 1756, in his sixty-second year, he
was still publicly active and well known. In that year he is
mentioned as a Trustee of the Town, and in 1758—true son
of his father that he was—we find him making deeds of prop-

---

[a] In English history a purveyor is an officer who exacts or supplies
provisions for the sovereign under purveyance.

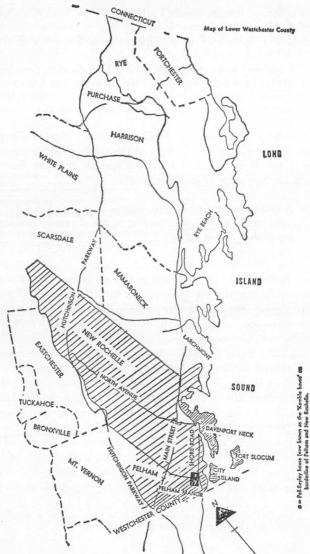

Map of Lower Westchester County

CONNECTICUT

RYE

PORTCHESTER

PURCHASE

HARRISON

WHITE PLAINS

LONG

SCARSDALE

RYE BEACH

MAMARONECK

PARKWAY

ISLAND

HUTCHINSON

NEW ROCHELLE

LARCHMONT

EASTCHESTER

NORTH AVENUE

SOUND

TUCKAHOE

BRONXVILLE

DAVENPORT NECK

MAIN STREET

SHORE ROAD

FORT SLOCUM

MT. VERNON

HUTCHINSON PARKWAY

CITY ISLAND

PELHAM

PELHAM MANOR

WESTCHESTER COUNTY

⊕ = Pell-Bayley house (now known as the "Kemble house" on borderline of Pelham and New Rochelle.

erty sales to various residents! Nor was he lacking in patriotic duties, having served as lieutenant of the militia in 1740.

One very interesting example of Le Conte's prominence in the town is shown by the following historic incident best given in the words of the account carried in the *New York Journal* of Monday, December 24, 1733:

> On this day Lewis Morriss, Esq., late chief justice of this province, was, by a majority of voices elected a representative from the county of Westchester. The election of great expectation; the court and country's interest was exerted to the utmost . . . Nicholas Cooper, Esq., high sheriff of the said county, having by papers affixed to the Church of Eastchester and other public places, given notice of the day, and place of election, without mentioning any time of the day when it was to be done, which made the electors on the side of the late judge very suspicious that some fraud was intended—to prevent which about fifty of them kept watch upon and about the green of Eastchester from 12 o'clock the night before till the morning of that day. The other electors, beginning to move on Sunday afternoon and evening so as to be at New Rochelle by midnight, their way lay through Harrison's Purchase, the inhabitants of which provided for their entertainment as they passed each house in their way, having a table plentifully covered for that purpose. At midnight they all met at the house of William LeCount, at New Rochelle, whose house not being large enough to entertain so great a number, a large fire was made in the street, by which they all sat till daylight, at which they began to move . . .

This "house" was, in all probability, the tavern which William had bought from Francois Le Conte some time after his father's death. Tavern keepers were men of high respect and good reputation, and certainly, of considerable means. In New Rochelle, all town meetings at which laws and community projects were to be discussed were held at this, or one of the other two taverns until 1829, when the first town hall was erected. Madame Knight testifies in her famous *Diary* to the accommodations she received in December, 1704, when she had to stay overnight in New Rochelle:

> Here are three fine taverns within call of each other, very good provision for Travailers.

The three taverns mentioned were, without doubt, those belonging to the Besleys, the Allaires, and Francois Le Conte. The latter building stood near the present southeast corner of Huguenot and Mechanic Streets. All three were important centers for social and civic gatherings of all kinds, as well as hostelries for travelers.

A most humanly charming touch is given by one such guest during the period of William Le Conte's ownership. One hot day in August, 1744, Andrew Hamilton, a physician from Maryland, stopped at Le Conte's for dinner. This is his account of the episode:

> I had a long ride before I arrived at New Rochelle, where I dined at the house of one Le Compte, a Frenchman, who had a daughter that is a sprightly sensible girl.[b]

Less than fifty years later the words "sprightly and sensible" will apply equally well to a description of Ann's grandniece, Elizabeth Ann Bayley, who will inherit not only the Le Conte hair and eyes, but also the lively manner of her French ancestors.

In or about the year 1720, William married Marianne Mercier, daughter of Isaac Mercier, and niece to Mme. Bonnefoy by her first marriage to Bartholomew Mercier, thereby strengthening the ties that already united these two families. The baptism of their eldest daughter Ann is recorded for Wednesday, October 23, 1723, her godparents being her Aunt Hester, her father, and her grandfather, Isaac Mercier. Two more girls were born of this marriage— Susanna and Maryanne.

---

[b] Le Conte had three daughters, but Ann was undoubtedly the one referred to as the other two girls were already married. Ann would have been twenty-one at the time of this incident.

William did not live to see his eldest daughter settled in life. Despite her sprightliness, Ann did not marry until rather late, in her forty-first year, just ten years before her grandniece Elizabeth was born. The account of her wedding to Peter Flandreau, grandson of a Huguenot who had fled from La Rochelle, gives the impression that it was one of the social events of the season. Her pastor, Rev. Jean Carle, has recorded the ceremony in these words which have been translated from the French of the original entry:

> Today, the 14th of April, I have married by a licecse of M. Cadwallader Colden Lieutenant Governor, given on July 1, 1763. I have said I married Peter flandreau and Ann LeConte in the home of the said LeConte young lady, in the presence of M. and Mad. guerineau, her brother and sisters, M. Besley and his daughter Manon, the beautiful Besly daughter, M. and Mad. Alaire, and others, registered today 15th April by me . . .

Although the license was obtained in July, it is apparent that the marriage did not take place until April of the following year. The Flandreaus had one son, Adam, one of the young cousins Elizabeth Bayley would visit in New Rochelle.

William's second daughter Susanna was "presented for baptism by her father Monsieur William Le Conte after the Morning Prayer on Wednesday, February 8, 1726." Her godparents were her uncle Pierre Le Conte, come from Staten Island for the happy occasion, and her mother, Marianne Mercier. Unlike the fate of so many "middle" sisters, the fortunes of this baby seemed destined both by nature and by circumstances to preserve the Le Conte strain in its most nativistic aspects. According to all the records, she grew to be a beautiful young woman, whose large dark eyes and black curly hair, so typically French, made her the cynosure of every other maiden in New Rochelle, and no doubt, the torment of all the youths.

In her seventeenth year, Susanna married a William Bayley from Fairfield, Connecticut, an Englishman considerably older than herself. The couple took up residence in Fairfield, and in the following year, 1744, their son Richard was born. A second boy, William, Jr., was born the next year in New Rochelle.

Maryanne, the third girl, also married an Englishman, one John Boyd, who later owned a store on Maiden Lane in New York City. Rivington's *Gazette* for July 29, 1773, advertised his "blue caps with scarlet rims, men's gray mittens, carpets, stockings, shambrick gloves."

William had now reached his sixty-fourth year, which he considered "advanced in years." Accordingly, he made his will on October 9, 1758. In his directives, he asked that his executors sell all his real estate, dividing the proceeds equally among his three daughters. Two months later, on December 13, his will was probated. Between these two dates William Le Conte died. No mention being made of his wife Marianne, it is to be assumed that she had predeceased him.

In a final gesture of affection for his two small grandsons, he left them his spirit embodied in his dearest possessions:

". . . I leave to my two grandsons, William and Richard Bayley, £20 and all my clothing, and my gun, sword, and watch . . ."

HUGUENOT FAMILY NAMES
IDENTIFIED WITH THE HISTORY OF NEW ROCHELLE
DURING THE COLONIAL PERIOD

THIS TABLET ERECTED BY
THE NEW ROCHELLE TWO HUNDRED-FIFTIETH ANNIVERSARY COMMITTEE

The area known as Hudson Park is located on the mainland of
New Rochelle on ground at one time owned by David Bonnefoy,
second husband of Guillaume Le Conte's sister-in-law, Katharine
Mercier Bonnefoy. Le Conte himself lived on adjoining Bonnefoy
Neck (Davenport Neck), now a select yachting and shore club
center. The Shore Road (Pelham Road) runs from the Pelhams to
the double entrance of these two recreational areas.

Of the names listed on the monument, eleven were directly related to Elizabeth Ann Bayley by ties of kinship:

Bayeux	Coutant	Le Conte
Besly	Flandreau	Mercier
Bonnefoy	Guerineau	Pintard
Bonyot	Lasty	

Other names represent close and trusted friends whose signatures
occur on baptismal and wedding records of the family as godparents
or witnesses, on deeds and wills as executors for the deceased, and
in the New Rochelle town records as business and civic associates
of Le Contes and Bayleys.

It is interesting to note also on the tablet several names famous
in early American history: Des Marest (Demarest, New Jersey),
Faneuil (Faneuil Hall, Boston), Fresneau (early American poet).

II
The Pattern Takes Shape
1745-1801

VI

A Chapter
on Bayleys

1

ONE SUNDAY IN 1788, Elizabeth Bayley being then in
her fourteenth year, she was sitting in the front room of her
uncle's house on the Shore Road, the family Bible open on
her lap. Directly after dinner that day, when her sister Mary
and their Bayley cousins had scampered off to spend the
afternoon by the water, Elizabeth had asked Aunt Sarah
for permission to remain indoors. She was experiencing a
growing desire to spend Sundays more quietly and now, with
everyone away, she might have some time for thinking. She
played the spinette for a while, and then she bethought herself of the Bible—this was the opportunity she had been wait-
ing for so that she might examine it to her satisfaction and
without interruption. She lifted the big book reverently onto
her lap and unfastened the large metal clasp. As she turned
now to the family entries on the front pages, a folded paper
attracted her attention. Carefully she smoothed out the
crackling parchment and spread it on the table. Written in
French, under the heading of Trinity Church, New Rochelle,
was this record:

Sunday 25 August 1745 was baptised William LeConte, son
of Mr. William Bayley and Mme. Susanne his wife, born
August 8, 1745 and presented for Holy Baptism by Mr.
William LeConte his grandfather, by Mr. Olivier Besly his

uncle and Mme. Susanne Besly his aunt, Parents and others.

William Bayley	C. Stouppe
William LeConte	
Ollivier [sic] Besly	Isaac Guion anc.
Susanne Besly	Jean Soulice (ancien)

"Why," Elizabeth exclaimed to herself, "this is Uncle William!" She read the baptismal record again, her wonder and curiosity growing with the rereading. Thoughtfully she gazed at the account. This simple declaration of fact was deceiving. The coldly recorded ceremony gave no hint of the powerful and far-reaching drama thereby set in motion. Nor did it conjure for its young reader the exciting background of affairs that had brought William Le Conte Bayley to the font of a New Rochelle church.

Elizabeth suddenly realized that she knew very little, almost nothing, about her father's family. He had always been too busy with his professional duties and with other matters regarding her education to talk to her about the Bayley history. Of the Le Contes and their part in the Huguenot foundation of New Rochelle, she had heard a great deal, for these people were all around her. The young Bayley girl had the average person's interest and pride in her family—and well she might—for it was an absorbing tale of adventure and achievement, the chief characters not being so far removed in time but that their very children and grandchildren remembered their exploits. Elizabeth might study her English history from school books, but American history was being lived out before her eyes. Yet the story of her English ancestors was still a closed chapter to her. She decided to ask Uncle William about it that very day.

It is ruefully true that time's perspective is more often than not the gauge of our estimation for another, and Elizabeth's forefathers were no exception in this regard. With typical British reticence they went about their work, avoiding fanfare, merging into the life of the colonies without attracting undue attention. Regret may well be felt for the dearth of factual information about these now important ancestors. However, events have yielded enough facts for us of the twentieth century to reconstruct with reasonable sureness, the interlacings of the human pattern that formed the warp and weft of this interesting story.

* * * * * *

Some twenty years before the coming of the Huguenots to New Rochelle, there lived at Fairfield, Connecticut, an English gentleman, Mr. Thomas Pell, who had fled England after the downfall of Charles I, of whose court he had been a prominent member. In 1654, Pell obtained a grant of land from the Indians, embracing the present sites of Pelham, New Rochelle, and Eastchester. Upon his death in 1668, he left his estate to his nephew, John Pell, still residing in England. This young man apparently lost no time in claiming his legacy, for he arrived here early in 1670 and became the second Lord of the Manor of Pelham. His great-granddaughter, Sarah Pell, married William Bayley on June 10, 1771.

A favorite picnic spot for the Bayleys was a grassy meadow that skirted the Hutchinson River between Eastchester and New Rochelle. Besides the excitement of fishing, and eating out-of-doors, the place held a mysterious fascination for the young people because of its tragic history. Every child in the country was familiar with the story of the massacre of Anne Hutchinson, the first white woman to settle in Westchester.

In 1642, Mrs. Hutchinson and her five children, fleeing Puritan intolerance in Rhode Island (some say that she was banished), settled on the banks of the thinly meandering stream that today bears her name. This site, the center for a small colony of sixteen people, was first known to its Dutch neighbors as "Annie's Hoecke," and then for a long time, designated as the "Manor of Ann Hoeck's Neck." It happened that at this time Governor Kieft, administrator for New Amsterdam, had aroused Indian fury against the whites by his inhumanity. When fifteen hundred warriors swept over Long Island, Manhattan, and lower Westchester, Anne Hutchinson and four of her children were massacred. Wampage, the Indian responsible for the attack on Mrs. Hutchinson, according to native custom, took the name of his principal victim, thereafter calling himself "Annhook." He even went so far as to give the name Ann to his daughter, the Indian princess who was to marry John Pell's son, Thomas. For the Bayley children this tale bore the stamp of family history. Thomas was their great-grandfather, and did not everyone know that they were the great-grandchildren of an Indian princess?

When Elizabeth found the occasion to question her uncle about the history of the Bayleys, he did not answer her at once, but going to the highboy, he removed a safe-box which he opened with a key attached to his watchfob. He lifted out a flat envelope and handing it to Elizabeth, he remarked, "We may start with this." Fairly holding her breath with excitement, she carefully drew from the envelope a reproduction of a heraldic device in red, blue, and silver. Under it was engraved the legend "Bayley of Hoddesdon, Hertfordshire, 1634."

"How strange," said Elizabeth. "While one side of our family was being persecuted by a French king, the English monarch was honoring the other side with an elevation of rank."

"We Bayleys," said Uncle William, "have not the colorful history of the Le Contes. It looks as though we just lived courageously and served our King well. My father came to America very near the turn of the century, probably about 1690. Some, however, fix the date as late as 1726. I never heard him say much about it except to recall certain kinfolk and friends back in Hoddesdon, a little village in Hertfordshire County, where he was born and where he grew up.

"They were evidently an old and respected family in those parts, for long before they received their coat of arms, the head of the house was always referred to as Esquire."

"What would that be?" asked Elizabeth.

"In Britain, Esquire is the title given to an English gentleman, ranking next below a knight. My father told me about two monuments to our ancestor John Bayley—or Baily—he spelled it both ways—in the church of Hoddesdon. On one of these tablets Baily is referred to as "Gentleman," on the other as "Esquire." Another interesting point about this man, Eliza, was that he had a son Richard and a daughter Elizabeth. So, you see, you and your father are keeping up the family traditions."

"Where did your father go when he came to this country, Uncle?" Elizabeth asked.

"To Fairfield, Connecticut," answered Bayley. "Most of the people there were from Hertfordshire, especially the Pells. My father was a great admirer of Thomas Pell, who treated him like a son and so did his wife, the Princess Ann, after whom our little daughter is named. Your cousin Joseph is named after your Aunt Sarah's father, Joseph Pell."

"And William is named for—guess!" laughed his niece.

"You're wrong, missy," declared her uncle. "I named him after our great ancestor, Guillaume Le Conte. William is a glorious name in our family, my girl."

2

As William Bayley had remarked to his niece, the history of the English half of their family seems commonplace beside the romantic story of the French side, and this is due, in part at least, to the nebulous and meager

information which these Britishers have left us. Most
biographers of Elizabeth Seton have followed the Archbishop Seton manuscript entitled *The Record of the Bayley
Family in America* in which the author emphatically states
that his branch of the family "had no connection with that
founded by one Richard Bayley who came over in the *Bevis*
for New England in 1638." This seems to be a correct position, for all the Bayleys of that line remained in Massachusetts and Rhode Island, whereas the Bayleys of Long
Island and Westchester form a contemporary group with
them, figuring prominently in the development of the last
two mentioned localities.

In the list of emigrants from 1600-1700, we find numerous references to Bayleys who sailed from England
to the New World. There are Richards, Williams, Johns,
Josephs. One William Bayley sailed to the Island of St.
Christopher in the West Indies in 1635. It will be recalled
that Elizabeth's French ancestors, Jacques Lasty and Guillaume Le Conte, also went to this same island after they
had fled from France. The imagination would like to toy
with the suggestion that here might have occurred the first
contacts between a Le Conte and a Bayley.

Establishment of the authenticity of Hertfordshire as
the county seat of Elizabeth's forebears has not been too
difficult. *Hertfordshire Biographies* gives interesting sketches
of several groups of Bayleys, spelled variously Bailey, Bayley, and even Baly. There is mention made of one Stephen
Bailey, a monk in the nearby monastery of St. Albans before
its dissolution in 1538. How interested Elizabeth would have
been in the monk Stephen had she heard about him! Here
was a kindred spirit for this girl who would, in her eighteenth
year, "have many thoughts of running away to such places
overseas in disguise . . . where people could be shut from the
world and pray, and always be good."

An examination of the histories of the Bayleys of Hertfordshire discloses that they were of the upper middle class
of society, probably squires to certain local knights. A

Hugh Bayley was entrusted with the care and upbringing of the Lady Frances Cecil, daughter of Sir Robert Cecil, Earl of Salisbury and Lord High Treasurer of the Realm. This fact would confirm the opinion that the Bayleys were well-born, well-known, and of high repute.

It would seem probable that Elizabeth's branch of the family was closely connected with one John Bayley who arrived in Westchester in 1654, the very year that Thomas Pell, Sr., received his grant of land there. The Pell and Bayley names are coupled in many circumstances of their early history: both came from Hertfordshire; Walter de Pelham held the Lordship of Pelham in Hertfordshire, England, in 1294 under Edward I. His descendant called himself William Pell of Walter (Water) Wellingsly. Archbishop Seton tells us that the elder William Bayley sailed from Lynn Regis. We read in the Pell genealogy that John Pell Esq. (1527-1607) was Lord Mayor of Lynn Regis. Both families arrived in Westchester, in Pelham, almost simultaneously. Finally, a Bayley married a Pell.[a]

Whether we take the stand that this John Bayley, or some other whose identity will never be established, was the first to bring the particular strand of British color to the family loom already set up and partially filled in by the Le Contes, there still remains the long and honorable roster of Bayleys the length and breadth of Westchester, from its earliest days. In 1656, the Dutch Commissioner reported that "at a gathering of 15 men and ten or twelve women, Mr. Baly said the prayer ... as they had as yet no preacher." In 1691, on December 1, among others who appeared at the Court of Sessions as one of the Grand Jury, was John Baly, and in 1693, he was present at a meeting of the trustees of Westchester. A Joseph Bayley was one of the trustees for the building of a townhall in 1700, and in 1701, "Vestryman John Pell and alderman John Bayley

---

[a] Interesting to the reader might be the fact that there is a Hertford Street in New Rochelle not far from the Bayley property.

were chosen." In 1719 this John Bayley died and left to his wife Elizabeth (!) among other properties "all the rest of my lands lying on Throgmorton's Neck."

Whichever one of these plausible possibilities may be chosen, it cannot be, in any case, too remote from the truth, for it seems incontrovertible that many, if not all the West-chester Bayleys (or Baileys) were inter-related. The County records abound in Bayleys: in Somers, North Castle, Peeks-kill, Salem, Pelham, Rye, and New Rochelle. In many of these branches certain names appear again and again, as if they were being cherished for sentimental reasons: Cather-ine, Rebecca, Susanna, William, Richard, Ann, Sarah, John, and Joseph. It is provocative to note that there was an Ann Eliza in the family of Theodorus Bailey of Peekskill. It would indeed be a strange coincidence to find so many families of long residence in the same area, bearing the same names, without having at least a modicum of common background.

It is safe to assume, therefore, that, though the prem-ises on which the case for Elizabeth Bayley's British an-cestors rests may not have been indisputably established, the Bayleys of New Rochelle were in close connection with at least one branch of those mentioned in the early history of Westchester, and many of its members have contributed in service and prestige to the growth of that community.

One other fact can be settled beyond question. The Bayleys that were to weave in the first English threads on the loom of Elizabeth's background were closely associated with the town of Fairfield, Connecticut. There her father was born in 1744.

VII

The Doctor

1

FAIRFIELD IS A VENERABLE OLD TOWN, dignified by its historic background and the quiet beauty of extensive lawns and spreading shade trees. Settled by English colonists in 1639, it is rich in the traditions of colonial days and retains even yet much of the quaint flavor of the seventeenth century.

This town was directly opposite Southold on the Long Island shore, the most frequent point of disembarkation for British arrivals prior to the Revolution. An hour or two by sailboat across the Sound in either direction would bring the newcomers to any one of a dozen or more thriving settlements, where, in all probability, the immigrants would be welcomed by relatives already established in the New World. So it had been with the foundation of Fairfield, which received vitality and growth from the constant stream of Britishers seeking their fortunes in a new way of life. In 1779, during the Revolutionary War—that strange anomaly of brother against brother—Tory and Hessian troops burned the town as a punitive measure for the boldness of its inhabitants in resisting English tyranny. The town hall in Fairfield, remodeled from the old county court house, bears the following inscription:

Built A.D. 1720: Destroyed by the British A.D. 1779: Rebuilt A.D. 1794; Remodeled A.D. 1870.

But in 1726 (if we accept Archbishop Seton's date) when William Bayley Senior, arrived there, it was a peaceful village resembling in many ways the more rural shires of his native England. It would be a likely destination for a traveler from Hertfordshire since here he would be among his countrymen. This entire area was strongly Hertford (pronounced Harford). In 1636, two Protestant clergymen, Rev. Samuel Stone and Rev. Thomas Hooker, established a colony in Connecticut which was called after Hertfordshire, the birthplace of Rev. Stone, on the River Lea, England.

A strong representation of "County" men had been early established at Fairfield by such adventurers as Thomas Pell and his nephew John, who later married Rachel Pinckney of Eastchester. These pioneers had died before Bayley's coming, but John's son Thomas, with his Indian wife Ann Hooke and their eleven children still made their home there. Shortly after this date, the Pells took up permanent residence on their Westchester estate of Pelham Manor.

Owing to the close relationship existing between Westchester and Connecticut, and, as has been pointed out, between the Pells and William Bayley, the latter would feel free to visit the homes of these friends in both places. Bayley was a mere youth when he came to America, probably seventeen or eighteen, just the age in those days for "going abroad." In this young man's life the finger of Providence in furthering the Divine plans is markedly evident. Intrigued, we view the progress of the English lad from his home in Hertfordshire to a colonial settlement in Connecticut, and his subsequent arrival in New Rochelle, apparently the result of a friend's change of residence. But there are no accidents in the designs of God and, though unwittingly, William Bayley was going forward to his future destiny, the founder of a family line.

Thomas Pell's home became the social center for the leading names in Westchester, and Bayley, with other Fairfield friends, was often in attendance. In one of the balls given by his friend, William met Susanna Le Conte, in what may well have been her first appearance as a belle of society. It can be said that Bayley, now in his thirty-fourth year, and a man who seems to have cherished his bachelorhood during the seventeen years since his arrival, was swept off his feet by the vivacious French beauty of Mademoiselle Le Conte. Within a short time they were married, in 1742/43. It is with this union that a new chapter in the Le Conte history is opened. From this point on the Bayley pattern prevails.

William took his seventeen-year-old bride to Fairfield where, in 1744, their son Richard was born. Sometime between this date and August, 1745, the couple returned to New Rochelle for the birth of a second son William, who, as we have seen, was baptized in Trinity Church. It appears from the town records that the Bayleys remained in New Rochelle after this event. William Sr. owned an extensive farm on the borders of Yonkers and Eastchester, in an area still known as Mile Square. Susanna, as William Le Conte's daughter, had, no doubt, received a rich land legacy for her marriage dowry.

2

So it was in New Rochelle that Richard Bayley and his brother William grew up. Here they climbed trees and jumped fences, roamed the fields, and assuredly, swam in the Sound. As small boys they did all the things that their grandfather Le Conte used to do over on Bonnefoy Neck. Being so nearly of an age, the brothers were boon companions, and owing to the diversity of their temperaments, complemented each other very well. Together they flew their kites, performed the chores around the farm, and visited their cousins. We do not know of any Bayley relatives at this period, but on their mother's side there were aunts, uncles, and cousins all over the town. There was Aunt Ann, the maiden aunt whom all the younger people loved for her generosity to them and for her gay, sprightly manner. Great-Aunt Hester Bonyot, grandpere's sister, made the most delicious spice cakes in the county. She used to tease William and Richard saying that "Bayleys they might be, but they had the Le Conte trick of always turning up when something good was on hand." There were Merciers and Coutants of almost every age and degree of relationship. No kin of the Le Contes could lack playmates.

Their father, with true English love for the hunt, early taught his sons how to handle a shotgun, how to bring down a partridge, how to track a bear. When they were older, Grandpere Le Conte occasionally allowed them to use the blunderbuss that his own father had left him. This grandfather's natural disappointment in not having sons of his own to perpetuate his name and family, he had borne chivalrously, proud in being father of the three most beautiful and eligible girls in New Rochelle. But Susanna's sons, as the first grandchildren, tyrannized over him, while dogging his every footstep. They would walk into the village where Le Conte still managed the tavern, and squatting in the shade outside the door, would wait until their grandfather was free to join them. There he would entertain them by the half-hour with the mechanism of his enormous gold watch, which he wound with a key. His father's initials, fortunately the same as his own, were engraved upon the case with a tiny reproduction of La Rochelle Tower painted in blue under the figure twelve. Or they would arrive at his home with a trapped muskrat which he would be expected to remove and skin for them. They might browse around his room, examining this, asking about that, but they were never allowed to touch the great sword of the first Guillaume Le Conte that hung against a piece of red velvet in a position of honor over the fireplace. Grandpere said he did not think it right that anyone should use for trifling purposes a weapon already hallowed by so many deeds of valor.

From their grandfather the boys heard the thrilling story

of the Huguenots' escape from La Rochelle and other cities
of France. They knew well the narrative of their great-
grandfather's flight from the shores of Normandy and his
second flight from the West Indies. They listened spell-
bound as grandpere described for them, just as he had received the account from his own father, the terrors that
reigned in France during those dreadful days of persecution.
He repeated his father's descriptions of those far-off cities
with their thick walls and fortified castles, their hustling
market places and soaring cathedrals. To these boys, living
in an open, friendly country, beside deep cool woods and
clear streams, where no high walls shut out the stars at night,
nor obstructed a wide sweep of the blue skies in the daytime,
these stories must have sounded like fantasies.

By the time the Bayleys were nine or ten years of age,
bilingual homes had become a common-place. As Britain
gained more and more control over the colonies, French was
rapidly replaced by English. From their Huguenot mother
the boys learned Norman French which they would have to
know in order to converse with some of the older relatives.
Their English father tutored them in the refinements of his
own language. Formal education was provided in a limited
way by the school maintained by Rev. Pierre Stouppe, minister at Trinity Church, who also kept a boarding school in
the parsonage. Here boys of more well-to-do families were
taught Latin, French, and some other subjects. By 1745
New Rochelle was probably the only place in the English
colonies where French was still spoken, and wealthy parents
sent their sons here to learn the language in its most cultured form. Peter Schuyler, later to be one of the great
generals of the Continental Army, came from Albany in
1748 to attend Mr. Stouppe's classes. Josephus Bleecker, son
of a mayor of Albany, also came and remained to become
one of the town's leading citizens. In 1753, John Jay, aged
eight, arrived from New York City to stay for three years
in the minister's school, receiving from the lips of this
simple but cultured gentleman, the first steps in the train-

ing that would fit him to become the first Chief Justice of
the United States. Later, as Ambassador to France, he used
the French learned in the New Rochelle schoolroom to
negotiate the Treaty of Paris. Richard and William were in
good company in Mr. Stouppe's school, and years after,
Richard's name would also be included in the list of great
Americans, his contributions being in the field of medicine.
Dr. James Thacher, who wrote a memoir of Dr. Bayley in
1828, tells us that he had "an acquaintance with the Latin
classics which the constant pre-occupation of his after-life
prevented him from renewing or continuing...."

The day came, when Richard was fourteen and William
thirteen years old, on which Grandpere Le Conte died. For
both boys it was a grievous loss. After his affairs had been
settled, they received a note from Aunt Ann Le Conte asking them to come to the tavern on the following afternoon.
Mystified, but delighted to see their aunt, the boys arrived
on time. Ann received them solemnly, asking them to sit
down in the front room for a moment. Uneasily the boys
awaited her return from the next room—Grandpere's old
room. When she re-entered the parlor, she was carrying in
one hand their grandfather's watch, in the other, the blunderbuss. Over her arm were thrown several waistcoats,
breeches, and silk hose. Then going to the fireplace, she
lifted the great sword from its hooks, taking it down lovingly, and placing it beside the other objects on the table.
To the boys, now speechless and troubled at this unwonted
action, she said: "My father wanted you boys to have these
things he valued so much. He made special mention of you
in his will. I shall send them over to you this evening by
black Samuel, but I did want you to receive them personally
as his legacy. I shall not designate which of you is to receive
each definite thing; that disposition may be made in its own
good time."

And so it was. Circumstance of education and professional need gave Richard the watch; William kept the blunderbuss—and the sword. And though he was a Bayley, his

grandsire and great-grandsire would rest contented to see them still in the hands of another William Le Conte.

When the boys were in their late teens, their father died after a comparatively brief sixteen years of married life. The widowed mother kept the home together for four years; then in 1762, Susanna still young and beautiful, married John Guerineau, a carpenter, whose people had been among the early settlers in New Rochelle. We do not know how this marriage affected the lives of the two brothers, but there was little now to bind them to their home. When, shortly after her second marriage, Mme. Guerineau and her husband moved to the farm at Mile Square, which by legacy now belonged to Richard, the boys did not accompany her. Both had passed into young manhood and were capable of conducting their lives along lines of their own choosing.

3

Richard Bayley was twenty-one when he left New Rochelle to seek his future in New York City. A brilliant, ambitious young man, he was also filled with a nervous energy that would have its outlet in responding to his high calling to the medical profession. Through friends and family connections, he had been recommended to the famous Dr. John Charlton, physician to the socially elite of New York City, as a promising understudy and assistant in his practice. Young Bayley went directly to Staten Island to his mother's cousins, Pierre Le Conte's children, who introduced him to Dr. Charlton at the latter's home in the Richmond area of the Island.

The Charltons were descended from a family of distinction in Ireland. They came to New York by way of England where Richard Charlton was ordained for the Episcopal ministry. Shortly thereafter he was sent to the Leeward Islands, and then stationed as a missionary of the Ven-

erable Society for the Propagation of the Faith at New
Windsor. From 1732 to 1746 he was a Catechist at Trinity
Church in New York City. In 1747, in his forty-second
year, he was called to the rectorship of St. Andrew Episcopal
Church in Richmond, Staten Island. During the thirty years
of his incumbency, this church prospered in various ways.
He expanded the size of the building to 40' x 80' and erected
a steeple. He began the keeping of records, the earliest extant for this parish. His missionary zeal carried on the work
of evangelization with increasing numbers of conversions.

To this distinguished English grandfather may be traced
several of Elizabeth's most salient characteristics, her interest
in erecting and improving the foundations of her Institute
being not the least of these. But the strongest bond between
this revered minister and his foundress granddaughter was
their love for the poor and a desire to teach them. Perhaps
on this point Elizabeth Bayley comes closer to Richard
Charlton than to any other member of her family.

Dr. Charlton was particularly noted for his interest in
the Negro slaves whom he gathered together for instruction
after divine services. Nor did he believe in segregating these
unfortunate members of his fold. According to the statement of his curate, Rev. William Harrison, Dr. Charlton
"found it most convenient to throw into one the classes of
his white and black Catechumens." Even when himself a
curate at Trinity Church, Charlton had shown his deep interest for this work by taking over the Negro mission previously established there in 1704 by one Elias Neare, an
elder of the French Church. He became personally interested
in a Negro child known as Bill Richmond. This boy, but
fourteen years of age at the time of his patron's death, later
became a famous prize-fighter in England.

The charitable work now done under the auspices of the
Department of Public Works appears from the records to
have come under the supervision of this generous clergyman.
During the Revolution, while he remained loyal to the King
and served as chaplain to Lieutenant-Colonel Billop's bat-

talion of Staten Island Loyalists, he had the distress of several times seeing his churchyard overrun by British troops and the edifice itself fired on by the Continental Army.

Dr. Charlton continued to minister to his flock until a few months before his death, the last baptism he performed being recorded for February 25, 1777. He died October 7, of that same year. The Bible he used has been preserved and may be seen in the Public Museum. His obituary notice in the daily paper paid him a glowing tribute, describing him as "sincere and steady in friendship; charitable to the distressed, hospitable to *all*, deservedly esteemed and respected."

Rev. Charlton's son, John, a short, stout, florid gentleman well known by sight to all New Yorkers, had studied medicine in England, and had been a prominent surgeon at the Court of George III before he returned to America with the British Army of Occupation. He married Mary De Peyster, daughter of the wealthy Abraham De Peyster, onetime mayor of the city.

Historians tell us that Dr. Charlton and his young assistant were rivals with Dr. McKnight, a professor of anatomy at Columbia College, for the moneyed clientele of New York. The former were the first physicians to ride to visit their patients. This would mean, of course, to use a carriage. Dr. James J. Walsh gives us a colorful picture of physicians of pre-Revolutionary days:

> Physicians making their rounds might wear a scarlet cloak, a three-cornered hat, a blue velvet coat with gold buttons, buff vest, lace ruffled shirt, knee breeches, colored stockings, silver shoe buckles, a wig and queue tied by black ribbon.

On January 9, 1769, in his twenty-fifth year, Richard Bayley married his mentor's sister Catherine Charlton. The ceremony was performed in St. John's Episcopal Church, Elizabethtown, New Jersey, by the well-known Loyalist minister Dr. Charles B. Chandler. The record of this marriage includes the information "both of Staten Island."

This early connection of Dr. Bayley with Staten Island is interesting in the light of the great work he was to do there some day as Health Inspector of the Port of New York. It would also affect the first years of Elizabeth Bayley's married life when she and her children spent their summers in Tompkinsville at her father's cottage, from the upper porch of which she might look out to sea "fifty miles beyond the Hook."

In that same year of his marriage, Dr. Charlton sent Bayley to England to study anatomy under the renowned Dr. William Hunter. This trip covered the first two years of his married life. He returned to a lonesome wife and a year-old daughter, Mary Magdalen, named for her mother's sister, Mary Magdalen Charlton, who had married Walter Dongan, grandnephew of Thomas Dongan, the former Catholic Governor of New York State.

In this episode Richard Bayley must have had to make a choice to which he seems to have adhered throughout his life—his first love would ever be his profession. Family affections and home ties would yield to what he must have felt was a higher calling. He made his profession the center and motivating force of every decision. In this regard he may have been over-zealous, especially in the more personal concerns of family life, as subsequent events will show. But whatever else he may have neglected, he never failed in a call to duty, particularly where the poor or plague-stricken were concerned. In this regard he deviated from the practice cultivated by Dr. Charlton, known to his contemporaries as the "society physician." Bayley devoted a great deal of his time to the care of the ailing poor. "No risk was too much for him to take in his professional capacity."

He was, moreover, a natural-born doctor. When only a student under Dr. Hunter, he won that great man's praise. In a letter to his wife, Richard wrote that Hunter had commended him for his "uncommon dexterity with the knife." As early as 1774, when Bayley was barely thirty, he set forth a new theory on the causes of croup and its deadliness:

"Death is not caused by suffocation but by a circulatory disturbance."

For a little less than four years, he practiced with Dr. Charlton, but shortly after the birth of his second daughter, Elizabeth Ann, he returned to England for another year, 1775-1776, to further his knowledge of the treatment of croup. At the time of his departure for London, the hard feelings that had been growing between the Mother Country and her colonies appeared to be coming to a head, but it was generally agreed by most Loyalists that the trouble would soon blow over. When this supposition, certainly a most shallow and short-lived one, proved false, Dr. Bayley returned on a British man-of-war as staff surgeon to Lord Howe. This was a very natural decision for him to make. As the son of an English squire, the student of an English doctor, in view of his close contacts with the Mother Country, and with most of the members of his social class siding with England in the struggle, he cannot be impeached for disloyalty. In a letter of General Hazen to General Schuyler, both Rebel leaders, the former remarked:

> With respect to the better set of people, both English and French, seven-eighths are tories, who would see our throats cut and perhaps would readily assist in doing it.

It should be noted here that after the Revolution Bayley declared himself an American citizen and proved that he meant it.

Dr. Bayley's skill was put to good use for the British army. In 1776, a note issued from "Ward's House, British Headquarters near the Brunx [sic] 27th Oct." gave this recommendation:

> Mr. Bailey, Surgeon's Mate in the Hospital, to do duty with the Brigade of Guards till their own Surgeon joins.

and again in March of that year:

General Sir William Howe's orders—62nd Regiment—Lieut.
Richard Baily [sic] of 23rd Regiment to be Captain.

A third promotion followed, but the rank was not designated in the dispatch. At the time of his service under Lord
Howe at Newport, Bayley was able to convince the inter-
nationally famous Hessian surgeon Michaelis, already an un-
disputed authority on croup, to such an extent that the
distinguished doctor adopted the "opinions and practices of
a young American physician, the unknown Bayley."

Dr. Thacher, his official biographer who knew Dr. Bayley personally, gives an interesting sidelight on his reason
for joining Lord Howe's staff—"a step of necessity rather
than of inclination . . . for like genius in every clime, Bailey
was poor; and the necessity of a lovely wife and beloved children will often dictate a course which sober reason might not
approve." A bitter outcome of his decision to take service
with Lord Howe was the refusal of the British headquarters
to pay him for any of his work . . . though "he had min-
istered to five or six thousand troop at Newport" . . . because an army regulation forbade payment for any period
of time less than a full term. Dr. Bayley was asking for
retirement before that date that he might return to New
York to care for his sick wife. So irritated was he by the
situation, and so worried about home matters, that he gave
up his commission. However, the one thing he derived from
his army career was the affection and esteem of his fellow
officers, and the high regard in which he was held by all the
citizens, even those who did not agree with his political
affiliations.

4

The Bayley brothers seem to have been basically different in their temperaments and way of life. Richard ob-

viously inherited predominantly French traits: the bold,
venturing, derring-do spirit of his great-grandfather, Guillaume Le Conte; the impetuous quick-tempered disposition
of his mother's people together with a certain French
restlessness of mind—a quality which was to take him across
the ocean three times in search of knowledge and also carry
him far ahead of his contemporaries in medical research.
His life and letters give evidence of independence of thought,
the true key to his work as a pioneer in his profession, and
to his bent as a free-thinker.

It may be presumed that Richard and William had been
brought up in an atmosphere of staunch Protestantism.
Everything in early New Rochelle life and history centered
in the Church. Bayley's lack of religious belief, or even of
interest, removed as he was only two generations from ancestors who endured persecution and exile rather than
change their tenets, is strange and could scarcely be accounted for in any way save for the agnostic influence which
the study of medicine makes upon the minds of certain
people.

Dr. Bayley's impetuous and fiery temper may be listed
as the more immediate cause of his contracting yellow fever
in 1801. He had left orders that the crew and passengers
from a contaminated vessel just arrived in the harbor be at
once removed from the ship to Quarantine, leaving their
baggage on board until fumigated. In the morning, when
he went to inspect the cases, he was chagrined to find that
his orders had been disobeyed; the crew and passengers—
with their baggage—were huddled together in one apartment
where they had passed the night. Bayley rushed into the
chamber, forgetting his mask, and although he remained
but a moment, it was sufficient time for the germ to strike
its lethal blow. He died seven days later, in his fifty-sixth
year, ending abruptly a life of extreme usefulness and
charity.

Dr. Richard Bayley was a great man, exhibiting in the
achievements of his profession the intelligence and moral

fiber of both his French and English forebears. He was one
of the promoters of the New York Dispensary. In his capacity as Health Physician to the port of New York, he was
chiefly responsible for the adoption of the State Quarantine
Laws. He it was who advocated a place of quarantine at a
distance from the city or port of entry where suspected
vessels could be inspected. Dr. Bayley was the first surgeon
in this country to amputate the arm at the shoulder. Besides
being an active member of the Medical Society of the State
of New York, he served with Dr. Bard, Dr. Charlton, and
others on several important commissions. In the Minutes of
the New York State Medical Society of 1794 we read:

> A number of medical gentlemen, wishing to associate for
> the purpose of promoting friendly professional intercourse,
> determined to meet at the City Hall in the evening of
> November 14, 1794, where there appeared (among others)
> Drs. John Charlton ... Samuel Bard ... Richard Bayley ...
> Wright Post. .... Dr. Charlton was appointed chairman.

A similar entry for the following year refers to a letter from
the Governor of the State to the members of the Medical
Society "on the subject of the present alarm in consequence
of the disease in the upper part of the City." As a result of
his appeal, we are told that a committee including Dr. Bard
and Dr. Bayley was appointed to answer the Governor's
letter.

In 1796, Drs. Bayley, Post, and Tillary

> ... recommended suitable provision against further
> epidemics and at a meeting in that same year these three
> were appointed as a committee to protect the city against
> infectious diseases.

Dr. Wright Post, Mary Bayley's husband, had been Dr.
Bayley's understudy for several years. He was, by the time
he took part in the above-mentioned activities, rapidly approaching the peak of his professional career and was the

constant companion of his father-in-law for whom he felt a son's devotion and admiration. He was also, with Dr. Bayley, an instructor at Columbia College where his tall handsome person, his grave and dignified manner and his "luminous and perspicacious teaching" aroused the devotion and enthusiasm of his pupils.

Dr. Bayley had also delivered lectures on anatomy at King's College, later Columbia (University) College, and had been on the attending staff of New York Hospital for thirteen years. According to Thacher, he was "startlingly modern-minded in his conception of infection and contagion," and he was a pioneer in ophthalmic and general surgery, croup, and yellow fever. This same biographer has left the following thumbnail-sketch of his fellow practitioner:

> ...he expired leaving behind him a high character as a clinically instructed physician, an excellent bold operator, a prompt practitioner of rapid diagnosis and unhesitating decision.
>
> In demeanor a perfect gentleman; honest and chivalrously honorable; of perfect integrity, and therefore, little tolerant of obliquity in others: ever ready to serve the cause of his profession; inflexible in his attachments; invincible in his dislikes and unbrooking of insult; in temper, fiery yet suddenly cool, a fault which he knew and regretted; thoroughly fearless, somewhat too strongly partial to certain patients, but withal charitable to a fault.

Dr. Arthur Jacobson, at one time editor-in-chief of the *Medical Times*, wrote to Sister Aurea, of the Mother Seton Guild, St. Joseph's, Emmitsburg, in 1939:

> I think that an understanding of Bayley has a bearing upon the career of Elizabeth Ann Bayley Seton, since there are obvious character traits that are similar in the two personages.

Indeed, these traits shared by father and daughter are striking. One is impressed by their common spirit of courage in facing the new, in making courageous "and bold" decisions. The keenness of intellect that enabled the parent to make a rapid diagnosis served his daughter in a like capacity in her relations with others and in the manifold problems that beset her every step in later life. The refinement and culture of Dr. Bayley became the adornment of all his children; his uprightness and readiness to work hard at his professional duties also characterized his favorite daughter. Even her father's fiery temper Elizabeth claimed as her birthright, though she appears to have been more successful than he in restraining it. His concern for the troubles of humanity became her shining virtue, softened and spiritualized by her conversion to Catholicity. One characteristic of her father Elizabeth did not inherit: his harshness and intolerance with the mistakes of others or with those who may have offended him. Elizabeth felt only pity and sympathy for the erring, love for the sinner, pardon and understanding for her critics.

Elizabeth has left us an affectionate and reverent testimony to her father's noble character:

> ... to all these sufferers and almost countless numbers that came in several vessels—my Father was a Father—in offices of humanity he never wearied, every rising sun found him already 2 and 3 hours engaged in them—and except for the indulgence of an hour's rest by the side of my Piano—his labors were unceasing.

Dr. Richard Bayley, in his position midway between distinguished ancestors and his daughter, now so universally known and loved, was worthy of them both. In the words of his ardent admirer Dr. Thacher:

> ... his name must not be lost from the records of American physicians and surgeons, when his practice did so much at so early a period to bring their profession honorably before foreigners . . .

VIII

The Merchant

1

DR. RICHARD BAYLEY CONSULTED his large gold watch, the family heirloom he so highly prized, and decided that he had a few minutes to spare before reporting back to Dr. Charlton on the cases he had visited during the course of the afternoon. These few minutes would give him the long-denied opportunity of dropping in on his brother William at the latter's store on Beaver Street. Richard and William had not seen much of each other through the years, though the old bonds of affection were as strong as ever.

Both Bayleys had done well in fulfilling the high promise of their inherited, as well as their personal, talents. Richard had achieved medical fame in New York City and had benefited by two years of study in England. He was now, in the fall of 1774, the father of two little girls, his second child, Elizabeth Ann, being but three months old. William was a successful merchant and an influential citizen.

Bayley stopped his carriage before his brother's establishment, noting with approval the enlarged accommodations of the building that had formerly housed Parker's Printing Office. Though he had occasionally been to the store's former location opposite the Coffee House Bridge, this was the first time that the doctor had seen this new place. He looked around with interest. Neat arrangements of every variety of household goods met his eye: japanned ware, tea urns, and trinkets. He scarcely had time to take all these in with one sweeping glance before William emerged from the rear of the store. The brothers greeted each other warmly and for some moments discussed family matters. While they were so engaged, a wagon drove up before the shop. William's two blacks jumped down from the high seat of the carry-all, one of them approaching the brothers respectfully to report that they had obtained the shipment from Captain Lawrence. At once William was all eagerness and business. As the men unloaded the goods, he explained to Richard that he was lucky indeed to get these things from England in such good time, for with warclouds looming, shipping was certain to be the first area to suffer. "Importing has its risks as well as its returns," he assured his brother. Richard, however, was of a different mind—more inclined to brush off the bitter clashes that marked the recent relations between the colonies and the Mother Country.

"In fact," he remarked earnestly, "I am considering another visit to England early after the turn of the year. I have completed a paper on the causes of croup, and if I can get Dr. Hunter to support it, I may be fortunate enough to have it printed in one of their medical journals."

William showed some surprise at the announcement of the proposed trip, but he knew how useless it would be to argue with his elder brother. If Richard had come to tell him about it, then his plans were already well laid. It was now November. The Doctor would probably leave in February—good sailing time. With a shrug, William abruptly turned to pick up a highly ornamented steel collar, so much in vogue among stylish young women of the period.

"My compliments to your wife, Dick," he remarked genially, handing the neckpiece to him. "Tell Catherine that she will be the first lady in New York to own one of these."

Richard was looking at some beautiful French plate.

"Some day I may be able to buy a set like that," he sighed. "Just now it's pinch and squeeze every penny." Then as he turned to go, "If you see Jim Barclay, Will, ask him to send up to the house several jugs of his West India rum, and some molasses. Dr. Charlton always stocks up on the rum against winter colds. My wife will be glad to get the molasses, and-er-the necklace."

That evening William told his wife about the visit and of his brother's desire to return to England. Sarah was silent at first. Then she remarked pityingly: "I am glad you sent her the necklace, Will; the poor thing will not get much for herself *this* winter."

2

Rarely had a more disparate pair of brothers set out together to meet the world than Richard and his brother William Bayley on that day in 1762 when they had turned eager faces toward New York City, the Mecca of the American colonist.

There was in William's nature a curious combination of Le Conte and Bayley traits which would develop in him a twofold vocation in life—the city merchant and the country squire. Unlike his grandfather and great-grandfather, he would not engage in these occupations simultaneously. In point of fact, on that very morning he was turning his back on the farmer's life to struggle for success in the mercantile world.

Young Bayley needed but to mention his whole name, William Le Conte Bayley, to have doors opened to him and helping hands extended to the descendant of a man whose reputation was still highly regarded among the city leaders. Judged by his later success, William evinced the same shrewdness and business ability that marked the affairs of three generations of ancestors, so that before too long, he was arranging for his own establishment, and setting himself up in rivalry to the already prosperous hardware dealer, James McBride.

On May 1, 1773, just eleven years after his arrival in
the city, Bayley was able to move his business from the
Coffee House Bridge location to better quarters on Beaver
Street. About this time, he also opened another store in the
Fly Market "at the house of the Widow Tucker." From
this time on, his advertisements appeared regularly in *Rivington's Gazeteer* and the *New York Gazette and Weekly
Mercury*. Bayley was what might be called today an "im-
porter" in hardware and a general line of smaller objects.
Widely assorted stock seems to have been the usual practice
of that day. Similar shops were kept by John J. Roosevelt
around the corner on Maiden Lane. The firm of Jay and
Barclay sold West India rum and molasses, coffee, snuff, and
grindstones "at their store on Hunter's Quay, opposite
Messrs. Curson and Seaton" who advertised Indian blankets,
pig iron, candles, and Port wines.

William Bayley was an astute business man. Beaver
Street, where he set up his new store was, prior to the Revolution, a populous and thriving thoroughfare; Fly Market
was a public square where most of the citizenry of New York
did their shopping. He was alert to new products on the
market, and through his agents in London, received ship-
ments promptly and regularly. His advertisements invariably
contained some such phrase as "of the newest fashion now
used in London." All these considerations point to his obvious prominence in the mercantile world of his city, and
his probable financial security—no small achievement for a
man of twenty-eight!

Young Bayley was extremely busy during these years,
for not only was he making his name in his chosen work, but
he was courting a childhood playmate of New Rochelle. In
this, too, he was successful. On June 10, 1771, in his twenty-
sixth year, he had married Sarah Pell, daughter of Joseph
and Phoebe Pell, and granddaughter of the Indian Princess
Ann Hooke. Apparently, he took up residence in New York.
How pleased his father would have been to see this union
between the Bayleys and the Pells!

From time to time business demands gave way to those of social life, for a man in William's position would receive many invitations to functions of one kind or another. Both Pells and Bayleys were on the society roster of their day. The young people with whom they had grown up in New Rochelle were also marrying, giving balls, and visiting their city friends. One such gala affair which the Bayleys attended was the wedding of Sarah's cousin, Theodosia Bartow, to the handsome, clever Captain Aaron Burr. This couple's daughter, another Theodosia, became the childhood playmate and life-long friend of William's youngest daughter Anne Bayley. Perhaps the finest and most talked about social event of the year 1773 was the marriage of Frederick Jay and Ann Margaret Barclay, daughter of Andrew Barclay, a well-to-do merchant of Wall Street.

An extremely popular form of relaxation for the gentry was attendance at the Theater in John Street and at the Theater Royal in Drury Lane. Playbills of the day testify to the high type of drama demanded by these early New Yorkers. There were presentations of many Shakespearean favorites: *Catharine and Petruchio, Hamlet, Prince of Denmark, The Tempest,* and *The Merchant of Venice.* Also included in the repertoire of a season's showings were Milton's *Masque* and the comedy *She Stoops to Conquer,* Goldsmith's latest production. William and Sarah, thoroughly British in their love for a good play, often attended these performances in which Major Andre, Capt. De Lancey, and other British officers sometimes took leading roles at the John Street Theater.

No doubt the Bayleys also bought the "best sellers" of that time: *The Tatler,* Thompson's *Seasons, The Rambler,* Capt. Cook's "new and authentic *Journal of a Voyage Round the World."* Our modern pocket editions are not so modern as we think. In 1773, the printer Rivington advertised *"Gentlemen and Lady's Pocket Almanack,* necessary to everyone, in and out of Business, and useful in every Colony upon the continent."

By 1774 Bayley seems to have gone in heavily for iron ware, especially stove grates and screens of ornate designs. The enterprising William advertised these grates by a line-cut in the *New York Gazette and Weekly Mercury*, an example of the very few illustrated advertisements carried in the newspapers of those days. From this line of goods, his Beaver Street store became known as the Stove-Grate Ware-house. He also carried a variety of portable printing presses, tool chests, paper hangings, toys and trinkets. One such advertisement closed with the succinct summary ". . . a number of other articles too tedious to mention." As a sort of after-thought, he adds, "Ready money for bees-wax and old brass."

3

During the years preceding the outbreak of the Revolution, business men of the status of William Bayley searched their consciences in an effort to determine which side of the struggle they should espouse. Decisions were for them doubly difficult, embodying not only the peace and future of the country, but also their own individual fortunes. As they read their newspapers, they sensed the growing ridicule and public feeling expressed by both camps. *Rivington's Gazeteer,* a Rebel paper, carried frequent diatribes in doggerel against the Tories. The following appeared in the January 5, 1775 issue:

> On Calvert's plains new faction reigns
> Great Britain—we defy, Sir;
> True liberty—lies gag'd in chains
> Tho' freedom is the cry, Sir:
> The Congress, and their factious tools,
> Most wantonly oppress us,
> Hypocrisy triumphant rules.
> And sorely does distress us.

On April 13, 1775, the following pair of political advertisements were printed side by side in the same paper.

In the Press and Speedily will be published	In the Press and Speedily will be published
The Republican Dissected: or the ANATOMY OF AN AMERICAN WHIG in answer to the Farmer Refuted written by A. W. Farmer	A REPLY To an address to the author of a CANDID EXAMINATION of the MUTUAL CLAIMS of Great Britain and the colonies

Pamphlets were distributed by either party bearing such
titles as: "What think you of the Congress Now?" or "The
Friendly Address to all reasonable Americans on our present
political confusion." Several papers printed the almost complete text of Edmund Burke's *Speech on Conciliation* as well
as the debates in the House of Commons on the rights of
taxation, quartering of soldiers, and other problems that
vexed England in her dealings with the growing rebellion
in America. Even daily business matters were geared to the
political disturbances springing up everywhere. Charles
Bruff, who had hitherto advertised gentlemen's dress suits,
published this:

> Those gentlemen who are joining themselves into Com-
> panies, in Defense of their LIBERTIES and others, that
> are not provided with
>   SWORDS
>   may be suited therewith by applying to
>   Charles Oliver Bruff

Which side of the affair William Bayley decided to
favor is uncertain, but there are evidences of Tory leanings.
He is listed with others "who for one reason or another"

signed a petition addressed to General Lord Howe, October 18, 1776—"to restore the colonies to the peaceful protection of His Majesty." An interesting sidelight on this item is the concurrence of the date of this petition with that of the death of William's great-grandaunt, Catherine Bonnefoy Coutant, with whose solemn funeral rites, the landing of Lord Howe in Pelham so sadly interfered.[a] It is not likely that there was any connection between these two incidents, so widely separated in place, but it does serve to point up the twofold effects of war on one family.

Again, at the close of the War, William is given as a claimant for damage to property by the American Army. This would refer to both his New York home and business assets, and his property in New Rochelle which probably suffered depredations during the fighting in Pelham between Lord Howe's forces and the Continental Army.

In November of 1774, a most startling announcement appeared in the *New York Gazette and Weekly Mercury* to the effect that

William Bayley

intends to remove from his store in Beaver Street, New York, to his store in Newport, Rhode Island, early next spring. . . .

He put his stock up for sale at "prime cost for cash." The advertisement was repeated in three subsequent issues of the paper, and then—silence. But "in the spring"—in April, 1775—Bayley gives this account of himself in the same daily:

William Bayley

is removed from his house in Beaver Street, into the house where Messrs. Mercer and Schenck formerly lived, in Hanover Square. . . .

Whatever the reason for his initial decision to close

---

[a] See Chapter 1, p. 21.

out his New York business, and the subsequent reversal of that decision, we at least have learned through his announcement, of his store in Newport. It will be remembered that the battles of Lexington and Concord took place in April, 1775. It may well be that William considered Newport too near the scenes of warfare, little suspecting at that date that within the year New York City would itself be the center of hostilities. That Bayley's business was still prosperous at this time is certain from the location of his new quarters. Hanover Square was the center of retail trade from 1757 on. Various well-known dealers had their shops there, notably Gains, the printer, and the Bank of New York, of which William Seton Sr., was a director while the younger Seton was the cashier.

4

The record of the Bayleys as public-spirited citizens compares favorably with that of the Le Contes. Certainly Dr. Richard Bayley might well claim to have been the most energetic of New York City citizens during the plague years, when, according to Elizabeth's account, his family scarcely saw him, his days being spent without rest or food, ministering to the needs of the stricken. William's career, on the other hand, was not by its nature spectacular, nor does he himself give evidence of any taste for the dramatic or exciting. He was a steady, quiet and earnest merchant, yet he was not lacking in spirit or goodwill.

William's first recorded decision to join himself to a civic group occurred in 1770 when he was admitted as a charter member into the newly established Marine Society of the City of New York, "a guild of seamen whose only object was charity." Membership was of two types. The first group consisted of those who like young Bayley, admitted under the heading "Not Masters of Vessels" were gratuitously called "Captain," a privilege which William made use of in later years. The second group was classified as admitted "with vessels." A member of the last-named type, whose date of admission coincides with that of William, was his famous cousin, Catherine Bonnefoy's grandson, William Mercier, soon to distinguish himself in the naval history of the Revolutionary War.[b]

Among the earliest subscribers to this philanthropic organization, Bayley was soon to find himself in excellent company, and perhaps the measure of his business and social success may be judged in the reflection of the Society's roster: Thomas Barclay, British consul for New York; Frederick Jay; Stephen, Oliver, and James De Lancey, wealthy Huguenot leaders—to mention just a few. Some years later, honorary membership would be granted to Chief Justice John Jay, to General Washington, and to Governor Clinton. On April 13, 1789, the barge which conveyed Washington from Elizabethtown Point in New Jersey to New York for his Inauguration was rowed by thirteen captains with Captain Randall (Randall's Island) acting as coxswain. It is interesting to recall that of the twenty-eight battalions of enlisted American loyalists who fought on the Tory side of the Revolution, many claimed membership in this Society which they had joined before the struggle.

In 1788 Bayley may have journeyed down from his estate in New Rochelle whither he had retired, to witness the participation of the Marine Society in a public procession. In this demonstration, held by the Federalists to approve the proposed constitution of the United States and to urge its adoption, a 22-gun frigate, manned by 30 seamen, was drawn through the streets of the city.

In such a congenial and busy atmosphere William Bayley pursued his first vocation, successful, happy, and probably desirous of continuing for long years as he had begun. But late in the night of September 21, 1776, he was

[b] See Chapter 4, p. 53.

aroused by a mad pounding on his door and frantic cries
of "Fire!" seeming to come from every direction at once.
Leaping from bed, William dashed to the window and looked
down upon an inferno of smoke and flames. It is quite
likely that his living quarters were over his store. His first
care, therefore, would be to see his young wife and their
infant daughter to comparative safety. It was hopeless to
try to save anything except whatever money they had on
the premises. William joined the brigade of workers who
were trying vainly to bring the blaze under control. The
fire, generally conceded to have been started by the Patriots,
was thought to have begun in a small wooden house on
the Wharf near the Whitehall slip. Not many people lived
in that area, and the fire was not detected until it raged into
nearby streets. Alarms could not be sounded because the
rebels had carried off the bells of the city. A high wind
added to the hazards of the conflagration. Lord Howe, under
whose protection the city lay, ordered the boats of the fleet
to be manned and to stand by to evacuate the citizenry, for
from the looks of things, the entire city would be razed
to the ground. All the houses in Beaver Street were wiped
out. Flames roared through the buildings east of Broadway
and north of Morris Street, many of the shops adding to
the blaze by the very nature of their merchandise. Finally,
when all the southeast section of the city, including Trinity
Church, had been gutted, the open fields on Mortkill Street,
now Barclay Street, stopped the fiery rampage. The fire had
had its way without interference for ten hours! An eye-
witness of the burning of Trinity Church gives us a glimpse
of the frightening experience the whole episode must have
been:

> The steeple, which was 140 feet high, the upper part of
> wood, and placed on an elevated situation, resembled a
> vast pyramid of fire, exhibiting a most grand and awful
> spectacle. Several women and children perished, their
> shrieks, the crash of falling houses and ruin everywhere . . .
> Only gaunt and blackened walls lined all the downtown
> section.

When the catastrophe had subsided somewhat, it was ascertained that 493 buildings, houses, and stores had been reduced to ashes. Many of the wealthy citizens were now poverty-stricken and homeless. Added to the distress already caused by the British occupation, the affairs of the war, and the sad divisions between members of the same family in support of the Tory or Patriot causes, this last tragedy seemed to sap the very spirit of the people, many of whom were forced to resort to living in tentlike structures until their future could be determined upon.

After a time some of the shopkeepers erected temporary stores, not much more than lean-tos, on Lower Broadway on the East Side, in a pathetic effort to resume trade with whatever stock they had been able to salvage, or had been since able to purchase. In the face of such disaster, however, the attempts were apathetic, and on the whole, unsuccessful. After a brief trial, many were abandoned, their makeshift walls and clapboard signs left like scarecrows, flapping in the breeze.

Two such flimsy structures, Nos. 58 and 59 Broadway, bore the name "Wm. Bayley—Tinsman," sorry memento of a successful mercantile career.

IX

Dark Skeins

1

ONE OCTOBER DAY IN 1778, when Elizabeth was four years old, she was sitting on the front steps of her New York City home, her elbows on her knees, her chin cupped in her hand. The tall hoop, which up to now she had never tired of rolling, leaned neglected against the stoop. Beside her lay a well-thumbed copy of *Goody-Two Shoes*, a favorite nursery story—now unopened. The solitary figure sat still as a statue while the trouble in her eyes deepened, and the little face, usually vivacious and merry, was gravely thoughtful. Time and Eternity were having their first meeting in this child's life and her bewildered mind struggled to grasp the intangible truism of death.

All about her was very quiet. Only a low murmur reached her through the slightly opened window of the front room, the blinds of which were drawn in. She knew that inside the darkened parlor her two-year-old sister Catherine lay in a long white dress—dead. As Elizabeth sat quite still, following the lazy motion of the clouds with a far-away look in her dark eyes, she recalled another occasion like this, when those blinds had been drawn, when visitors tiptoed in and out as they were doing today, and when her father had been sternly silent and strange. Then it had been her mother who had lain in that room. She remembered looking down at her from the comfort of her father's arms, for she had scarcely recognized that thin, pale form as belonging to the happy, tender, warm personality that had been Catherine Charlton Bayley.

Now it had happened again. Her little sister Kitty, that laughing, fair-haired playmate with her mother's name and face, was gone—to heaven, they had told her, to be with their mother. Then why could she not go too, and their big sister Mary? Surely their mother would want all her children to be with her. How Eliza ached now to see again that precious smile and those outstretched arms! There was this new mother toward whom she was trying, as her father had told her, to be polite and kind, but sometimes it was hard, and always it was so different. Just as the little girl had decided that she did not like these goings-away, these separations, and that she would not let her father nor Mary ever go away without her, her sad thoughts were interrupted by the appearance of several ladies in the doorway. Seeing the forlorn figure on the step, one of them asked her, "Aren't you crying, Eliza, because your little sister Kitty is dead?" Shaking her dark curls emphatically, the child answered quickly, "No, because Kitty is gone up to heaven,—I wish I could go too with Mama. . . ."

Thus unwittingly Elizabeth gave utterance to the thought that was to overshadow her all through her life. Though she was to close the eyes of most of her loved ones in death, she grieved not so much because they had gone, as because they had left her here in this valley of tears. This little incident, sketched for us by her own pen, indicates perfectly what was to be the pattern of her life and the ever-increasing longing of her soul for the life to come. More and more frequently as she grew older, she was to be aware of the passing quality of the things of this earth, and she would often exclaim with deepest yearning, "Oh, to be in our grand, unchanging Eternity!" Separations were to be the constant sorrow of her life. To such a degree was this true that we may safely say that, with the exception of one short interval after her marriage, Elizabeth

never completely emerged from those dark shadows cast by
her first early contact with sorrow.

Evidence of the deep scar left on her memory by these
childhood griefs comes from another incident recorded for
us by Elizabeth long years after. The occasion was a visit to
New Rochelle when she was eight years old. Eliza had been
playing with her Bayley cousins and the more remotely related Besley children in the meadows. It was probably her
cousin Joseph, or perhaps Oliver Besley, who had thought
of the age-old boyish prank of robbing birds' nests; this
may well have been Elizabeth's first experience with the
cruelty of small children, and the impression made on her
sensibilities was vivid and permanent. She says:

"(I) . . . cried because the girls would destroy them. I
gathering up the young ones on a leaf, seeing them palpitate,
hoping the poor mother, hopping from bough to bough,
would come and bring them to life,—and afterward always
love to play and walk alone . . . admiration of the clouds . . .
delight to gaze at them *always with the look for my mother
and little Kitty in heaven* . . ." (italics added)

In her youth Elizabeth had not adopted the fad of keeping a diary though she did make numerous notes on her
wide readings. The above-mentioned and similar recollections of her early years were committed to writing as late as
1812 at St. Joseph's, Emmitsburg, under the heading "Dear
Remembrances," because, she said, "it would be ungrateful
not to take note of them." The fact that after the passage
of so many years and the weight of so many other heavy
sorrows, she still recalled how she had felt about the deaths
of her mother and Kitty, gives evidence of the depth and
poignancy of her grief at the time of their occurrence. For
four years this child had dwelt with lonesome desire on
the thought of her mother and little sister, and this at an
age when children most easily forget and adjust themselves
with remarkable ease to the changes in their lives. A two-

fold cause may be assigned to this rather unnaturally prolonged grief. It was an indication of an early maturity of
emotion and impression joined with fervent loyalty of
affections, traits which were to cause Elizabeth so much
pain all through her life. But it was also an indication of
the failure of the circumstances of her life to heal the wound
her sensitive nature had suffered. The pathetic picture of
a child of eight walking alone through the meadows and
looking wistfully at the sky which seems to withhold from
her the two dear ones she so misses, speaks more eloquently
of the bleakness of her family life at that time than anything
she herself could have told us.

When Dr. Bayley made his second trip to England in
1775, Elizabeth was just a few months old. Before his return
in the following year, war had broken out between the
colonies and the Mother Country. The little family he had
left behind could not have had much of this world's goods
even before this disaster, for Thacher assigns as Bayley's
reason for joining Lord Howe's staff the usual one for
young doctors—poverty. What their condition now was
one can easily imagine. Added to this financial difficulty
for the young mother was the extra anxiety of being separated from her husband during these critical days. Dr.
Bayley had been ordered to Newport, Rhode Island, where
he was stationed for over a year. During his absence,
Catherine and the children must have missed him sorely,
and no doubt, it increased his wife's worry immeasurably
to think of his danger. These fears, and the fact that Catherine was expecting her third child, made serious inroads
on her probably not-too-rugged constitution. It would appear that Mrs. Bayley went to Newton, Long Island, to re-
cuperate under a change of air. There in the spring of the
year and at the height of the War, Richard Bayley was
summoned to the deathbed of his wife who left to the distracted father a delicate babe named for her mother, and
soon to follow after her.

Did Dr. Bayley regret now his earlier decision to give

himself so completely to his work? We do not know, but we do know that for one year he cared for his three children, and he did it well. For one year Elizabeth and her sisters enjoyed their father's devoted attention, and then— their world was shattered. The infant Catherine, so frail at birth, never attained full health. When at the end of her first year, she was even more sickly, Dr. Bayley realized that the children needed a woman's care. One month after the prescribed period of mourning was over, he remarried.

The haste with which he entered into this second marriage may be further explained in the light of his professional duties. A busy doctor has no time to care for little children, and though we know from Elizabeth's accounts of their relationship that he continued to interest himself in her education, he still left the girls pretty much to themselves and to the ministrations of their stepmother. Charlotte Amelia Barclay bore him four sons and three daughters. One cannot help feeling, however, that there was trouble in the Bayley household. That this trouble was serious and prolonged is testified to by the letters and notes left by both Elizabeth and Mary. The latter, after a lapse of twenty years, shudders at the remembrance of those days. She says in a letter to Elizabeth after a visit to the old scenes in New Rochelle:

> I can scarcely describe the state of mind I was thrown into by recalling scenes and persons that every year of my life seems somehow to have been connected with. Beginning with the unhappy situation of our Mother—taking refuge in the same place on our Father's going to England, the *very very* painful events that succeeded our leaving there until we married. Even that eventful step scarcely enabled us to shake off all that was disagreeably attached to our situation before.

In 1811, Elizabeth was to assure Henry Seton, her husband's half-brother, that she understood perfectly his emotion in questioning whether it would not have been better for him to have lost his life in a recent shipwreck. She said:

"I had just such a moment twenty years ago in which I asked myself the same question, dictated by that anguish of soul which can find no relief." Elizabeth would have been but seventeen at the time of this experience. Although we know by her own declaration that she occasionally suffered from attacks of moodiness at this time, the attacks in themselves must have been aggravated by external circumstances to have caused in one of so buoyant a nature the mental depression above referred to.

Five years after her marriage, Elizabeth speaks frankly of the rift between her father and stepmother. In a letter to her girlhood friend Julia Sitgreaves Scott, she says:

> My poor sister, Emma, is released from her terrible doubts and anxieties and I suppose her wedding will now take place as soon as she pleases. For myself, I cannot but reflect on the perverseness of human affairs for Mrs. Sadler's arrival (from Europe) once so much an earnest wish, is now converted into I could almost say a misfortune, except as far as respects her personal safety; for my father perseveres in his resolution that I shall never admit a reconciliation with Mrs. B—. And in that case intercourse with Mrs. Sadler will be so mixed with vexations, our difference will be a source of so much mortification to her, that I can never visit her without expecting to meet those I do not wish to meet.

It is difficult to decide from this passage whether the "reconciliation" referred to Elizabeth's efforts to bring her father and stepmother into more kindly relationship, or the desire she herself may have had to forget the past and to establish some more friendly rapport with Mrs. Bayley. It does prove beyond question how unyielding Dr. Bayley could be. Later, on the occasion of Emma's wedding, June 19, 1799, Elizabeth wrote to Julia Scott:

> I return home on Monday next, as Emma's wedding takes place on Wednesday, the nineteenth, and I hope, notwithstanding the difficulties, I shall be present, and forget the past as far as possible.

It would seem, furthermore, that Dr. Bayley, strong-willed and hot-headed though he might have been, was completely dominated by the second Mrs. Bayley in domestic and financial decisions during the first years of his marriage. Ten years after this second marriage, and thirteen years before his death, he made a will in which he left all his property and money to his wife and her children while omitting all mention of his two daughters Mary Magdalen and Elizabeth. This will remained unaltered at the time of his death. Had undue wifely influence been brought to bear? Elizabeth was only sixteen at the time it was drawn up, and two more years must elapse before Mary's marriage to Dr. Post. The incident points to the suggestion that Dr. Bayley, for all his protestations of affection for Elizabeth, had left her and her sister unprovided for.

Elizabeth was docility itself where the commands of her father were concerned. In later years, she could say that she had never knowingly disobeyed him. And it may be assumed that she did all in her power to please him in the matter of the second Mrs. Bayley. But that there was deliberate unkindness on her stepmother's part, and that Elizabeth was shocked and grieved by it, we may know from the latter's statement at the age of sixteen:

> Family disagreement, could not guess why, when I spoke kindly to relations, they did not speak to me. Could not even guess how anyone could be an enemy to another.

One is forced to the conjecture that one or more of the older half-brothers or sisters sided with their mother in whatever these unpleasant situations were.

Several references to Dr. Bayley's foibles appear in Elizabeth's letters to Mrs. Scott, who, from long contact with the family, would be in a position to appreciate them:

> He has been dancing attendance on the Legislature these three weeks and is likely to do so; but he is well and in a situation perfectly agreeable to him, at the Lieutenant

Governor's where he finds those attentions and formalities he is so fond of receiving.

and again:

He never can lose his interest in your welfare though as is very common with him, he takes little pains to show it.

Regarding her failure to write for some time, Elizabeth offers this reason to her friend Julia:

. . . and in truth, so much attention was required by my father during the summer and so earnest was I in fulfilling every attention to him (more so than ever from some particular circumstances which happened in the spring). . .

Dr. Bayley himself seems to have recognized the strangeness of his own character as the following passage attests:

I love to think on the oddity of my life. What words afford the most inconsolable affliction to another person, that which afford the aching heart to most people seem to me as a matter of amusement. Dear heady temper go on. Hail to the period when I shall be at rest.

Dr. Bayley's marriage was decidedly unfortunate; his household unhappy. It would further appear that an actual separation of some sort took place within the first four or five years of Elizabeth's married life which began in 1794. From ample testimony in her letters, we know that this was the period in which she and the grandchildren spent the summers with her father in his home on Staten Island. After reading his daughter's comment on the building of this house, one must conclude that Dr. Bayley was actually separated from his family at this time. In March, 1799, Elizabeth writes:

My father has obtained permission from the Legislature to perform all his plans he has contemplated on Staten Island. He is building a dwelling house, but I fear not to receive his family. Emma's marriage will be; but when is uncertain.

It would seem that poor Emma's health was suffering, probably as a result of the difficulties attendant upon her marriage to William Craig. Always thoughtful of the needs of others, Elizabeth wrote to her father, urging him to receive Emma at his new Staten Island home:

> Think of Emma . . . if it is not indispensable to offer her the air of Staten Island.

There is a striking omission of any reference in her letters during this period to the presence of Mrs. Bayley or of the half-sisters and brothers, with the exception of Helen, who seems to have remained closer to Dr. Bayley than any of the other children of this second marriage. Elizabeth writing to her father inquires:

> Is my Helen well, and will she be pleased to remember her sister with affection . . . If you would sometimes direct Helen's pen to Bloomingdale it would be a most grateful substitute for your own.

After the Seton fortunes had begun to wane, and William and Elizabeth had given up their Battery Place home, they themselves went to live with the Doctor on the Island, Providence so arranging that Elizabeth would be with her father when he died on August 17, 1801. She gives a detailed account of his last three days. . .

He called her to observe the beauty of the sunset "and the view of a bright rainbow"; he fed little Kit (Catherine, Elizabeth's youngest child) "with a spoon from his glass of drink, making her say 'Papa';" Elizabeth played all his favorite music to him after tea and then he retired. On the next day he took sick, a victim of that plague from which he had saved countless others. A young lad who had apparently been taken in by Dr. Bayley in the capacity of valet ten years previously "was with him and capable of executing every direction." After two days of intense suffering, he "put his hand in mine, turned on his side and sobbed out the last of life without the smallest struggle. . . .

"Two wagons full of relatives and friends paid the last respects. I, his dear, his darling child, whose soul doated [sic] on him, without a perceptible struggle, and with the calmness of a subdued spirit after once the soul was departed, saw all, did all that was to be done, and now review with wonder, and with grateful praise that I live, much less that I have lived through it."

There is no mention whatever made of any definite relative or member of the family being present during his last hours, nor of his asking for any of them. Yet Mrs. Bayley did not die until 1805, her will being probated in Surrogate's Court in November of that year. A most amazing denouement to this unhappy history is given us by Elizabeth herself in one of her letters to Mrs. Scott:

> I have had the indescribable satisfaction of attending Mrs. Bayley in her last hours. I believe I have expressed to you my pleasure in receiving from her since my return home [from Italy] every mark of peace and reconciliation, which also gives me the double enjoyment of the confidence, and affection of the dear girls, Helen and Mary. [Her half-sisters] Their situation is truly melancholy; indeed I feel more than I can tell for them.

* * * * * *

Elizabeth at eight hungered for a mother's love and understanding. This, her stepmother either could not or would not give her. His ever-increasing family usurped her beloved father's time and interest, so much of which had previously been devoted to the development of her own character and studies; this, no doubt, smote the heart of Elizabeth who, sensitive and affectionate, fretted over this new and distasteful situation. At that time the brooding child may have presented a drawn look which, to the professional eyes of her father, warned of physical reprisals if steps were not taken to restore her inner happiness. She may at this juncture have given some indication of that enervating disease that would waste her body at the early age of forty-six. Her father may simply have wished to relieve the domestic tension by removing one of the causes of friction. Whatever the reason, Dr. Bayley sent Elizabeth and her sister Mary to spend some time (almost a year) with their Uncle William, who shortly before, had purchased a vast piece of property in New Rochelle.

This is the way in which God worked to mold the character and to form the soul of Elizabeth Bayley for the great work He had in store for her. Already she was showing signs of those rare qualities in the young—thoughtful introspection and seriousness of purpose. In the overcrowded household, opportunities for reading and thinking were non-existent. Elizabeth daily becoming more reflective, felt a growing desire for solitude in proportion as she saw it slipping away. During those longer visits to New Rochelle, she saw a different aspect of life from that to which she had been accustomed. Here were tranquillity, good humor, comfortable living, room to move around without intruding on others' rights. From her youngest days, Elizabeth had a deep love for all that pertained to nature. Now amid the silence of a rural landscape, in the enjoyment of solitude of a sort, and in the relaxation of personal freedom, her soul stretched up to embrace these blessings, while her personality grew and deepened in those qualities best suited for nourishing the piety which would ever characterize her from these days forward.

Though a child of eight might not be too aware of the development of her spiritual life, yet it seems not too much to say, in view of Elizabeth's own utterances, that this was the seeding time of her long quest for truth. In these peaceful hours spent near to God in the natural beauty of the countryside, sitting by the water's edge, or in long solitary rambles under the shady cedars along the Shore Road, Elizabeth Bayley took her first steps toward Him for Whom her young soul was already yearning.

X

"At Uncle William's"

1

FOURTEEN-YEAR-OLD ELIZABETH ANN peered through the banks of white fog that rolled in moist billows past her window, submerging the countryside in a wet silence that hung miserably over everything. The only objects visible were a few trunkless branches suspended above the swirling mists.

Early mornings in New Rochelle were frequently like this, she knew, yet Elizabeth could not accustom herself to this sense of being cut off from the rest of the world. Idly she ran her finger along the window ledge, pushing little drops of moisture into canal-like crevices in the wooden frame while her thoughts borrowed something of the morning's chill. Her curly hair lay in tight ringlets around the lovely oval face with the Le Conte features and eyes. A description of her little daughter written many years later might have suited the mother as well at this time:

> Anna Maria is close beside me, and I will cut for you a lock of the beautiful hair that curls in a hundred ringlets on her head. She is one of the loveliest beings eyes ever beheld. . . . I only have the least influence with her, because her disposition is exactly my own.

But the dank heaviness of the weather had found its reflection in the present mood of the child and settled there with unwelcome tenacity. Elizabeth sometimes had passing spells of melancholy, it is true, but today's depression was not one of those. There was a reason for this sadness, and it was a good one.

Just one year before, in 1788, Dr. Bayley had brought his two eldest daughters to his brother William's home, and had bidden them goodby. Several days later he had sailed for England on professional business. During all the intervening time neither girl had received one line from him. Mary took the matter philosophically enough, but Elizabeth, always much closer in thought and sentiment to her father, was both hurt and anxious. Years later, referring in her *Dear Remembrances* to this period, she recalls how she had felt:

14 yrs.—at Uncle B's in New Rochelle, again . . . Joy in God that He was my Father. Insisting that He should not forsake me. My father away and perhaps dead, but God was my Father, and I quite independent of whatever might happen.

This feeling of having been put to one side was not new to Elizabeth. From her earliest days the frequent absences of her father from home was an issue which his family had learned to accept. Trips to England, sick calls day and night, classes at Columbia University, strenuous hours of professional duty during several plagues that harassed the city— all these necessitated repeated separations from his family and formed the domestic pattern to which the growing child had endeavored to accustom herself. Yet Elizabeth had never quite succeeded in this, for her ardent and affectionate nature missed her father's loving attentions and his deep interest in all that concerned his favorite daughter.

Moreover, on these previous occasions there had always been notes, verbal messages, and the daily expectations of a quick return. This time it was different; days stretched into weeks, the weeks rolled into months, and the

months into a year—and still no word—still no hope of returning to her own home and a more settled way of life.
Not that she was unhappy. No one could be sad in the kindly,
fun-loving household of which she and her sister Mary had
formed a part on so many occasions. Elizabeth smiled in
spite of herself as she thought of the pranks her twelve-
year-old cousin Joseph loved to play on the three older
girls. Only last evening—and she giggled outright at the
recollection—he had blown up a paper bag directly behind
the settee where Mary, a prim young lady of eighteen, was
entertaining her first serious beau, the young medical student, Wright Post.

Cousin Susanna, thirteen, was Eliza's close companion
for all teen-age activities. The two girls looked enough alike
to pass for sisters, and their interest in dresses, dances, and
partners was equally keen. Nor did they lack eager escorts.
An attractive young lady of fourteen—in a day when girls
matured early and set up their own homes before they were
twenty—would never be at a loss for an invitation, especially since the Bayleys themselves and their close relations
formed a large portion of the socially elite of New Rochelle.

The numerous younger members of these families were
proud to take such a pretty girl ice-skating, horseback-rid-
ing, or boating. Adam Flandreau, Anne Le Conte's son, was
eight years Elizabeth's senior, and skillful at handling a
sail. John Peter Guerineau, her father's half-brother by
Susanna Le Conte's second marriage, was just turned twenty
—and handsome. Another cousin, Charlotte Coutant, who
was the same age as Mary, often visited them; while young
Jeremiah Schureman, who anyone could see loved Susanna,
came as often as he dared.

The eldest Bayley boy, also a William, seemed delicate
and little inclined to enter into much of the fun that went
on around him. And, of course, the darling of the family
was six-year-old Ann, a pixy-like child, with the olive skin,
blue-black hair, and strong features of her Indian great-

grandmother, Princess Annhooke, for whom the little girl was named.

Elizabeth became aware that while she had been lost in her thoughts a little rift had appeared in the fog. Through it now she caught a hasty glimpse of sunlight on gray-green waters, and then the mists closed again.

"How like my life," she mused, "fog and shadows, sunlight and joy, ever interchanging, never at rest."

With a sigh she turned from the window, and taking up her basket of needlework, and a copy of Thomson's *Seasons,* she went slowly downstairs to join Aunt Sarah and the others in the living room.

"Yet," she decided as she went along the hall, "if I cannot be home, there is no place else I would prefer to be than here at Uncle William's."

2

We have seen how William Bayley, after the loss of his business in the great fire of 1776, made an attempt to revive his previous mercantile status. However, it was at this point that Providence introduced him to his second vocation—that of a farmer.

One of the happier results of Dr. Bayley's unfortunate experience on Lord Howe's staff was the resultant respect and good will of the officers and populace, regardless of their political attachments. He was, therefore, in a position to obtain favors for his friends. It was in this way that he procured for his brother a large estate in New Rochelle, and William, though only thirty-one years old, welcomed the excuse of giving up a business for which he had lost all heart. So it was that in 1781 the obscure workings of the Divine pattern through the fortunes of war brought him into possession of one of the most interesting houses in the County of Westchester.

Built in pre-Revolutionary days by Joseph Pell for his
son Jacob, the property originally comprised 250 acres of
the best Shore front in New Rochelle and Pelham, together
with Hunter Island (now Travers Island) and David's Island
(now Fort Slocum). When, however, young Pell became
a captain in the British militia, his lands were confiscated, in 1779, by the New York Provincial government.
At the close of the War, Pell fled to Halifax to escape reprisals. According to the then existing law, patriot relatives
of Tories might redeem the latter's property from the Board
of Forfeitures. William Bayley, whose wife Sarah was
the younger Pell's sister, bought his brother-in-law's mainland estate, without the islands, for $5.20 an acre. Pell
himself returned to New Rochelle in 1818, seven years after
Bayley's death, to reclaim part of his land, but he never
succeeded in procuring the farmhouse which Bayley had
sold with some of the land to Elbert Roosevelt in 1801 at
the handsome profit of $25 an acre!

This is the house in which Elizabeth visited and where
she built up, along with her health, a deep fondness for
"Uncle William" and all her New Rochelle relatives. The
structure, remodeled in 1860, is a two-story clapboard dwelling typical of the colonial farmhouses of the Revolutionary
period. Large bay windows flank the wide door reached by
a flight of rough stone steps. This entrance opens onto a spa-
cious hall extending from front to back and giving egress
to a sweeping lawn—just the right sort of lawn for croquet,
or turning somersaults, or romping with the dog. A broad,
self-supporting staircase rises straight from the main hall to
the second floor. What fun six children could have coasting
down its polished baluster, arriving with a joyous swoop in
the rather stately dining room at the right, with its open
fireplace and dormer windows; or collecting themselves
with nervous giggles outside the arched doorway of the
parlor at the left whither they had been summoned to meet
family guests.

Over a first-floor bedroom is a small chamber that may

have served as a trunk room, or even as a child's bedroom, from the window of which Elizabeth herself may have looked out on the Sound. When central heating was installed in 1937, a secret room was discovered in the cellar. This gives rise to some extremely interesting conjectures as to the need for and uses of such a room. Did the Bayley children know about it, and did they invent fantastic tales of horror about what was in it? The supports of the house are large ships' timbers still to be seen in their raw condition, probably among the few remnants of the original structure. Thirty-three acres of this holding were eventually sold for an Anglican priory, and in 1927, the city of New Rochelle claimed a wide piece of the front yard for broadening the Shore Road.

When the Bayleys lived there, however, and during the years of Elizabeth's visits to her Uncle William, gently rolling meadows terraced the house, its rooms were swept fresh by the salty breezes of Long Island Sound, and tall shade trees rustled a friendly welcome to the little city-bred girl. Elizabeth and her sister Mary would find here what seemed to be lacking in their own home: a tranquil family life with plenty of loving care. We do not know just how warmly Sarah Bayley received her brother-in-law's two girls, but judging by the nostalgia with which Elizabeth later spoke of her New Rochelle sojourns, it is safe to conclude that Mrs. Bayley shared her husband's spirit of hospitality.

There would be many advantages for Dr. Bayley's two girls in being part of his brother's household. For Elizabeth, the freedom and the beauties of nature would have been ample charms in themselves, but beyond these, and far stronger, was the deep calling of like to like, the certainty of "belonging." To a child of Elizabeth's unsettled home-life, this sense of security offered by strong and numerous family ties was stimulating and aroused in her a justifiable pride in the long unbroken contribution of her people to the history of New Rochelle.

These contacts with her relations who constituted the

backbone of social and political life in the town, stirred
her curiosity regarding their history. She would ask Uncle
William about this one or that, and would listen carefully
as he sketched for her the lineage of her people. He would
show her the sword left him by the will of his grandfather,
William Le Conte, while he traced for her the history of the
first Le Conte to come from Normandy to New Rochelle,
Aunt Sarah, too, would fill the romantic mind of her niece
with wonder at the strange story of Wampage, the Indian
chief, who was really Sarah's great-grandfather. There
would be fun in examining heirlooms, letters, jewelry, and
trinkets treasured as mementos of a former life in England,
France, or the West Indies. And all the time Elizabeth, together with her young cousins, was absorbing into her veins
the traditional spirit and ways of her ancestors.

3

With William Le Conte Bayley the family name occupied a distinguished place in the town life of New Rochelle.
British in his way of life, he attended the Episcopalian
church, administered his estate in the manner of a country
squire, and like his Le Conte grandfather and great-grandfather, took a personal interest in the politics of his locality.
We judge him to have been an even-tempered, genial, and
active townsman.

In 1779, two years before he secured the Pell property,
Bayley must have been a resident of New Rochelle for at
least part of the year, for he is listed in the Town Records
with one Samuel Wooley as "two of the Justices of the
Peace of the Town and County of Westchester. . . ."

At a town meeting held in Pelham in 1801 Bayley was
elected to the office of Assessor, Commissioner of Highways,
and Commissioner of Schools. That must have been a busy

year for Squire Bayley! We read in the minutes of a Town Meeting of 1808:

> It unanimously resolved that the present Overseers of the poor take Council, Respecting the money paid, and a note given by W. Baley [sic] of the Town of Pelham to the Overseer of the poor of this Town before it be refunded.

This business is not again referred to and therefore remains hazy. But after his death we find further testimony to Bayley's generosity toward the indigent in a resolution adopted to put $600 left by him for the support of the poor "in the chest for safety."

In "Westchester County, Pelham Town" occurs the name of William Bailey [sic] as head of a family comprising: 1 free male over 16 (himself); 2 free white males under 16 (Joseph, William); 3 free white females (Sarah, his wife, Anne, Suzanne); 6 slaves.

The matter of the six slaves is somewhat surprising. Only one other person on the list had more—James Pell with seven. Many of those mentioned had none at all. It may well be that Bayley required the help of such a number for the cultivation of his extensive property. Whatever the reason, he was kind to them. One of these slaves, Sarah by name, was amply provided for in his will; he asked that "she be maintained in decent and comfortable manner out of my Estate." Another Negro, a young boy named Isaac, was taken care of by the following quaint clause:

> I give the use of my negro boy Isaac otherwise called Ike to my said wife so long as she remains my widow and at her death or marriage whichever happen first the Value of him to be ascertained by an equitable apprisement and that he have his Election to live with whichever of my said Children he may think proper such child paying the amount of such apprisal.

Eloquent testimony to the kindly, grateful nature of this genial man! It is also an insight into his shrewd business instinct that left nothing to chance.

Although British influence probably predominated in Bayley's home (his wife was a Pell), the homes of relatives and friends were just as decidedly French. William's children grew up with an easy fluency in both languages. We are told by the Reverend William Hague,[a] Bayley's grandson, that even in his generation—

> The younger children of the family spoke of her as "Aunt Molly Bayley"[b] and were obliged, each in turn, to take a lesson on the different spellings of French words that sounded alike . . . She would place her hands upon my temples, then, kissing me upon the forehead, would pleasantly allude to the old French mode of salutation . . .

Elizabeth herself must have come under the influence of this same "Aunt Molly" and her charming French lessons. The opening of one of the notes in Elizabeth's *Dear Remembrances* reads: "New Rochelle—Miss Molly B's—at eight years of age." Whether this heading indicates that Elizabeth was actually staying with Aunt Molly Bayley or was merely visiting her for a few hours, is not clear from the incident that follows. Uncle William was in possession of his Shore Road estate at this time. Therefore it seems likely that his niece would be with him.

Hague has left us a well-outlined sketch of his grandfather whom he delighted to be with as a small boy. Bayley is remembered as a good talker who enjoyed sitting on his "piazza" in his easy chair looking out "over one of the finest

---

[a] Reverend William Hague—youngest son of Ann Bayley Hague, minister of the Presbyterian Church.

[b] Molly Bayley—really Besley—the oldest living member of Oliver Besley's family—a Huguenot related to the Le Contes and Bayleys by marriages into both families.

of landscapes taking within its scope Hunter's Island, Pelham Creek, the expanse of long Island Sound." He was handy in whittling toys for his children and later for his grandchildren. His personality must have been vibrant, for at an advanced age, this grandson easily and affectionately recalls all that his grandparent had meant to him from the age of three. In an eloquent tribute, Hague sums up these impressions:

> The image of my grandfather, associated as it is with the old homestead . . . has never become dim; so that he has ever represented to me the ideal grandpa of poetry or song, of fiction or graphic art. . . . Thus has he ever been to me in thought "a living presence." . . .

To appreciate fully the impression that William Bayley had made on his grandson, it will suffice to recall that the latter wrote this testimony seventy-one years after his grandfather's death!

William Bayley's signature on an original document in the possession of the New Rochelle City Hall of Records shows large, clear, perfectly formed letters, the signature of an educated man, and if writing means anything, of steady, amiable character.

4

Such was the household to which Elizabeth Bayley came for visits of varying length—as an impressionable child, a developing, sensitive girl, and as a mature wife. In the freedom, spaciousness, and informality of the New Rochelle environment, she found the complement of her artistic nature, so deeply imbued with a consciousness of all things beautiful. She loved nature, but she was no naturalist, as she indirectly avers:

Every little leaf and flower, or insect, animal, shades of
clouds, or waving trees were objects of vacant unconnected
thoughts of God and heaven.

These lines, written later by Elizabeth in her *Dear Remembrances*, express her sentiments at the age of eight! Although so young, she already evinced the attraction of her
heart for heavenly things and the constant winging of her
soul to God upon every and any occasion. Nothing seemed
too trifling to elicit the act of love, the sigh of gratitude
to Him Who provides "all things, both great and small."
God builds His spiritual bastions upon nature's clay, and
from the dry dust of our human qualities He brings forth
the fruits of His vineyard. Thus He used Elizabeth's innate
love for creation to raise her heart to the Creator. All her
life she was to find it but a half-step from earth to heaven.
    This granddaughter of the Le Contes came most natur-
ally by her love for growing things. Her Huguenot ancestors had been farmers for the several generations in which
we know them, and we cannot conjecture for how many before that. Huguenots were reputedly skilled husbandmen,
bringing to this country in their mass immigration from
France and the West Indies, a system of gardening and
vine-dressing that had been their inheritance from generation to generation, and which has not been equaled in our
land. Though her own father had early become a city-
dweller, her grandfather Bayley had been a farmer, and as
has been seen, her Uncle William took great pleasure in
viewing his beautiful surroundings. Elizabeth would scarcely
have been a true daughter of either side of the family if
she had not a deep appreciation for all the lovely things of
nature. A little sidelight on Elizabeth's own "green thumb"
and her love for living things is glimpsed in a brief note
to her friend, Julia Scott, on the occasion of a visit that
had been expected but had not taken place:

The bird cages were dressed, the flower-pots replenished,

the children all tip-top, and their mother smoothing all the care-worn wrinkles from her forehead, anticipating a day of most perfect pleasure.

On another occasion writing to her friend Mrs. Sadler she says:

> Last Sunday morning before breakfast, I retraced the honey-suckle walk, and to my great astonishment found that those bushes with buds on them which grow near the honey-suckles bear the sweetest flower you can imagine, with the greatest profusion. Its fragrance is beyond any wild flower I ever saw. . . . I will transplant a great deal of it next month.

The picture which Elizabeth has left us of these days at New Rochelle is graphic in its delineation of her solid piety and almost premature earnestness. She tells us, that at the age of fourteen, she delighted "to sit alone by the water-side, wandering hours on the shore, singing and gathering shells." She would take her copy of Thomson, and walking through the fields, surrounded by sheep and lambs, she would read her favorite poems and sing her best-loved hymns. When she became thirsty, she drank the sap of the birch trees and afterwards gathered stones on the shore.

In the evening she walked under the cedars while she gazed at the stars, picking out the constellations—Orion and the others. She has also given us a recollection of herself in a winter setting:

> Hymns said on the rocks, surrounded with ice, in transports of first enthusiasm. The Bible so enjoyed, and Thomson and Milton.

She tells us further that she "took pleasure in everything, coarse, rough, smooth or easy, always gay." In this same spirit of gayety she leaves us a pen-picture of how she spent one lovely spring morning:

In the year 1789 when my father was in England, one
morning in May, in the lightness of a cheerful heart, I
jumped in the wagon that was driving to the woods for
brush, about a mile from home; the boy who drove it began
to cut and I set off in the woods, soon found an outlet in a
meadow, and a chestnut tree with several young ones growing around it; found rich moss under it and a warm sun.
Here, then, sweet bed—the air still, a deep blue vault
above—the numberless sounds of spring melody and joy—
the sweet clover and wild flowers I had got by the way, and
a heart as innocent as human heart could be, filled even
with enthusiastic love to God and admiration of His works—
God was my Father, my all. I prayed, sang hymns, cried,
laughed, talking to myself of how far He could place me
above all sorrow. Then I laid still to enjoy the heavenly
peace that came over my soul; and I am sure, in the two
hours so enjoyed, grew ten years in the spiritual life.

These vignettes, so appealing in their simplicity, are
framed against the poignant shadows of Elizabeth's youth.
It is odd to hear a child of fourteen speak of "sorrow"
yet it was no stranger to Elizabeth. Now in this respite provided by a sojourn in New Rochelle, how her young spirit
expanded and soared in the freedom of the great outdoors
where every sensory impression was also a spiritual experience. Elizabeth reveled in the solitude of shore line and
wooded path where opportunities to think, to read, to pray
were golden nuggets to be stored away against the days—
before and after—when life was crowded, shrill, and
bustling.

She was now on the threshold of young womanhood,
her soul keenly aware of those first serious touches of religious insights that were to engulf her before long in the
great decision of her life. Her thoughtful mind was gravely
concerning itself with the things that really mattered: her
soul's ideals and the curbing and forming of her character.
She made earnest efforts to balance the wide extremes of
her nature—its exuberance and its proneness to moodiness.

Or we might look at the conflict as the clash of vastly different national backgrounds—a French sprightliness as opposed to English doggedness.

It was while roaming the fields that she gave her young mind to thoughts far beyond the level of her fourteen years. No doubt these precious occasions for reflection had to be snatched from the demands of normal life in the midst of growing children in Uncle William's household, between the times appointed for little duties, attendance at school, the games and festivities of her cousins and friends. The extent of her enjoyment in these hours of solitude is token of their rarity. They were the seeding times, the early springtime of the spiritual life that would flower only after the winter of trial.

5

Of all the members of the Bayley family, Elizabeth's affection went out most spontaneously to her little cousin Anne, born during the older girl's first prolonged visit to New Rochelle at the age of eight. Experienced as Elizabeth was in caring for little ones, she promptly took over from the busy Sarah Bayley much of the attention required for the new arrival. The resulting bond between the cousins developed into a strong friendship that was preserved for many years, the younger girl no doubt regarding Elizabeth somewhat in the capacity of a second mother. Anne's mind was quick, refined, and docile. She benefited immeasurably by her constant association with the exceptional mentality of her "sisterly cousin," a term used by Anne's son, Reverend Hague, to describe their close relationship.

There lived on an estate adjoining the Bayley farm "a man of large fortune, an educated gentleman, a bachelor just touching the border of middle life, Alexander Henderson." Every day he crossed Pelham Creek which separated the two estates, walking over the causeway and bridge to the Bayley homestead. There he would enliven his bachelorhood for a while amidst the happy family life of his neighbors, sitting on the front piazza in friendly conversation with Uncle William and any of the children who might stroll along. From his extensive library he often brought with him a book which he would leave for Anne to read. In this way she early became acquainted with the best of the English authors, and the most recent. It is almost inconceivable not to suppose that Elizabeth, too, was sometimes the recipient of like favors, for Mr. Henderson would quickly recognize in the young guest a trained mind of superior caliber.

Dr. Bayley returned home in 1790 and Mary and Elizabeth went back to New York. On June 10 of that year Mary was married to Dr. Wright Post, her father's young understudy. Elizabeth seems to have spent the greater part of the next three years, until her own marriage, with her sister at her home on John Street, New York City.

After her marriage to William Seton, Elizabeth continued to go to New Rochelle to see Anne. Reverend Hague tells us that they were "constantly interchanging sentiments as well as visits." This remark leads to the surmise that the young bride had frequently the pleasure of entertaining her favorite cousin in her own home in New York. Elizabeth was in her twentieth year, Anne had just turned thirteen, both apparently more matured and intellectual than many others of their day and age.

Having seen how deeply imbued with religious sentiments Elizabeth's mind was, we are not surprised to read that the chief topics of conversation between the two were the variant teachings of the Protestant churches. In the opinions formulated as a result of these discussions, Elizabeth greatly influenced the younger girl, drawing her more and more toward the personal love and knowledge of God which she herself experienced. These two earnest minds may also have examined certain Catholic beliefs, for we are told

Old Baily House, Shore Road, New Rochelle

The Bayley house is a relic of pre-Revolutionary days, being one of three homes built by Joseph Pell for his children. The line between Pelham and New Rochelle divides the property, the house having two street numbers. Originally it set in the midst of a wide lawn.

Side view. The chimney and dormer windows were new at a renovation carried on by Robert Emmett in 1860.

Graves of Captain William Bayley and his son Joseph in Trinity Churchyard in New Rochelle. The picture, taken in 1954, shows the stones to be in good condition.

that Elizabeth showed marked leanings in that direction even in her earlier years.

However, as Anne grew older, and Elizabeth's visits were curtailed by the demands of her growing family, the younger girl came under other influences. One of these may have been James Hague, captain of an Indian trading vessel, who was soon to become Anne's husband. She was also attracted by the preaching of a famous minister, Reverend John Mitchell Mason, of the Presbyterian Church in Murray Street, New York, who occasionally conducted services in New Rochelle. Perhaps Anne Bayley was as much influenced by the personality of the Rev. Dr. Mason as she was by his subject matter. One of his contemporaries gives the following picture of the worthy divine:

> His imagination was lofty, and yet carefully trained; his language choice, and yet exuberant; his conceptions clear, distinct, and yet flowing in a current as if he could not restrain them; and his bursts of feeling at times so overpowering that I have seen whole assemblies comprising rich and poor, learned and unlearned, bowed down before him with one impulse, till there was scarce a dry eye to be seen.

One of the most controversial questions discussed in the pulpits of that period was the relation of the sacraments to salvation. It was upon the answer to this question that Anne and Elizabeth's friendship suffered a severe blight. Hague tells us:

> The affirmation, sometimes eloquently argued, that the sacraments, administered through a regular priestly succession are the divinely appointed channels through which saving grace flows forth from the fountain of life into the human soul, took the strangest possible hold on the spirit nature of the elder cousin. . . .

Eventually Anne's religious explorations ended with her acceptance of the formal Protestant stand on the subject: justification by faith alone.

Early in 1803 Elizabeth, now the mother of five children, faced the double trial of her husband's fatal illness and severe financial reverses. As a last desperate effort to regain his health, William Seton determined to go to Italy where, he hoped, the soft mild climate might restore his wasted strength. Elizabeth and their eldest daughter Anna Maria would accompany him.

With a heavy heart, a short time before her depearture, Elizabeth made what was probably her last trip to New Rochelle. She had gone in a beautiful gesture of friendship, in spite of the little cloud that had arisen between them, to say goodby to Anne. Reverend Hague describes a scene that must have been freighted with deep and varied emotion on either side, in these few terse words:

> Sometime before her departure for Italy, the elder cousin visited the younger, sisterly cousin at Pelham; at the moment of taking leave, bidding her goodby while presenting her an article of skillfully wrought needlework as a love-token, she kissed her, and said, "I hope we shall meet in heaven."

Hague adds the cryptic remark: "They never met on earth again. Both lived, however, to an advanced age." What tragedy in these words so coldly penned.

What prompted Elizabeth to express herself so prophetically? Did she already sense in Anne the coolness, the silly fear that within the next year would terminate their long relationship? It is painful to consider the hurt that Elizabeth suffered upon finding this door, of all others, closed against her when she returned to America after William's death. The aloofness of her "sisterly cousin" cut more deeply than did the open scorn of others.

There are few episodes in Elizabeth's life that exemplify so strikingly her nobility of character as does this poignant visit to her cousin. The initiative she assumed in trying to repair the breach in their friendship, her generous impulse of a lovely gift, the delicate farewell in her last words: these portray for us the real Elizabeth, so loyal, tender-hearted, and forebearing.

While still in Italy, Elizabeth had been made to realize what her status at home would be if she took any steps toward Catholicity. She had written to Anne long, enthusiastic letters, filled with admiration and awe for all she saw and heard in her thoroughly Catholic surroundings. Almost at once Anne's letters intimated the mounting alarm and disapproval with which this correspondence was viewed by the Bayleys and their relatives. One can almost feel the tightening of Anne's sympathies as family pressure was brought to bear; then ensued the gradual breaking-off of the interest and the affectionate tones of their younger days. Finally came Anne's last letter—stiff and suppressed; after that—silence.

When the twenty-nine-year-old widow sailed into New York Harbor upon her return voyage in June of the following year, she came almost as complete a stranger as her great-great-grandfather Guillaume Le Conte had been a little more than a hundred years before. Society friends would abandon her because her fortunes had sunk so low; her family would shun her as a traitor and a rebel for her inexplicable desertion of their ancestral traditions in favor of a Church that, in their eyes, had already offended so gravely.

In the dark hours of embarrassment, loneliness, and privation that were to follow, Elizabeth, scarcely still a Seton, very nearly ceased to be a Bayley.

III

We See The Design
1774 - 1821

The loom is filled. No thread in its vast expanse has been left unfastened. Laborious weaving of warp and weft accomplished over the years has fashioned a design which those who worked behind the fabric could not see, conscious only in their workmanship of the importance of weaving straight and true—with strong threads—for those who would mount the loom in future years to finish out the pattern.

The tapestry is now reversed and we see, delineated in lifelike proportions, the figure of Elizabeth Ann Bayley, valiant and beautiful in her full-blossomed maturity. Looking upon her there, against the handiwork of her French and English ancestors, we are impressed by the richness of the over-all design, its gay and sombre hues, its intricate web of human achievements.

The American Elizabeth evinces in her own nature the dual quality of her national background. As two diverse strands merged to form the pattern, just so do these two elements imbue her personality and temperament with distinct traits that characterize her alternately as a Le Conte or as a Bayley.

XI

A Daughter
of the Le Contes

1

THE MUSIC HAD FADED TO A STOP. Partners curtsied and bowed. Some retired to chairs in alcoves, others to the punch bowl. In the drawing room of the De Lancey home was gathered that evening in the winter of 1792 all of New York's fashionable society. Periwigged gentlemen in richly colored brocades stood around the fireplace and discussed matters of current interest: Dr. Bard's plans for his newly established New York Hospital and Dispensary; the story that a man from Yale had made a machine by which a slave could produce fifty pounds of cleaned cotton daily. Gentlemen of French extraction were disturbed by the news that the proclamation of a French Republic was imminent. The talk then drifted to the probable re-election of Washington and Adams in the fall, and its effect on the growing feud between Hamilton and Jefferson. On this last question the opinions of the gentlemen were severely divided. Earnest and loyal supporters of both parties seemed to be equally lined up on either side.

Their ladies, seated in friendly groups, were possibly more distressed by the threatened execution of King Louis XVI of France. Tories among them were aghast, and all felt that that Revolution was getting completely out of hand. Feminine sympathy went out to the beautiful, if improvident, Marie Antoinette, as with shudders, they dis-

135

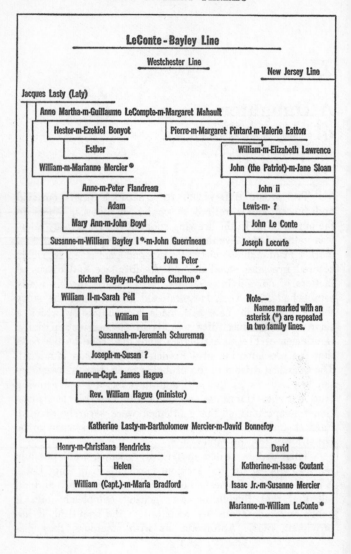

LeConte - Bayley Line

Westchester Line

New Jersey Line

Jacques Lasty (Laty)

Anne Martha-m-Guillaume LeCompte-m-Margaret Mahault

Hester-m-Ezekiel Bonyot

Esther

Pierre-m-Margaret Pintard-m-Valerie Eatton

William-m-Elizabeth Lawrence

William-m-Marianne Mercier *

John (the Patriot)-m-Jane Sloan

Anne-m-Peter Flandreau

John ii

Adam

Lewis-m- ?

Mary Ann-m-John Boyd

John Le Conte

Susanne-m-William Bayley I*-m-John Guerrineau

Joseph Lecorte

John Peter

Richard Bayley-m-Catherine Charlton *

William II-m-Sarah Pell

William iii

Susannah-m-Jeremiah Schureman

Joseph-m-Susan ?

Anne-m-Capt. James Hague

Rev. William Hague (minister)

Note—
Names marked with an asterisk (*) are repeated in two family lines.

Katherine Lasty-m-Bartholomew Mercier-m-David Bonnefoy

Henry-m-Christiana Hendricks

Helen

David

Katherine-m-Isaac Coutant

William (Capt.)-m-Maria Bradford

Isaac Jr.-m-Susanne Mercier

Marianne-m-William LeConte *

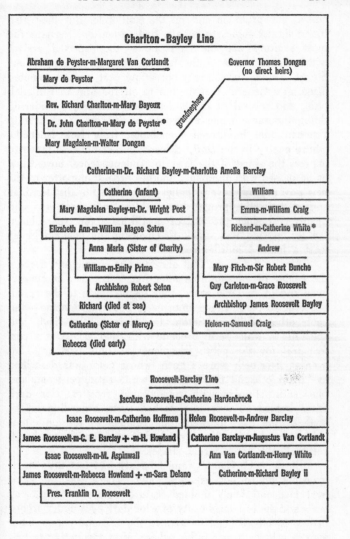

Charlton - Bayley Line

Abraham de Peyster-m-Margaret Van Cortlandt   Governor Thomas Dongan
                                                          (no direct heirs)
    Mary de Peyster

    Rev. Richard Charlton-m-Mary Bayeux
                                                    grandnephew
        Dr. John Charlton-m-Mary de Peyster*

        Mary Magdalen-m-Walter Dongan

            Catherine-m-Dr. Richard Bayley-m-Charlotte Amelia Barclay

                    Catherine (Infant)   William

            Mary Magdalen Bayley-m-Dr. Wright Post   Emma-m-William Craig

        Elizabeth Ann-m-William Magee Seton   Richard-m-Catherine White*

                Anna Maria (Sister of Charity)   Andrew

                William-m-Emily Prime   Mary Fitch-m-Sir Robert Bunche

                    Archbishop Robert Seton   Guy Carleton-m-Grace Roosevelt

                Richard (died at sea)   Archbishop James Roosevelt Bayley

            Catherine (Sister of Mercy)   Helen-m-Samuel Craig

        Rebecca (died early)

            Roosevelt-Barclay Line
            Jacobus Roosevelt-m-Catherine Hardenbrock

        Isaac Roosevelt-m-Catherine Hoffman   Helen Roosevelt-m-Andrew Barclay

    James Roosevelt-m-C. E. Barclay -+- -m-H. Howland   Catherine Barclay-m-Augustus Van Cortlandt

        Isaac Roosevelt-m-M. Aspinwall   Ann Van Cortlandt-m-Henry White

    James Roosevelt-m-Rebecca Howland -+- -m-Sara Delano   Catherine-m-Richard Bayley ii

        Pres. Franklin D. Roosevelt

cussed her probable end on the guillotine. But they also
found lighter topics to engage their attention. Perhaps the
most exciting was the latest news—the expected arrival
within a few weeks of the famous portrait painter Gilbert
Stuart. Rumor was already spreading that he had solicited
Mme. and General Washington to sit for him in Philadelphia, and several of the ladies were seriously considering
doing the same while he would be in New York. Philip
Freneau, that handsome Frenchman from New Rochelle,
whose poetry in the *Daily Advertiser* had done so much to
express the spirit of the War for Independence, bowed low
as he passed with John Jay, another ardent supporter of the
new government. Several ladies of staunch Loyalist leanings
sniffed their disapproval, but nothing unpleasant was said
openly, for since the end of hostilities a few years back,
the losing side was quick to cover up its chagrin by at
least a feigned indifference.

Among the guests that evening one couple had become
the center of considerable attention. Attractive in appearance and of enviable grace, they seemed even to the casual
observer to be enjoying immensely both the dancing—and
each other. William Seton, tall, fair-complexioned, and
splendid in white satin brocade with gold lace, was a perfect foil for the petite lissomeness of his partner. That
evening Elizabeth wore a gown whose color was described
as "plain celestial blue" over a white satin petticoat, and
blue satin slippers with rose-colored rosettes. Her dark
hair, dressed all over in detached curls, according to the
style of the day, allowed four ringlets to fall on either
side. Around her neck was softly draped a large gauze hand-
kerchief with satin border stripes.

Susanna Le Conte's famed beauty had lost little in its
transmission to her granddaughter. There was the same
oval face and finely molded features, the same clustering
curls and the lustrous beauty of wide dark eyes under arched
brows. Elizabeth herself refers to the size and color of her
eyes in a letter to her father where, after recounting to him

how she had overheard high commendation for his article on yellow fever, she adds: "I imagine my eyes were larger and blacker at that moment than usual." During the period of William's courtship, Elizabeth's eyes again figured in a little note—this time not so brilliantly! With charming whimsey she wrote:

> Your Eliza's eye is very ugly but not very painful, but it will prevent the possibility of my going out—therefore you must devote a great deal of your time to me—Come as early as possible.

William Magee Seton and Elizabeth Ann Bayley had been childhood playmates. Six years her senior, William had gone to Italy, when she was fourteen, as a guest of his father's business associates, the Filicchis. By the time he returned, a few months before the ball, Elizabeth had grown into a charming young woman, vivacious and beautiful, the darling of New York society. Off and on during the next two years, William would pay her his admiring attention. The romance bloomed into love and the pair became engaged. Often during the months that followed, Dr. Bayley's houseboy (calley Bayley) was dispatched by his young mistress on love's business—the bearer of tender little messages from Elizabeth to William, then a cashier of the Bank of New York. Like all lovers the world over, the mere nothings of daily life became important whenever either one was involved. In this vein Elizabeth hastened to apprise William of a change in their plans for an evening:

> My dearest Will—Mrs. Sadler is not going to the Concert and wishes very much to see Us there this Evening—do not be too late—   Yours, E. B.

or with a sudden spurt of energy, she announced:

> My dearest Will—I have resolved to do my duty and go to see Mrs. Knight this afternoon and if the weather remains

clear it is my intention to pass an hour with Mrs. Wilkes in
the Evening where you may have the honor of seeing me if
you please—   Yours, E. B.

William's obligations sometimes kept him from visiting
Elizabeth for several days. Sweetly, appealingly, she reminds him:

> Your Eliza is well—and would be perfectly happy if she
> could enjoy the Society of her Friend.
>   I have wished very much to see you, and know that Indis-
> position only could have prevented my wish—Tomorrow I
> will wait in anxious expectation.
>   Believe me   Your *own*

Eager to have cordial relations between William and her
father, she wrote to the former regarding an appointment
for the same day—

> My Father dined with us and has gone I don't know where—
> I do not think you will meet him until the Evening—Your
> *apology* is already made by one who is most earnestly in-
> terested in his good opinion of you.
>   Your E. will be on Wall Street by five o'clock and you
> shall then know more on the subject.

The wedding of William and Elizabeth took place on the
evening of January 25, 1794, the ceremony being performed
by the Episcopal Bishop Provost.

There were few things Elizabeth enjoyed more in her
younger days than dancing, although in later life she confessed to having had serious regrets on more than one occasion for having frittered away her time so idly. It brought
her, she said, "the most innocent cheerfulness both in public
and in private," but the remembrances of the pleasure later
distracted her at her prayers. Yet she was careful to provide
dancing lessons for her eldest daughter Anna. She who had
enjoyed the reputation of being the "belle of every ball"

could scarcely ignore the development of these social graces in her own children. Elizabeth had no doubt imbibed much of the French *joie de vivre* during her numerous visits to New Rochelle where families but two generations removed from their native France still lived her life, spoke her language, and possessed her gayety.

2

Elizabeth's cultural background was predominantly French, both in her ability to read and converse fluently in the language and in her tastes for aesthetic pleasures—the beauties of nature, poetry, music, and as we have seen, the dance. When a small child, "Bette", as her father called her, objected to the time required for mastering these subjects. Dr. Bayley, however, saw to it that his little daughter lived up to her birthright. "French and music," he said, "must have their time." And they did. Elizabeth became an accomplished musician, retaining her skill at the piano even through the most distracting phases of her married life. A brief visit to the Long Island home of her friend, Mrs. Sadler, brought the comment: "I have all the enjoyments of books, music, walking, etc. that my most romantic fancy ever formed." On another occasion, after remarking that all the family were busy elsewhere, she says: "So I have all my pretty library and my music to myself."

Before her marriage, a little note to William informed him that

> An unavoidable Something obliges Mrs. Sadler to drink tea with Mrs. Constable. If you are anxious to see your Eliza, you will find her at Mrs. Atkinson's at the piano.
>
> Your own.

In a letter to her friend Julia Scott, Elizabeth bears

testimony to how well she had carried out her father's command. Speaking of the distribution of her time so that she might have more leisure to help her children at their studies, she says:

> . . . that I may be able to give a large portion of my time to Anna in communicating to her what I know of music and French, which is as much and perhaps more than she would attain in another situation. . . .

Later she would give a progress report to her friend: "Anna is making rapid progress in her music. She often plays off simply when I am obliged to study."

Through Dr. Bayley, in whom the French influences were also marked, Elizabeth acquired an early acquaintance with the contemporary literature of France, especially the works of Voltaire and Rousseau. The latter exerted for some time a powerful influence on her philosophical ideas, his comments remaining fresh in her mind even in later life. There is the letter written to her youngest daughter Catherine Josephine on the subject of reading romances in which she says: ". . . or to speak the sentiment of Rousseau himself, 'No chaste woman can read romance.'" Elizabeth's own quick mind and fertile imagination no doubt made her more sensitive to the dangers inherent in this kind of reading which was so much in vogue at the time. We may gather what type of "romances" was referred to by Elizabeth in her letter if we take a look at the list of books advertised by leading dealers such as Gains and Nutter.

> Just Published—*The Italian* or the Confessional of the Black Penitents, a Romance by Ann Radcliffe in 2 vols.
>
> *Evelina*—Or the History of a young Lady's Entrance into the World—recommended by Dr. Samuel Johnson—written by Miss Burney, a young lady of sixteen—a novel.
>
> *Juliet Greenville* or the History of the Human Heart—Brooks.
>
> *Charlotte Temple* (an exceptionally popular sentimental novel) by Susanna Rowson.

Even the books for children were abridged—and, we hope—expurgated editions of the adult best sellers. Nutter's advertisement in *Rivington's Gazeteer* announces that "at his shop are sold the following books":

> *Little Books for the Instruction of all Good Boys and Girls*: abridged editions of *The History of Tom Jones, Joseph Andrews, Pamela, Clarissa*

along with the more edifying companionship of

> *Pilgrim's Progress* and the *Christian Companion*.

Elizabeth herself had probably read all of these at an early age, since we know from her own words that reading was her favorite pastime. Speaking of Anna's progress in her studies and in needlework, she says:

> She is very neat at her needle and her pen, and translates French with facility and pleasure. She is fond of occupation, but like her poor mother, only attached to reading and writing.

Her early contacts with French authors was, no doubt, sparked by discussions with the older generation of relatives in New Rochelle whose parents had received their education in the schools of France, and who had often recalled for their children the works and sayings of their national writers. There was, as late as Elizabeth's young adulthood, a virile French culture extant in New Rochelle, the last citadel of Gallic colonization. William Bayley's grandson, Rev. William Hague, tells us that "at the opening of the nineteenth century, the French language, spoken in purity and elegance, still lived on as the vernacular of home-life." When Elizabeth attended Trinity Episcopal Church with the Bayley family, she saw all around her, relatives and close friends— Badeaus, Merciers, Flandreaus, Besleys, Le Contes, and

Coutants—names so rooted in the soil of France that it would take several generations to complete their grafting onto the new America.

3

Guillaume Le Conte's behest concerning the education of his children was carried out by his descendants beyond what could have been his most cherished hope. As we have noted in an earlier chapter, the name Le Conte is an honored one in the annals of higher education; it has been borne by botanists, doctors, professors, and scientists. Joseph Le Conte, the great naturalist, traced his lineage directly to Pierre Le Conte of Staten Island, Guillaume's son by his second marriage. According to Professor Le Conte, Pierre became a physician, as did his grandson Louis, who was graduated from Columbia College Medical School in 1799. It is quite likely that he studied anatomy under his cousin Dr. Richard Bayley, who was teaching there at this time. Elizabeth, too, must have met this young kinsman, who, it seems, would have been about her own age. In his autobiography, Professor Le Conte included a number of portraits of Le Conte relatives. All are distinguished-looking intellectuals having the same refined features: sweeping brows, deepset and thoughtful eyes; the straight, well-shaped and rather long nose.

No descendant of Guillaume Le Conte's, however, was more faithful to this tradition of learning, nor left to posterity a greater legacy of accomplishment for its promotion than his great-great-granddaughter Elizabeth Bayley who appears to have been occupied from her earliest years in instructing others. At the age of six she took her two-year-old half-sister Emma to the highest window of the house and showed her the setting sun, telling her that good children go up to heaven to God. She also taught Emma her prayers.

As a young mother of five children, caring also for several of her husband's half-sisters, she gives an account of how she spent most of her mornings:

> Suppose yourself a teacher of reading, writing, sewing, for I devote the whole morning, that is from ten until two to my three girls;

and again—

> By ten o'clock all is arranged, and the round table covered with different books used by my darlings—Cecilia begins grammar, reading, writing, spelling large and small words, marking, sewing and figures. You doubtless smile at the idea of my being her directress . . . Anna Maria follows Cecilia as nearly as her inferior age allows and discovers a capacity and amiability of mind that gives me a peaceful satisfaction —for a mother always "rejoices with trembling." William and Richard say their lessons, little pieces, names of the United States, divisions of the globe, some of the commandments. All this employs the morning completely.

Later she writes:

> William makes his letters very well and Anna begins to join hers. They spell very well and would read, but I promised my father the first of last summer that I would keep them back for twelve months.

Evidently Dr. Bayley did not believe in hurrying his grandchildren through their baby years.

But her great work in life, after the founding of her religious community, was the opening of schools, both free and private, and setting up, out of her own wide experience, a system of classroom management and curriculum organization that remains today a model for all who would make the profession of teaching the noble calling that it should be. Some of her advice to the young women whom she trained may be recalled with profit. The following extracts are from her notebook of instructions:

> . . . it is to be observed that to avoid the confusion of perpetual changes, the course shall not be changed without a deliberation on the subject, no more than the uniform mode of teaching—as for the distribution of the children in the classes and the choice of the mistresses, as they depend in some measure on the improvement of each scholar and other variable circumstances, Mother shall be consulted and determine it alone.

> Every one of the girls belonging to each class shall have one copy of every one of the books taught in her class for which her parents shall be charged.

> No girls shall be permitted to absent themselves from any class to which they belong on any pretext whatever; even of taking a lesson in Music; but in case their parents insist upon their learning it, they must leave off one of the classes at the choice of the parents and always the same, or else take their Music lesson during recreation, if it is possible, as it is impossible for them to do their duty in class if their study time has been taken from them.

> Of course they can neither be employed by the Sisters or be called out of their class by any Sister without a positive order from Mother which is to be given only in case of urgent necessity.

> Every one of the teachers of writing must have her pens, copy books, ink, and ink horn, and copy plates ready before the respective classes of writing begin.

> During the time of classes and particularly during the writing classes the greatest silence must be observed, no children may be allowed to speak except to the Sister, and in whispers so as not to disturb the others.

Every Sister is bound to keep her class in order, and punish delinquents immediately or in the next recreation.

The girls shall not be permitted to do anything during class which would distract from their main object, such as sewing, knitting . . .

No girl can be sent out of any class even by the Sister on the pretext of carrying a message to another Sister, when it is not a case of urgent necessity.

The greatest attention shall be paid to the behavior of the children in class, they shall not be permitted to loll, sit where they please, stoop too low, with crossed legs, leaning upon one another—impudent manners or behaviour towards the Sisters shall be punished instantly—they shall not be permitted to come to class in a rude noisy manner.

Stubbornness, disobedience, shall be punished immediately when habitual or frequently repeated by the same child; no Sister shall ever yield to the importunities or obstinacy of the child—if mild advice will not do, needed punishment will succeed. If the child has not been subdued by any, she shall be referred to Mother, who will direct a severer punishment. If this will have no effect the child must be dismissed from St. Joseph's.

Once a month Mother will endeavor to attend every class herself, choosing for it a time which will suit her best and least foreseen either by the children or even the Sisters in order to witness herself not only the talents, applications and dispositions of the pupils; but also the capacity, mode of teaching, attention and success of the different teachers on the whole. She will take notes that she may be able to judge better of those which will be taken by the Sisters.

From these passages, it may be seen with what exactness Mother Seton organized and supervised the educational work of her community. The methodical system of classroom management inaugurated by this eighteenth-century educator has become a precious inheritance for every teaching Sister of Charity in the United States.

Mother Seton was wise in her knowledge of the partiality of parents toward their children, probably because she was a mother herself. In this regard she comments to her Sisters:

> I will tell you in what I know American parents to be most difficult—in hearing the faults of their children . . . in twenty instances when you see the faults are not to be corrected by the parents, but rather by good advices and education, it is best not to speak of them to papa and Mama who feel as if you reflected on their very *self* and while to you it will be "Yes sir, I know, I perceive," in the heart they think it is not so much, and they will often excuse to the child what they condemn to us and our efforts avail very little.

Another example of her adroitness in dealing with parents showed itself in a letter to Mr. Elder about his daughter Elenor:

> Your letter enclosing the order on Mr. Grover for sixty and one-half dollars is received. I was going to write Mrs. Elder by return of Rev. Bishop Flaget to tell her that your dear child was presented particularly to him before we knew her wish expressed in her letter to Elenor, who is always a good child and for her age uncommonly attentive to all her duties. Our Superior Bp. Du Bois thinks her the most intelligent child in her class of catechism and we have no reason to complain of her want of diligence in anything. She has some odd little ways as her dear Mama knows and is not always as docile as we could wish when she happens to be vexed—but in that she is not singular, and among our fifty odd children, we have very few as good as Elenor . . . I believe she will make an Excellent Woman and will be a real comfort to you. When you write to her you will speak to her of the necessity of silence in her class, diligence at her needle, and condescension to her playmates. These three points she is most deficient in tho' really not materially

faulty. If you really wish her to learn music we will apply her to it immediately but she must in that case sacrifice a part of the time allotted to needle work as by an arrangement of the classes lately made she could not be spared at any other time without great sacrifice of reading, grammar, spelling or arithmetic so essential at her age.

Jan. 18, 1813   To Mr. Elder. Baltimore

A touching example of children's loyalty and devotion to Mother Seton, and her fondness and interest in them has been left us in the exchange of letters between Jerome Bonaparte and the Reverend Mother. The lad had made his first Communion at Mount St. Mary's where he was privileged to read the Baptismal vows for all the others. In this letter he asks a favor, confident of being kindly received:

Mount St. Mary's Seminary
June 21st

My dear Mother,

I am anxious to get an Agnus Dei before I go home in order to preserve me in the vacation from the dangers that will surround me in the vacation. I will keep it as a memorial of kindness and love for your little child who always thinks of you with respect and love and who will think of you with gratitude also, especially if I will have an Agnus Dei as a present from you.

          . . . Your dear child in God

Jerome N. Bonaparte

Mother's answer:

Dear Jerome, It is a great pleasure to me to send you the Agnus Dei—I wish that I had one handsomely covered but you will mind only the Virtue of the prayers our Holy Father has said over it.

I earnestly beg Our Lord to preserve in you the graces he has so tenderly bestowed on you—take care yourself not to lose them. Pray for us and I will for you.

Your true friend
EAS

A charming example of the effective methods used by Mother Seton in disciplining the young minds entrusted to her care is the incident of "General Harper's daughter." One day little Mary Diane Harper said to her playmate Clotilde Brawner: "Do you know who I am?" "No," answered Clotilde, "I don't know." "Well, I am General Robert Goodloe Harper's daughter!" Someone told Mother Seton about Mary's boastfulness. She sent for the child and bade her sit for half-an-hour under the picture of "The Redeemer" in Mother's room and reflect who General Robert Goodloe Harper's daughter really was!

4

In nothing was Elizabeth more truly a daughter of the Le Contes than in her fervently religious spirit. Guillaume Le Conte and his great-great-granddaughter might not hold the same tenets, but what they believed in, they held to with equal tenacity. Guillaume fled his country to escape persecution and to find religious liberty. Elizabeth, returning to her native land after the death of her husband, and on the eve of her conversion to Catholicism, faced bitter persecution and social ostracism. Opposition did not shake the faith of her ancestors; it would not shake hers.

Viewed from the standpoint of her Huguenot forebears, there is something ironical about Elizabeth's becoming a Roman Catholic. Actually, however, her ancestral background, so rich in its appreciation of supernatural values, was the very source of the pious strain that urged Elizabeth toward a closer and closer contact with God through His Church. One recalls the early dawn processions of faithful Huguenots from New Rochelle, making the long trek to services in a New York City church, singing hymns and psalms along the way to enkindle their spirits. And the mind instantly conjures another picture of a frail little widow, hurrying alone

through empty early morning streets to keep a rendezvous
with the God of her heart—

> How bright the sun, these morning walks of preparation!
> Deep snow, or smooth ice, all to me the same—I see nothing
> but the little bright cross on St. Peter's steeple.

Spoken surely with the Le Conte spirit!

Elizabeth's predilection for the psalms was another
Huguenot legacy. One reads repeatedly of their pilgrimages,
processions, and services—always beginning, continuing, and
ending with psalms and the hymns of Marot.

The preponderance of French traits in the physical and
temperamental life of Elizabeth Bayley is to be expected
when one considers how many times that strand had woven
itself in and around the ancestral tapestry. The early Le
Conte marriages with the Merciers, Flandreaus, and Lastys
had deepened the strain of pure French brought across the
ocean at the time of their exile and stretching far back into
limitless generations of ancestors. Elizabeth's maternal
grandmother was Mary Bayeux, daughter of Thomas Bayeux
and Madeleine Boudinot, both of the original two hundred
Huguenot settlers in New York City. Her paternal grandmother was Susanna Le Conte whom Elizabeth herself so
strongly resembled. Through both sides of her family she
inherited salient French traits. The very philosophical, questioning, and logical reasoning of her mind was typically
French!

Elizabeth was by nature—her French nature—eager and
impetuous, yet inclined to be somewhat stubborn, with a
Gallic tendency to extremes of temperament. Her usually
sunny and gay disposition was occasionally clouded with
spells of melancholy. She recorded her own impression of
this failing as follows:

> There is a certain temper I am sometimes subject to—it is
> not sullenness or absolute discontent, 'tis a kind of melan-

choly; still I like it better than those effusions of cheerfulness, that hilarity of spirits, which a good night's rest and a
fine morning often inspire. I prefer the sadness, because I
know it may be removed; it may change to cheerfulness.
The gayety, I am sure, will change to sadness, before
the day ends, and perhaps to sorrow; 'tis not the natural
temper, but the influence of situation. I trust the day will
come when I may show a more regular Christian disposition.

How perfectly Elizabeth was to learn the lessons of evenness
and self-restraint, even she could not guess!

Dr. Bayley was quick to notice these tendencies in his
daughter and set himself to correct them. Writing to her on
one occasion, he advised:

... But calm that glowing of the soul, that warmth of spirits; impressions will then be less readily admitted, but they
will last longer.

At another time, regarding her little fits of sadness, he wrote:

I hope you have made up your mind to laugh at all imagi-
nary evils; it will smooth your path through life.

Her father was probably conscious of these same tendencies
in himself, his disposition also being impulsive and stubborn.
His advice to Elizabeth was unfortunately based on French
rationalism rather than on religious principles. He had assured her on one occasion that idle speculation about God
had no place in the life of a practical Christian. It certainly
had little place in his strenuous days, nor did he foster in
Elizabeth any of those weak emanations of piety to which
her ardent disposition might have led her. There was a viril-
ity and forthrightness about Elizabeth Bayley which could
readily be traced to her close and tender associations with
this great man. Religious belief he may not have had, but
assuredly, his own boundless solicitude for the poor passed
into the soul of his observing daughter, there to burgeon
forth into the charitable works that were to crown her last

years. But Elizabeth would have a long thorny path to traverse between these days of French influences and those far-off years when at last she would be free to answer the beckoning finger of her sublime destiny.

It was as a daughter of the Huguenots that Elizabeth wounded her family and friends most deeply by her conversion to Catholicism. To them it was tantamount to betrayal, rendering void all the long years of suffering and exile they had endured for their beliefs. "To have gone over to the Church that persecuted her ancestors" was for her sister Mary the most harrowing sorrow that Elizabeth could have inflicted upon her. It was possibly in this respect that she herself suffered the most refined pain. This young woman who looked, felt, and acted as a Frenchwoman, could not have lightly sold her birthright.

It is one more proof of Elizabeth's heroic stamina that— to a different end—but in the same spirit—she acted as a Le Conte!

XII

Elizabeth
Ann Bayley

1

AN ERRONEOUS IMPRESSION that Elizabeth Bayley was the favored child of Fortune, a beautiful, gay, and carefree young woman, has gained prominence in certain accounts of her life written for popular appeal, and for the young. Nothing seems further from the actual truth when the documents of her background, most of them in her own handwriting, are thoughtfully examined.

Elizabeth was the child of sorrow: her mother's sorrow first, and then, her own. During the months preceding the birth of her second child, Catherine Charlton Bayley experienced the gnawing pain of anxiety. Once already in their five brief years of married life, she had bade her husband "Godspeed" on a professional trip that extended over two years. Now again she was being asked to make that same sacrifice. Richard had informed her of his intentions to seek recognition for his work among the medical leaders of London. Unselfishly, courageously, she had tried to hide her distress. Besides the painful separation from her husband just at a time when he would be most needed, there was the financial strain of another mouth to feed, of another ocean voyage to pay for. According to Dr. Thacher, the Bayleys were poor; at least, struggling. Dr. Bayley was still apprenticed, as it were, to Dr. Charlton, and though many of their patients were no doubt beginning to appreciate the skill of

154

the young assistant, it would take some years to build up a large, well-paying practice. But Catherine did not feel equal to the scene that might follow if she were to protest Richard's proposed trip. She knew only too well his impulsive, determined disposition, and though she never doubted his genuine love for her, she had learned to accept the fact that the first love of his life was his profession.

On the morning of August 28, 1774, Catherine held her infant daughter in her arms and marveled at the perfect loveliness of the child. At once she knew that this little one was different—very different—from her other little girl, four-year-old Mary Magdalen. The mother's heart welled up with pride and joy as Richard bent to kiss them both. Then a sudden stab of realization went through her like a knife. They could be so happy with their children . . . why did he have to go? After Richard had left the room, Catherine turned her face to the wall and wept.

*　　*　　*　　*　　*　　*

Elizabeth saw her father for the first time when she was nearly two years old. He had but recently returned from England in company with the British Army, whose uniform he now wore. Dr. Bayley had felt that the expenses of his trip, the exigencies of the times, and the needs of his growing family called for this step which would assure him a regular salary for the duration of the War. What his wife thought of it we do not know, but her sympathies were probably Loyalist. Her joy in her husband's return was, nevertheless, clouded by the necessity for his reporting to Newport, Rhode Island, within a short time.

Catherine now faced a third separation. Her situation on this occasion, however, would be more desperate than during either of the preceding ones. The British were soon to lay siege to New York. Pitiable scarcities of food and fuel, black market prices for what little could still be purchased, the flight of thousands of Loyalist friends and neigh-

bors, the treachery of others—all these were to be faced by
the young wife and mother—alone with her two small children. The first three years of Elizabeth's life were rich in
mother love, but they were decidedly impoverished in all
other respects.

Richard's departure for Newport left his wife and children quite unprotected at a time when the city was a seeth-
ing center of military activities. During his absence it is not
likely that he was able to send Catherine money for her
needs and those of his children. His contract with the British
War Office called for two years of service before payment.
This we know he forfeited completely when he left his post
to be with his dying wife.

There are several questions regarding Catherine's situation that provoke consideration. Where did Mrs. Bayley
live at the time of the disastrous fire of 1776? Was she involved, together with her little ones? That is a harrowing
thought. One would like to know, too, what contacts,
if any, Catherine had during these years with Richard's
brother William. Elizabeth herself does not speak of seeing
her uncle at this period, yet it would seem to be entirely
out of character for that genial man to have left his sister-in-
law and infant nieces to fend for themselves.

One certain friend the Bayley family had. That was
Catherine's brother, Dr. John Charlton. We have Elizabeth's
own words for the fact that he "loved me more than anyone
in the world." He it was, no doubt, who, out of his "immense fortune," provided for his sister and her children.
There is also the possibility that Catherine may have spent
part of the time with her father, Rev. Richard Charlton, at
his home on Staten Island. Circumstances point, however,
to Dr. John's special care of the little family. It was very
likely to his home in Jamaica, Long Island, that he brought
the ailing Catherine. There her third child was born and
there, on May 8, 1777, she died.

One duty the young wife seems to have fulfilled despite
loneliness, poverty, and ill health. Whatever Catherine's pri-

vate heartbreaks may have been, she instilled in her children a deep respect and affection for the father whom they hardly knew. To Elizabeth, bereft of her mother at the age of three, he came almost as a stranger, yet we find that she felt for him at once a deep tender love which was to be his comfort throughout life.

2

At the age of three, Elizabeth probably was an average child with keen intelligence and abounding vitality. Close association with her elder sister and with her mother, the shadows cast over her baby days by the continued absence of her father, her mother's poor health, and the disturbed times in which they lived had, without doubt, rendered her more aware of the currents of life than were carefree children of an older growth.

When Dr. Bayley could spare the time from his heavy duties, he delighted in sharpening the mind and training the character of his "Bette," as he fondly called his favorite daughter. Her sister Mary seems to have been content to learn the basic skills of good housewifery and the social graces. In this situation Elizabeth's mental powers were given lively impetus while her thoughtful nature readily absorbed the ever-challenging aspects of life around her. All children of that period seem to us, as we read about them, to have been precocious. Certainly, they were quaintly wise; their schooling began at the tender age of four when these mere babes were expected to sit on hard benches for many hours, and if we can trust the testimony of the pupils, all the mistresses were stern-eyed and inexorable! The curriculum included geography, spelling, writing, French, music, needlework, and arithmetic. Long sums requiring multiplication of fifteen numbers by fifteen numbers and long division of quintillions were laboriously worked out on slates. The

pupils made their own copy books from foolscap sewn into
book shape and ruled by hand with lead plummets sharpened
at the end. Elizabeth and her sister were sent to the school
maintained by "Mama Pompelion." It was probably from a
class in this same establishment that the little girl dashed out
into the street to greet her father as he rode by on his sick
calls.

The winter of 1780 was a most harrowing one for all
New Yorkers. The city was under siege by the British.
Redcoats shot down without quarter any male patriot abroad
within the city limits. It was a ghost town of women and
children—cold, hungry women and children. Although Dr.
Bayley's family suffered less, probably, than most other New
Yorkers because of his Tory affiliations and the high respect
with which he was regarded by both factions, still, the scarc-
ity of staple products must have caused some discomfort to
his household. In addition to these physical trials, the six-
year-old Elizabeth was struggling to accept her stepmother
and to welcome generously the half-brothers and sisters
which each succeeding year seemed to bring.

By the time she had reached her twelfth year, the War
had been brought to a close and the new nation was in the
throes of adjusting itself to a tentative government under
the Articles of Confederation. This was Elizabeth's most
difficult period of adjustment also. Speaking of herself at
the age of twelve she declares that she was "foolish, ignorant,
of childish heart." This, of course, was written in retrospect,
yet there are indications that her early teens were not very
different from what she pictured them. Her natural willful-
ness, high spirits, quick temper, and sudden moods of melancholy offered such a gamut of emotional activity as might
well have proved the ruination of a more flighty child. All
her life Elizabeth would struggle against her tendency to
independence; she would find subjection difficult, but in her
latter days, so complete had been her victory, that those
nearest to her would speak of her gentle and serene manner
as among her dominant traits.

At sixteen Elizabeth comments on "family disagreements" and refers to her own "folly, sorrows, romance, and miserable friendships; but all turned to good—and thoughts of how silly to love anything in this world." These were the days when the young Eliza began to realize the transient nature of joy and to perceive more clearly in her own life the ever-present reflection of the Cross. She was a soul marked for detachments and separations that would foster in her that abiding yearning for Eternity which was to be the theme and purpose of her life.

Accordingly, Elizabeth arrived at her eighteenth year after a somewhat disturbed and unsettled adolescence. She was now a beautiful young lady of great natural charm enhanced by a cultured and refined mind. At a period when the education of women was not considered a necessary adornment, Elizabeth Bayley must have presented a striking personality. She was able to converse fluently in French, had read and even translated some of the classics in that language; she could write passable poetry, was an accomplished musician, and she was deeply interested in religious and philosophical subjects. Her nephew, Guy Carlton, recalled that she wrote a "fair hand," and we who have seen the painstaking and laborious notebooks she kept in later life, have admired the clear and refined script.

To these intellectual qualities may be added Elizabeth's personal beauty, her love of dancing and gay society, her skill as a horsewoman. This last accomplishment marked her as an Englishwoman; in this she was predominantly a Bayley. Undoubtedly, she often rode the "fourteen-miles-around," a fashionable afternoon drive, whether by coach or in the saddle. The route led up the Boston Post Road, crossed Murray Hill (now the 42nd Street area) went west through McGown's Pass to Bloomingdale (100th Street and Broadway), a seven-mile trip from the lower end of the city. The return route was along the Hudson River to Greenwich Village into Broadway. This drive was a favorite one of General Washington whose cream-colored coach with its

green Venetian blinds and gilt trim was a familiar sight to
New Yorkers in the neighborhood of his Cherry Street home.

Elizabeth probably did her shopping at the Fly Market
off Maiden Lane. In the evening we know that she sometimes went to the Theater on John Street—a structure so
small "that the whole fabric might easily be placed on the
stage of a modern theater." She may have been present for
the first public rendition of "Hail Columbia" written by
Fyles, a German musician, as a tribute to Washington who
frequently attended this same theater with his staff.

Yet Elizabeth's mind was not entirely given over to the
social whirl of which she seems to have been the center. She
has left jottings in her diary in which she expresses regrets
for the frivolity of a Sunday afternoon which she should
have devoted, she thought, to more prayer and Bible reading.
She upbraids herself for thinking too much of the company
of certain people. One entry in her eighteenth year gives
evidence of the maturing woman:

> Fine plans of a little country home; to gather all the chil-
> dren around and teach them their prayers, and keep them
> clean, and teach them to be good.

In these lines she is unwittingly prophesying her twofold
vocation in later life: as a mother and as a religious teacher.

Elizabeth possessed a rare magnetic power to attract and
hold others. Constant reference is made to it—chiefly by
her enemies!—who attributed to it all the converts who followed her lead into the Catholic Church. Mr. Ogden's letter
to Harriet Seton is typical:

> Immured in the solitude of your retirement, you have lent a
> willing ear to the persuasions of Mrs. Seton, the only person
> in her situation in the United States; a constant witness of
> the external performance of her devotions, your heart has
> yielded to the delusion; your mind thus seduced had em-
> braced and answered *her* faith, not because internally con-
> vinced of its purity, but from the strong impression of her
> manner. . . .

This gift of impressing others was the keynote of her astonishing influence upon widely varying characters. All who met Elizabeth were charmed by her rare qualities—from little Rebecca, her sister-in-law, to the imposing figure of Archbishop Carroll of Baltimore.

3

During the period from her seventeenth year to her marriage at the age of nineteen, Elizabeth appears, from all accounts, to have led a very worldly life. There is a sad anomaly in this situation, for during this same period it is also correct to assume that she had no real home—at least not more than a transient one. Whatever the cause, it is evident that she did not live with her stepmother. Her letters are written from her married sister's home in John Street, from Staten Island, and occasionally, from wherever her father was living at the time. The announcement of her wedding, carried in the *Weekly Museum* of February 1, 1794, gave the John Street residence as the scene of the ceremony. Elizabeth was, therefore, not married from her father's house.

Her social success had, indeed, a Cinderella-like quality. It can be attributed to her own beauty and to her family connections. As a great-granddaughter of William Le Conte, she was a young lady of distinguished background. Her maternal aunt was Mary De Peyster, Uncle John Charlton's wife. Elizabeth was closely related by marriage to most of the leading families of New York. On her mother's side, she had Bayeux, Lispenard, Schuyler and Groesbeck cousins. By her father's second marriage, she claimed relationship with Roosevelts, Jays, Van Cortlandts, and De Lanceys. Dr. Bayley, by this time a highly renowned and successful practitioner, still had not the financial means that would have admitted Elizabeth to these select circles. He and his daughter were accepted for what they were rather than for what they had. This fact may account for the noticeably patronizing attitude first shown by William Seton toward his suggested marriage with Elizabeth.

* * * * * *

Shortly after becoming Mrs. William Seton, the young bride wrote ecstatically in her *Dear Remembrances*:

> My own home at twenty—The world and heaven too, quite impossible! So every moment clouded with fear, My God, if I enjoy this I lose You. . . . Delight in the continual contrast of all my blessings with the miseries I saw.

During one of the numerous epidemics that swept over New York, Elizabeth and her children were evacuated to the Seton family estate at Bloomingdale. From there Mrs. Seton sent the following wifely note to her husband, who had remained in the city near his business:

> My love,
> I send you the cloaths, [sic] Brush and comb which I forgot this morning and also to remind you of the Box of Silver and the Bread Basket in my Press which will not lock. Is it possible that I am not to see you again for so long a time? Heaven Protect you, and return you again in safety. Your darlings have enjoyed this cool day and are as merry as Birds they cannot understand that Papa is not to come tomorrow—nor next day—nor the day after—that is for their mother to feel. . . .

Set against the umbra of her early years, this extravagant mixture of joy and fear is completely understandable: joy in the possession of something entirely her own—a home where she is the mistress—where all the pent-up affection and deep emotions of her life may at last be poured out lavishly on her husband and her children—*her* family, her

very own! Fear clutched at her heart because of the newness
of her joy; remembrance of the long years of insecurity
tugged at her present tranquility with a sense of foreboding.
In spite of herself, the lessons of detachment which circumstances had forced upon her, intruded on this unusual happiness with their reminders of the transitory nature of all
things. For sorrow, not joy, was Elizabeth's "element" as
she was to write to a friend a few years later. Unalloyed
happiness was hers for a brief four years and then the
shadows closed in. In May, 1798, Mrs. Seton wrote to her
friend Julia Scott:

> Have I not remarked to you that the world would have too
> many sweets if we did not view disappointment forever in
> the background, and often pursuing us in our most favorite
> retreats of happiness? Do you remember the day we rode
> out as far as Hornbrook's on the East River? When we had
> ascended the hill and were viewing the delightful scenery
> in every direction, I told you that this world would always
> be good enough for me, that I could willingly consent to be
> here forever. But now, Julia—since that short span of time
> —so thoroughly is my mind changed, that nothing in this
> world, were all its best pleasures combined, would tempt
> me to be other than what I am—a pilgrim.

At the time of this letter Elizabeth had been married four
years, was the mother of two children, and was awaiting the
birth of her third child. There was no apparent reason for
Mrs. Seton's extreme change of sentiments at that period,
but early in the following month we find that her presenti-
ments were justified.

The first blow was the unfortunate accident suffered by
the elder William Seton when he fell on the front steps of
his own dwelling. While his fate remained in the balance,
Elizabeth wrote to her friend:

> I think I have never in my life suffered so much from the
> anticipation of evil as during the past fortnight, for in that

space of time we have every hour expected to lose our dear
papa Seton. . . .

Her grief was genuine, for a bond of deep affection had
grown up between Mr. Seton and his charming daughter-in-
law. He admired her virtue, her fidelity to her wifely duties,
and her native keenness of mind and sound judgment. He
looked on her as his counselor and adviser, his wife being
dead, his family still young.

On the 9th of June Mr. Seton died, at the age of fifty-
two. He had been twice married and left thirteen children.
Elizabeth epitomizes their situation in an account of the
tragedy written to Mr. Seton's sister then residing in Dub-
lin—"and with him we have lost every hope of fortune,
prosperity, and comfort, and shall feel his loss irreparably."

The elder Seton did not leave a will. As the oldest son,
and his father's business partner and confidant, William was
therefore confronted, at the age of thirty, with the management of a vast shipping house as well as the responsibility of
a double household. The young couple had lived with
William's father during the first days of their marriage, but
it is to be presumed that they had maintained separate do-
mains. Returning now in the capacity of guardian to his
seven half-brothers and sisters, he would find that the former
arrangement would have to be altered. Elizabeth mentioned
this situation in a letter to Aunt Cayley:

> Rebecca is the eldest daughter unmarried, and there are six
> younger than herself; but our beloved father brought up his
> family in such harmony and affection, that if William can
> but make them some comfortable maintenance, we shall
> yet have hopes of domestic enjoyment when the family gets
> in some degree settled.

Rebecca Seton was eighteen, her two youngest brothers,
eight and nine.

Elizabeth's sense of humor saved her from bitterness

during these trials. She was able to write whimsically of herself to Mrs. Scott:

> . . . Colonel Giles . . . will present you with the long-promised little pictures, which I hope you will like—though not the lively, animated Eliza Bayley, but the softened matron with traces of anxiety on her brow, and this is much more expressed in the large picture than in the small ones.

Her cheerful acceptance of the inevitable expresses itself sweetly in another note to the same friend:

> To be sure, to me, who so dearly love quiet and a small family, to become all at once the mother of six children is a great change when I consider *self*. But I have accustomed that to yield to affection for my William and when I consider his vexations and cares I bless my God who allows me to share and lessen them.

William's "vexations" were indeed multiplying. At this period, the erupting French Revolution caused disastrous setbacks in shipping. The young husband, who seems to have had weak lungs even before his marriage, felt his health declining under the unremitting struggle to keep his mercantile affairs from collapse. In spite of his efforts, however, things went from bad to worse. Before two years were over, he had lost his entire fortune. On January 3, 1800, Elizabeth wrote:

> My dearest Julia,—I write only to wish you a happy New Year and to tell you, if the news of our misfortunes have reached you, that you must do as I do: Hope for the best. My Seton is in distress of mind scarcely to be imagined; partly from the necessity of immediate statement of accounts, which is necessary for his personal honor and the satisfaction of his friends. . . . What is to become of his father's family, Heaven only knows, for his estate has the first claims because he was the principal partner. . . . For the girls I must use economy, and in case of unnecessary

demands appeal to their reason. Dear, dear Julia, how long
I have been tired of this busy scene; but it is not likely to
mend, and I must be thankful for what remain from the
ruins of Wall Street.

What Elizabeth's life was during these two years can be better imagined than described. Perhaps the best pictures of
what circumstances demanded of her are glimpsed in the
hasty, poignant letters to her dearest friend with whom she
was in constant contact. To Julia, who complained that she
had not heard recently from Elizabeth, the latter wrote:

> My Dear Julia may well ask what I am doing, and really I
> was never so busy in my life, or should not have passed six
> weeks without a line to you. My Seton has a great deal of
> private writing just now, which either he or I must do, and
> as I am doomed this winter to suffer a great deal of pain
> both of mind and body, and no employment helps me so soon
> to forget both as writing, I have taken to myself as a com-
> fort what would have been a great deal of trouble to him.
> Besides, my knowing all the whys and wherefores makes me
> a better companion to him: and I am his only one now.
> Ogden has gone in the packet, to settle as far as possible all
> difficulties with Maitland, and if it can be done, to dissolve
> the partnership. Until we know the event everything re-
> mains quiet except the pen, which as you may suppose, has
> little rest and keeps us up till one or two o'clock . . . We
> have not one line of explanation from Maitland; but Seton's
> bills, and all those indorsed by him, refused and returned,
> give an appearance not favorable, and make the prospect so
> serious that even *I* can not bear to dwell on it.

Elizabeth explained a similar lapse in her correspondence
with her sister-in-law, Rebecca Seton:

> If I could have written to my dearest Rebecca as often as I
> thought to, she would have received a volume by this time;
> but every thought that arises when I sit down with my pen

is the very contrary of what I should express to you, for what avail melancholy forebodings and an indulgence of feelings which can never alter the course of events. It is all easy to me, for I have never thought of my own comfort when there were others depending upon me. But to see my William struggle with fortune, and his constant reflections on what is to become of *us*—and "us" such a number, at times makes courage quail. . . . Never did mortal bear misfortune . . . with as much firmness and patience as my husband does . . . vessel after vessel arrives, and correspondents in London and Hamburg notify him that his bills are refused and his property detained there, and not one line of explanation from Maitland, good or bad. Here he is with funds seized on one side of the water, and one suit already against him on this side. Sweet world! how good you are to those who serve you.

A dismal picture of what was happening in the State Street residence is hinted at in a letter to Julia:

It sometimes lessens personal sorrow to compare our condition with that of others, therefore when you sit thoughtful of your crosses, turn your mind to your friend and view the changes of the last year in my lot. Figure to yourself Mr.— sitting in our library, taking inventory of our books, furniture, &. This is the anticipation for the following week.

One month after her father-in-law's death she gave birth to her third child, Richard. This little one's advent brought his mother so near to death that she was, as she expressed it, "within one pang more of that rest she has so often longed for, but which Heaven for good purposes has again denied." What utter truth in this unwitting remark, and how different the "purposes" of Heaven from those Elizabeth had in view at this time!

By November the mother was not only up and around but "occupied well with pantries, closets, store-rooms, and cellars." When winter set in, Elizabeth's hands were more than full with the education of Rebecca, Harriet, and Cecilia

Seton and the care of her own three small children. But the
arrangement of tutoring the girls at home was better for
Mrs. Seton because William's half-sisters were very delicate
girls. During the spring vacation in April, when all the
young people came home from school,[a] Elizabeth wrote:

> Every soul of our thirteen children, except little Will, has
> in turn had the intermittent fever.

And another more detailed account goes on to say:

> But this month I have had every variety of disagreeable
> circumstances, a sick chamber, dressing blisters, &. All our
> boys are at home and two strangers they brought with them
> to pass their vacation. Added to all this, being without a
> servant, I have been obliged to set my own table, and do all
> the work of a servant man, except cleaning of knives. As
> Richard has small-pox, the two women were obliged to con-
> fine themselves entirely to the nursery; and little Sandy
> was so far in a decline we were obliged to send him on a
> sea voyage. . . . You can have no derangement, no difficulty,
> that I do not endure every day.

Yet Elizabeth's unflagging courage never deserted her nor
were her spirits embittered by these excessive trials. She
bears eloquent testimony to the patient disposition she had
built up over the years:

> But Julia dear, the heart of nature cannot easily be changed,
> particularly if confirmed by the long habits of six and twenty
> years, and in that time I can not remember ever having ex-
> pressed suffering if I had the choice of silence.

To one of a sensitive and freedom-loving nature such as
Elizabeth's, the overcrowded household, the constant clamor
of youthful spirits, the compression of her personal prop-

---

[a] Mary and Charlotte Seton were attending an English boarding
School in Brunswick, New Jersey. Samuel and Edward were tutored
by a Protestant clergyman in Cheshire, Connecticut.

erties into space and circumstances to meet the needs of others—these were often more severe trials than the heavy work or the deprivations occasioned by her dwindling fortunes. She speaks plaintively of this matter:

> To feel all our old habits infringed or altered, to extend our ideas to the affairs of other people, and to make exertions we are unaccustomed to is not so easily to be reconciled. But acting well our part in present difficulties is the only way to insure the peace of futurity.

That these burdens were exacting a heavy toll from the young couple we would know even without the wife's comment:

> I am not yet five and twenty—but the last year has made both William and me at least ten years older.

Indeed Mrs. Seton was old before her time, and burdened beyond her physical strength. Frequently from these days forward, she would suffer from severe boils and abscesses, pains in the chest, and fevers. Yet it will be twenty-two years more, and a life-time of achievements, before the debonaire and indomitable spirit of this valiant woman will yield to the demands of her frail body.

One of Elizabeth's heaviest crosses was the unexpected death of her father, Dr. Bayley, in 1801. So deep an impression did this sorrow make on her that from this time on she gave herself entirely to the will of God. A marked change appears in the tone of her letters for she realized more intensely with each new holocaust that in God alone could be found her security and her joy. She was now in her twenty-seventh year. Although her whole life had been piously inclined, she had drifted away somewhat from the deeply religious sentiments of her younger days with scant practical application of some of the sterner duties of her creed. She had led as gay a life as her circumstances permitted, and aside from her natural goodness and personal religious exercises, she was as worldly as other young women of her station. It was at this time that her contact with the distinguished Rev. Henry Hobart, rector of Trinity Episcopalian Church, led to a revival of her former fervor. Two jottings of this period deserve quoting:

> This blessed day, Sunday the 23rd of May, 1802, my soul was first sensibly convinced of the blessing and practicability of an entire surrender of itself and all its faculties to God.

The other—

> Sunday, first day of August, 1802. Five o'clock in the afternoon.—Solemnly, in the presence of my Judge, I resolve through his grace to remember my infirmity and my sins,— to keep the door of my lips,—to consider the causes of sorrow for sin;—to check and restrain all useless words,—to deny myself and exercise the severity that I know is due to my sins;—to judge myself; thereby trusting, through mercy, that I shall not be severely judged by my Lord.

What beautiful preparation in her own soul for the work of training the souls of those who will come to her as her spiritual children!

Ironically enough, Reverend Hobart, the most vindictive of her opponents after her conversion to Catholicity, was chiefly instrumental in heading her toward that same decision, by himself drawing her into a more fervent way of life that prepared her heart to receive the culminating gift of Faith.

*   *   *   *   *   *

Since the greater number of Elizabeth's letters were true pictures of her day-by-day existence, they must, of necessity, be repetitions of sorrows, disappointments, and illnesses borne in the heroic spirit that ever characterized her. In the midst of her crosses, however, she evinced a most delightful sense of humor which helped to relieve the strain of her situation and which remained one of her striking traits, especially in her later years.

All of the passages here included were written to Julia Scott, with whom Elizabeth was completely at ease. They point up the playful teasing and whimsey that stole so naturally into her intimate letters. For Elizabeth's disposition was never gloomy; if there is a single salient characteristic that marked her from one end of her life to the other, it was her hopeful cheerfulness. This explains, in part, her ability to pass through the most devastating crises without breaking.

When Julia was remiss in answering Elizabeth's letter, she was asked:

> I should be happy to know if the key to your memory is lost, or if you have a felon on your finger. Something certainly must have happened to make you so indifferent to my wishes on the subject of hearing from you.

And in similar vein:

> . . . that there is some serious reasons for so long a silence, which if occasioned by your usual unwillingness to write and the coldness of your dear little fingers, might have been supplied by the warm heart of your gallant Jack, who I know would willingly relieve anxiety in anyone, and most readily in his old friend. Tell him I challenge him in prose or verse, short or long, any measure that will assure me you are well. . . . Oh, do, dear Julia, write me, if but in shorthand.

Elizabeth had been ill. With mock solemnity William and Julia (a widow) talked about their getting together when Eliza would be gone. After her recovery, Elizabeth wrote to her friend:

> He (Seton) is delighted with your claim, especially as he thinks I am likely to go very soon. Next September is the time I appoint for relinquishment; but if it is true, as we

have heard from an intimate acquaintance and relative of
yours, that you are to be married, I do not know what you
will do with (my) budget.

A certain troublesome acquaintance whom they humor-
ously referred to as "Chippy" announced her intentions of
visiting Julia in Philadelphia. Elizabeth quipped:

> I wish you joy of Miss Chippy. Pray get her a husband if
> you can.

William's expected arrival home after a business trip to
Philadelphia during which he visited Julia, occasioned this
delightful bit:

> To change a sorrowful thought, I charge you to send a kiss
> by my husband—one, mind, no more, or you will be putting
> notions in the man's head . . . He will be with you next
> Thursday, I suppose and then, next Saturday, I hope with
> me who will make your one many, by all the rules of
> multiplication.

Julia had asked Elizabeth to visit her with her children as a
respite from the cares and worries that surrounded her.
Elizabeth chided playfully for what was in reality her
friend's failure to appreciate the true condition of affairs:

> Dear little soul, who can bear no exertions even in common
> cases, require your friend, with all her "weights and mea-
> sures" to leave home, physician, and a thousand et-ceteras,
> to take a journey over roads almost impassable, and to re-
> turn when they certainly must be worse. You might as well
> say: Come, friend, we will take a trip to the moon.

Concerning an ambitious spinster of their acquaintance,
she writes to Julia:

> I have had a long letter from Miss Shipton, who I suspect is
> on the road to matrimony or disappointment; for I think it
> very evident by her expressions respecting Mr. Morgan that
> if he regains his health and returns from Lisbon he will
> marry her.

5

In the early part of 1803 William's health failed so rapidly that it became evident that if he did not at once seek a cure in a more temperate climate, he would not recover. The inevitable panacea for illnesses in those days was a sea voyage during which the patient might relax from his daily concerns while breathing in the curative salt air.

Despite the troubled conditions on the high seas at that very period, the Setons decided to try the customary remedy and go to Italy where friends and business associates would receive them. Elizabeth's half-brother, Carlton Bayley, was at that time employed in the counting house of the Filicchi brothers, Antonio and Philip, former banking affiliates of the elder Seton. Leghorn, the center of their business, was also the main port for United States sailing vessels.

Many of the Seton friends and relatives considered the voyage madness in William's weakened condition, and it may well be that his wife trembled before the thought of such a trip with her sick husband. William, however, was pleased with the prospect of the voyage and the hope it held for his recovery, particularly since their destination would be Leghorn. Previous to his marriage he had for some time enjoyed the health-giving climate of Pisa and Florence and the friendship of the Filicchis.

Antonio Filicchi and his elder brother Philip were well known at the highest echelons of both the United States government and the Catholic Church in America. Philip had spent several years in this country during which time he had become a close friend of George Washington and Bishop Carroll. Upon his return to Italy in 1788, he had been accompanied by the son of his business associate in the Bank of New York, young William Magee Seton, who had formed on this occasion a friendly relationship with the younger brother Antonio. Seton had again visited the

Filicchis in 1791, cementing thereby the friendship formed earlier.

In September, therefore, William and the children moved out of the State Street house to remain with friends and relatives until the sailing date in October. Elizabeth herself attended to all the packing, the temporary disposal of the furniture, and the closing of the house. The care of her own children and the Seton girls had also to be arranged for with generous relatives. Rebecca, the ten-weeks-old infant, was given to Elizabeth's married sister, Mrs. Wright Post, a trusted servant named Phoebe going along to care for the baby. This child was ailing when the mother sailed, and Elizabeth confessed later that while she was away she had often pictured the little one "with the angels." What a torture for the mother's heart, what anxiety for her wifely affections to be thus torn between two groups of loved ones so far apart!

On Saturday, October 2, 1803, William, Elizabeth, and their oldest daughter Anna Maria sailed on the brigantine the "Shepherdess." We like to think of these unfortunate people leaving their home and kin under the ministering protection of their Guardian Angels, even if that comforting truth was still unknown to them. Writing to a close friend, Mrs. Eliza Sadler, regarding their decision to take their daughter with them, Elizabeth gives these reasons:

> Do you like the plan of our little Anna going with us? Though she is so young, the voyage will have its use to her in many ways, and will probably be strongly remembered by her through life.

If the real reason were known, might it not be that Elizabeth wished the child to be with her as comfort in facing what she daily expected—William's death? It also served, as we know, to cheer both parents during their long painful trial in the Lazaretto.

A perusal of Elizabeth's letters during this family crisis

leaves the reader awed by the tremendous courage of the
young wife and mother—a courage that seemed to impart
new physical strength for her overwhelming tasks. One
wonders just what would have become of William Seton
and his seven half-brothers and sisters if his wife's devoted
care and her generous intelligent leadership had not encour-
aged, directed, and "mothered" them all through their numerous vicissitudes. The heroic stamina and lofty qualities
of the future foundress, the pioneer educator, and the spiritual mother are observed in their embryonic state during
the married life of this intrepid woman, whose last penned
words before leaving for a strange land with her precious
invalid were

> But I neither look behind nor before, only up. There is my
> rest.

*　　*　　*　　*　　*　　*

The Setons arrived in the port of Leghorn six and a
half weeks later on November 18, only to find that they
would be compelled to remain in a fortress-like Quarantine
or Lazaretto because of an epidemic of yellow fever that
had broken out in New York City after their departure. William's condition grew daily worse in those damp, cold quarters and when at length, on the morning of December 19,
the forlorn family was at last released, he had to be borne
to the Filicchi carriage in the arms of two retainers. For a
few days he rallied, but the exertions of the voyage, culminating in the trials of the Lazaretto, proved too much for
his wasted body, and on December 27, he died.

William, whose failure to attend church services and to
respond to religious inducements had so worried his wife
during the ten years of their marriage, had learned during
the long weeks of his last illness to love God; he passed
from this world a fervent Christian, his last articulate words
being the Holy Name repeated over and over. God received

his soul prepared for Eternity by the beautiful example of his wife, and purified by suffering. He was her first convert, even before herself, but in the designs of Providence, his death was necessary to free Elizabeth for her life's real work, which was about to commence.

After the funeral, Mrs. Seton and her little daughter were received with sincere sympathy and Christian hospitality by the Filicchis at their beautiful home in Pisa. Their delay there was prolonged until April owing to repeated illnesses of both mother and child. This circumstance was also part of the Divine plan, for it afforded Elizabeth ample opportunity to observe the Catholic faith lived in its most edifying purity by her kind hosts. She was especially impressed by the doctrine of the Real Presence and by the family's devotion to the Blessed Sacrament. In her *Journal* of these days she writes:

> ... how happy we would be if we believed what these good souls believe, that they *possess* God in the Sacrament, and that He remains in their churches, and is carried to them when they are sick. Ah! me. When they carry the Blessed Sacrament under my window, while I feel the full loneliness and sadness of my case, I cannot stop the tears at the thought. My God! how happy would I be, even so far away from all so dear, if I could find you in the church, as they do! (for there is a chapel in the very house of Mr. Filicchi) . . .

and further on:

> The other day, in a moment of excessive distress I fell on my knees, without thinking, when the Blessed Sacrament passed by, and cried in an agony to God to bless me, if He was really *there*. . . . A prayerbook of Mrs. Filicchi's was on the table, and I opened it at a little prayer of St. Bernard to the Blessed Virgin, begging her to be our mother, and I said it to her with such a certainty that God would assuredly refuse nothing to His Mother, and that she could not help loving and pitying the poor souls He died for, that I truly

felt I had a Mother, which, you know, my foolish heart so often lamented to have lost in early days. From the first remembrance of infancy I have looked, in all the plays of childhood and wildness of youth, to the clouds for my mother, and at that moment it seemed as if I had found more than her, even in the tenderness and pity of a mother, so I cried myself to sleep on her heart.

And so it is at last, through the instrumentality of Our Lady, as it must ever be, that Elizabeth Seton experienced the first substantial attraction to the Faith—through Her who will indeed show Herself to be her "Life, her Sweetness, and her Hope." It is highly probable that if Elizabeth had followed the bent of her mind at this time, she might have become a Catholic before returning to New York and would thus have spared herself a year of harrowing doubts and questionings.

As the time approached for her to leave Italy, the question of an escort arose. It was conceded that no respectable lady of her rank could possibly travel across the ocean unprotected, and it was probably from Amabilia, Antonio's wife, that the suggestion came to have Antonio himself accompany the young widow and her child. This good woman had formed for Elizabeth a lasting affection which was equally returned. A cordial correspondence between the two ladies preserved their friendship through many years to come.

It was typical of the generosity of both Amabilia and Antonio that they were willing to make such a costly sacrifice in favor of a friend so recently acquired. In reality, however, they were but supplying one of the most important parts of the great pattern of things now being so minutely worked out by Infinite Wisdom. It may be said, in view of the later events, that this gracious gesture on the part of Mr. Filicchi was the second reason for Elizabeth's sad voyage to Italy. It would be through this great Christian gentleman that the graces of conversion would be wrought in Elizabeth's soul and through his munificent regard that her community would be established.

Elizabeth arrived in New York in the first week of June. During her absence, her favorite sister-in-law, Rebecca, had succumbed to the Seton malady. She lingered just long enough for "the tenderness of her beloved sister to accompany her spirit in its passage to eternity." Mrs. Seton has left us in her *Journal* a picture of the mixed impressions of joy and sorrow with which she returned to her native land:

> Do I hold again my dear ones to my bosom? Has God restored all my treasures, even the little soul I so long contemplated an angel in heaven? Nature cries out that they are fatherless, but God himself replies :"I am the Father of the fatherless, and the Helper of the helpless. . . ."
>
> The home of plenty and comfort, the society of sisters united by prayers and divine affections, the kiss of peace . . . all gone forever! And is poverty and sorrow the only exchange? My husband, my sisters, my house: poverty and sorrow! Well, with God's blessing, you, too, shall be changed into dearest friends.

To this growing list of painful separations Elizabeth might have added her own dear father and the coldness of many of her relatives who disapproved of her Catholic leanings. The Divine Shearer had indeed been doing His work.

* * * * * *

During the voyage Mr. Filicchi had had many opportunities to discuss the truths of the Catholic Faith with Mrs. Seton whom he had good reason to consider ready for conversion. However, when Elizabeth found herself once more among her family and former associates, she permitted herself to fall again for some time under the influence of Rev. Henry Hobart. He used every persuasion to retain for Protestantism so promising a member. Furthermore, he lost no occasion of vilifying the Church to which she was attracted. Elizabeth remained in this state of religious inertia, listening to the arguments of her friends and acquaintances, for several months. Whereupon Antonio, who, at their first return to the city, had recommended her to the care of Rev. Matthew O'Brien of St. Peter's Church in Barclay Street, became alarmed and urged her to write to Bishop Carroll of Baltimore as the one most capable of resolving her difficulties. Elizabeth delayed, however, and as the time for Antonio's return to Italy drew near, he wrote to the Bishop himself. The latter's reply reads in part:

Baltimore, Jan. 13th, 1805.
Dear and Much Respected Sir;—Your last favor was from Boston, Oct. 4th. I did not answer it because you were not to remain there long, and my answer might therefore be left in the post office. . . . But no intelligence concerning you, or the very interesting subject of our correspondence having been received since your letter, already referred to, I could not defer any longer the expression of my acknowledgments for your favor, and at the same time to remind you of your promise to visit Washington this winter, and of course, to give me the pleasure of a personal acquaintance. Though, as is mentioned already, I have heard no more than is contained in your last concerning the estimable lady for whose situation and happiness you are so much interested; yet I have the fullest confidence, that after being put to the severe and most distressing trials of interior darkness, doubts, and terrors of making a wrong step, our merciful Father in heaven will soon send her relief, and diffuse light and consolation in her heart. . . . She ought to consider whether the tears she sheds and the prayers she offers to Heaven, are purely for God's sake, and arise solely from compunction for sin; and are unmixed with any alloy of worldly respects, or the inordinate solicitude for the attainment of some worldly purpose. Indeed, when I read the words you copied from her letters, and her letters themselves, I remain convinced of the sincerity of her endeavors to make herself conformable in all things to the Divine will; but afterwards a fear arises in my mind that God discovers in her some lurking imperfection, and defers the final grace of her conversion, till her soul be entirely purified of its irregular attachments.

After remarking that the usual way of Providence with converts is to reverse these dark trials until after their conversion is completed, the Bishop adds this comment:

> Perhaps in the case of your most esteemed and respected friend, it pleases God to suffer her to experience now, before her open union with His church, those agitations of conscience which will induce her to perform wth the greatest care and attention all previous duties necessary for her adoption into it. You will be good enough to ascribe this long letter to the solicitude with which you have inspired me for the subject of yours, and to my desire of adding my feeble cooperation to your charitable and earnest labors for her happiness.

The Bishop communicated with Mrs. Seton herself on August 20, 1804. Her reaction to his letter and the value she attached to it may be gathered from her words to Antonio to whom she reported receiving it:

> The Bishop's letter has been held to my heart on my knees beseeching God to enlighten me to see the truth, unmixed with doubts and hesitations. I read the promises given to St. Peter and the 6th Chapter John every day and then ask God can I offend Him by believing those express words. . . . God will not forsake me, Antonio, I know he will unite me to his flock.

Another renowned ecclesiastic whom Antonio enlisted in behalf of his protegee was Rev. John Cheverus, later Bishop of Boston. Bishop Cheverus' first letter to Elizabeth bears the date March 4, 1805. He says:

> Madam: I have received a few days ago your favor of the 19th of February, and have perused it several times, with the greatest attention. I have received also, by a private hand, a letter from our responsible friend, Mr. Antonio Filicchi, this morning:

After her conversion, Elizabeth wrote to Bishop Cheverus:

New York, 30th March, 1805.

Reverend Dear Sir,—My heart offers you the tribute of its living gratitude for your kind and charitable interest in its sorrows when I was oppressed with doubts and fears, and hastens, after the completion of its happiness, to inform you that through the boundless mercy of God and aided by your very satisfactory counsels, my soul offered all its hesitations and reluctances a sacrifice to God, and on the 14th of March was admitted to the true church of Jesus Christ, with a mind grateful and satisfied as that of a poor ship-wrecked mariner on being restored to his home.

Mrs. Seton assures Bishop Cheverus that though she had read many good books, directions "personally addressed from a revered source most forcibly impress":

These books and some others Mr. Filicchi, who has been the true friend of my soul, provided me with. If he did not encourage me, I do not know how I should dare to press such a long letter on your time so fully and sacredly occupied. . . .

Eight months later Elizabeth received another letter from Bishop Cheverus:

Nov. 30, 1805,—I received, through the hands of our worthy friend, Mr. Filicchi, your esteemed favor of October 10th. I am sorry that he will be the bearer of this and that we must bid him adieu. Duty has not permitted me to be in his company as much as I have wished, but I have known him enough to esteem him, and regret sincerely that he must live far from us. More than any other you will miss this true friend of your soul, but after an absence of few moments, true christian friends will meet in the heavenly kingdom to be parted no more.

After Filicchi's return to Italy, Mrs. Seton received this message from the Bishop:

I have received about ten days ago a letter from our respected friend, Mr. Filicchi, dated Leghorn, February 21st.

He and his family were happy and well when he wrote. . . .
This correspondence serves to manifest the high esteem in
which Antonio was held by several of our most prominent
church dignitaries. They reveal the apostolic spirit of this
Catholic layman—worthy indeed of a zealous missionary.

*   *   *   *   *   *

Letters from Mrs. Seton to Antonio's wife Amabilia
show the depth and spiritual quality of their friendship.
Writing early in 1805, two months before her actual conversion Elizabeth assures her friend:

> . . . you would not say we are unhappy, for the mutual love
> with which it is all seasoned, can only be enjoyed by those
> who have experienced our reverse, but we give it never a
> sigh. I play the piano in the evening for my children, and
> after they have danced themselves tired, we gather round
> the fire, and I go over with them the scenes of David,
> Daniel, Judith, or other great characters of the Bible, until
> we entirely forget the present. The neighbors' children, too,
> sometimes come in to hear our stories, sing our hymns, and
> say prayers with us. Dear, Dearest Amabilia, God will at
> last deliver. . . . I have tried so many ways to see Dr.
> O'Brien, who they say is the only Catholic priest in New
> York, where they say, too, Catholics are the offscouring of
> the people; indeed, somebody even said their congregation
> was a "public nuisance"; but that troubles me not. The
> congregation of a city may be very shabby yet very pleasing
> to God. . . .

And a few days before her conversion, her joy cannot be
restrained. She writes exuberantly:

> A day of days for me, Amabilia. I have been—where To
> the church of St. Peter, which has a cross on the top in-
> stead of a weather-cock—to what is called here among so
> many churches the *Catholic Church.*
> When I turned the corner of the street it is in—"Here, my

God, I go", said I, "my heart all to You." Entering it, how that heart died away, as it were, in silence before that little tabernacle and the great crucifixion above it. . . .

After all had departed, I was called to the little room next to the sanctuary, and made my profession of faith as the Catholic Church prescribes, and then came away light of heart, and with a clearer head than I have had these many long months. . . .

On the Annunciation I shall be made one with Him who said, "Unless ye eat the flesh of the Son of Man, and drink His blood, ye shall not have life in you." I count the days and the hours. . . .

On Lady-day Elizabeth made her first Communion, after which she poured out her soul to Amabilia:

At last, Amabilia, at last God is mine and I am His. Now let all earthly things go as they will. I have received Him. The awful impressions of the evening before! fears of not having done enough to prepare, and yet the transports of confidence and hope in His goodness. My God! to the last breath of life I will remember this night of watching for the break of day, the fearful, beating heart so pressing to be off; the long walk to town, but every step brought me nearer that tabernacle, near to the moment He would enter the poor little dwelling so all His own. And when He did come, the first thought I remember was: "Let God arise, let His enemies be scattered", for it seemed to me my King had come to take His throne, and instead of the humble tender welcome I had expected to give Him, it was but a triumph of joy and gladness that the Deliverer was come, and my defense, and strength, and salvation made mine for this world and the next. . . .

Elizabeth concludes this letter with a few short personal comments:

Your husband goes now to England, and will soon, I trust, be with you. He says much of my bringing all the children to you at Gubbio to find peace and abundance; but I have a long life of sins to expiate, and since I hope always to find the morning mass in America, it matters little what can happen through the few years I may have to live, for my health is pitiful; yet we will see. At all events, happen now what will, *I rest in God.*

But Elizabeth's "rest" was entirely of a spiritual quality. Certainly she enjoyed very little of that blessing in the midst of the barrage of abuse leveled against her by friends and relations when it became known that she had entered the Church of Rome. Among the most voluble of her critics was her sister Mary, Mrs. Post, who though remaining true to her younger sister, lamented to their New Rochelle cousin Anne Bayley Hague that "she had gone over to the church that persecuted her ancestors!" Mary's husband, Dr. Wright Post, was puzzled by Elizabeth's conversion and asked her to tell him the difference between the Protestant churches and the Catholic Church. When Elizabeth tried to explain to him the right of succession from the Apostles, he exclaimed, quite sincerely, "Church of the Apostles! Why, is not every church from the Apostles?"

Elizabeth wrote to a friend in Paris about what she was enduring:

If Mr. Wilkes had not taken so much interest in my situation, I would have left this country almost immediately on my return, on account of the coolness with which I was treated by my friends when my Catholic sentiments became known.

Elizabeth met this antagonism with her usual patient endurance, but victory was achieved on the battlefield of the spirit. A letter to Antonio at this time is significant:

You will congratulate me in being most earnest in seeking "the Pearl." It is best to be obliged to conquer the principle most apt to blind me in my pursuit; and my daily object is, to keep close to your first advice (with St. Francis to take every event gently and quietly, and oppose good nature and cheerfulness to every contradiction; which succeeds so well that now it is an acknowledged opinion, that Mrs. William Seton is in a very happy situation; . . . But Mrs. William Seton is obliged to watch every moment in order to keep up the reality of this appearance. You know, Filicchi, what it costs to be always humble and satisfied; though really when this disposition is familiarized, it is the true treasure. Do, do pray continually for the salvation of that soul whch has already cost you so much care.

As might have been expected, Antonio Filicchi remained the staunch supporter of the neophyte. Again in this country on business, he wrote to her from Philadelphia:

I shall be glad to hear of some effectual plan, and steps taken by your old friends and relatives in this new part of the world, for the independent settlement and comfort of yourself and children; but in their failure, be easy and rely on the sentiments and principles of your new friends in the old part of the world; they will prove themselves in deed what they boast of in words, and will thank God for it, from whom they derive the means and the will.

With this gracious letter came an offer of financial assistance and a promise of continued aid. Mrs. Seton, in delicacy, could not accept all that these kind friends put at her disposal, but devoid of that false shame that would have deprived her and her family of the very necessities of life, she accepted enough to see her through her darkest days with a modicum of security.

But Providence was about to provide the answer to all Elizabeth's problems, and her life, heretofore so entwined with domestic and material matters, was now to be cleaved in two. The future would be lived for God alone.

XIII

Mother Elizabeth Seton

1

IN THE SEQUESTERED VILLAGE of Emmitsburg, under the hazy shadows of the Blue Ridge Mountains, Elizabeth Ann Bayley lived out the last thirteen years of her life as Mother Elizabeth Seton.

After spending so many years on the flat shoreline of Long Island Sound, or in the narrow cobbled streets of old New York, what comfort it must have been to her, who loved the beauties of nature so much, to view from her window that gently sloping range named for the misty hues that envelop it. Maryland's dry sunny climate offered health as well as security to the young widow for whom the few previous years had been so disturbing. Peace she would have, and security, after a time, but her health was never to be completely restored.

Even before her arrival there her body, driven and harassed by numerous hardships and sorrows, already bore within it the incipient stages of the slow malady that would burn away her physical energies while it purified her soul for its entrance into her "grand Eternity." Yet with the same remarkable stamina and disregard of self that had characterized her during all the thirty-four preceding years, this valiant woman remained, until the moment of her death, the heart and head of the religious community she had founded. No step was taken, no decision reached that Mother

Seton had not prayed over and discussed with competent advisers. She displayed keen interest and sound judgment in all her transactions whether she was purchasing flour and textbooks for the school or instructing her pupils in matters of piety and good breeding.

One must keep in mind while considering Elizabeth Seton's role as a foundress that she never desired that office and that the actual foundation of a sisterhood was very nearly thrust upon her. When eventually it became apparent that the choice of the sisters for superior would fall upon Mrs. Seton, she was alarmed and expressed great diffidence. It had been one thing to have presided over the school and the institution, but now that a more definitely spiritual regimen was to be undertaken, she required strenuous encouragement to consent to accepting the office. She voiced her distress upon finding herself elected to the dignity of religious superior:

> Merciful God, thou knowest how unsuited I am to the charge that has been committed to me; I whose sins have crucified Thee so often, and who ought to blush in shame and confusion!

and

> How can I hope to direct others? I who am so wretched, so imperfect and at the same time so lacking in self-knowledge.

As far as Elizabeth was concerned, her essential vocation lay in the performance of her duty as a mother. Writing to Archbishop Carroll on this subject, she says emphatically:

> . . . I would gladly make every sacrifice you think consistent with my first and inseparable obligations as a mother.

And to her friend Julia Scott:

> . . . but the dear ones have the first claim which must ever remain inviolate. Consequently if at any period the duties

I am engaged in should interfere with those I owe to them
I have solemnly engaged with our good Bishop Carroll as
well as my own conscience to give the darlings their right
and to prefer their advantage to everything.

Writing to another friend on this subject, she says:

By the law of the Church I so much love, I could never take
an obligation which interfered with my duties to the children, except I had an independent provision and guardian
for them, which the whole world could not supply, to my
judgment of a mother's duty.

The financial distress of her situation after the death of
her husband had clouded the joy of Elizabeth's admission
into the Catholic Church in March 1805. A widow with five
very young children, whose husband had left her penniless,
she was compelled to put aside her pride and self-respect in
order to provide the common necessities of life for her little
ones. Mrs. Seton made four attempts to open small schools
in New York City; for she felt that by education and paren-
tal experience, as well as by natural aptitude, she was best
fitted for teaching. All four efforts failed through the evil
effects of bigotry and malicious gossip.

Her next thought was to apply for a teaching position
in one of the French Convent schools of Montreal where her
three girls might be educated while her boys were provided
for at Georgetown, in Washington. In this decision Elizabeth's French ancestry was exerting a strong influence. Not
only would her knowledge of French, learned in its purest
form at the very fountainhead of the language, be a ready
asset in obtaining such a position, but she herself would
easily feel at home amid the French culture of Montreal or
Quebec. But this was not what God wanted. He Who had
brought Frenchmen across the seas to bear the strands from
which her family ties would be woven, was not permitting
her to go off to French Canada at the very moment when
the work He had kept for her was about to begin.

One autumn morning in 1806, Elizabeth assisted at the Mass of a visiting priest in St. Peter's Church, Barclay Street. Profoundly impressed by her sensible devotion and piety at the moment of receiving Holy Communion, the visitor questioned the pastor a little while later at their breakfast. He barely had time to hear her name when the young woman herself was announced. This meeting between Father Dubourg, the first President of St. Mary's College in Emmitsburg, and Elizabeth Ann Seton was fraught with illimitable graces and the inscrutable designs of Providence for the young widow.

According to Elizabeth's own recollection of it in her *Dear Remembrances*, the period between 1806 and the spring of 1808 was "the most painful," yet probably the most fruitful in purifying graces for her soul. Her troubles during this time were of a different sort from the conscience-searching that preceded her conversion. Now she had to meet the hostility of her own family, contemptuous as they were in their attitude to all things Catholic. Stripped by His "uplifted stroke" of all that had formerly been hers by right of birth and association, Mrs. Seton found herself a social outcast, an economic derelict, an almost despairing mother. A few faithful friends and her sister, Mrs. Wright Post, assisted her as far as they could reasonably be expected to, but Elizabeth could not continue in this precarious way of life indefinitely. With her accustomed lack of bitterness, she wrote to Antonio Filicchi:

> Some proposals have been made me of keeping a tea store or china shop—or small school for little children (too young I suppose to be taught the Hail Mary). In short, Tonio, they know not what to do with me, *but God does*— and when His blessed time is come we shall know—

That "blessed time" had now arrived. Two years after the first meeting with Father Dubourg there occurred a second, again in New York. On this occasion the Sulpician proposed that Mrs. Seton go to Baltimore where she might open a school for girls on property which he himself would provide. Having consulted Archbishop Carroll, her friend and adviser, and submitting to what was the obvious will of God in her regard, Elizabeth gave up all associations with her beloved New York. Several relatives, still cordial after her conversion, and a few faithful friends gathered at the dock to bid her farewell when she sailed in a packet for Baltimore on June 9, 1808. There, next to the Church in Paca Street, in "a neat delightful mansion in the French style of folding windows and recesses," Elizabeth again opened a school in the following September. This time she was successful.

As yet, Mrs. Seton had no thought of forming a religious community. Assisting her in the teaching were several young ladies interested in education work, all of them, like herself, of deep piety, and each hoping in some way to dedicate her life to God in such work. But while her five children remained dependent upon her, Elizabeth had no real hope of doing any more than establishing a Catholic boarding school. However, her scruples in that regard were overridden by the concerted agreement of all her advisers, and before the year was out, Mrs. Seton's vows were received by Archbishop Carroll, who at that time bestowed on her the official title of Mother.

One cannot but marvel at the inevitable swiftness of events at this period in Elizabeth's life. She herself seems to have been carried along with unfaltering sureness in the rushing waters of God's Providence. It was almost as if the Infinite, having waited for so many generations for the finite to work its way to this point, could endure Its Divine thirst for souls no longer, but must propel and harry the instrument into her destined vocation.

In earlier days, William Bayley had been forced, through circumstances not of his own choosing, to abandon the work in which he was engaged, to take up a completely different manner of life. Now, a similar fate overtook an-

other member of his family, and she too found herself faced
with the necessity of abandoning what seemed to have been
her vocation in order that a second, and more important—
because God-chosen—work might replace it.

2

Once God had made clear His designs, Elizabeth gave
herself heart and soul to her spiritual and educational duties.
Six months after the establishment of her Community, she
wrote to a young girl in whom she thought she saw the
seeds of a religious vocation:

> I am already the Mother of some and have the prospect of
> receiving many daughters. We are going to begin our
> Noviciate [sic] in a beautiful country place in the moun-
> tains.

In the month of June 1809, Elizabeth, her daughter
Anna Maria, and one of the members of the new Community
went to Emmitsburg where they lived temporarily in a log
house about two miles from the village, their own quarters,
procured by Bishop Dubourg, not being fit as yet for occu-
pancy. The good Bishop writing to Elizabeth here three
months later expresses his concern at their still not being
able to occupy their new home, and judging by the number
of items he felt it necessary to inquire about, the patience
of the trio would be further tried. He says in part:

> In your next, inform me of the precise state of forwardness
> of your house. Are the floors laid, wash and chair boards
> fixed, stairs put up, windows all in and glass? Is the little
> chapel framed and weather boarded? Is the front door, or at
> least the casement of it, done? I do not ask about the filling
> between the logs, because I suppose it finished long since.

In July the little group was moved to better quarters in
what has been since termed the Stone House. This building

is also considered the cradle of the Community, Mother
Seton being joined here by all the members who had remained in Baltimore. Their poverty was indescribable, and
their hardships called for heroic endurance. Carrot coffee,
coarse rye bread, smoked herring, and if fortune smiled on
them. a few spoons of molasses constituted their regular
fare for the first winter. In addition to this pathetic diet,
there was the difficulty of procuring water from a distant
well, of having to go two miles to assist at Mass, (though
this hardship was soon adjusted by the erection of a little
altar), and the psychological and social difficulties attendant
upon the crowding of sixteen people into four rooms. However, these pioneers were women of heroic mold and all
crosses were met in a spirit of holy acceptance, if not of
actual joy. At last in March 1810, the Sisters moved to their
first real Motherhouse, where a high Mass of thanksgiving
was offered on the feast of St. Joseph. Strikingly enough,
Mother Seton's chosen title for her new Community was,
Sisters of St. Joseph.

A clear outline of life in the "White House," as the new
building was familiarly called, is given by the Foundress
herself:

> Our community increases very fast, and no doubt will do a
> great deal of good in our chief business. Like yourself many
> of our Sisters do not know their vocation, but they make
> no engagements till they have passed their twelve months
> Noviciate and then if they persevere they make simple vows
> in the hands of our Bishop which he can dispense with at
> pleasure whenever he has just cause for doing it. Ah what a
> comfort while the Church of God is reduced to such distress
> and seems as it were abandoned to its enemies he permits
> us to serve him in peace in this happy corner, where he
> stays with us even under our very roof—we have an elegant
> little chapel. Thirty cells holding a bed, chair, and table
> each, a large infirmary, a very spacious rectory besides
> parlor, school room, my room, working rooms. . . .

ELIZABETH BAYLEY SETON

Further description is contained in Mother Seton's *Memoirs* published by her grandson Monsignor Robert Seton. He says:

> The house first occupied by the community of Saint Joseph's was a small two-storied building with a high porch in front and an open passage running behind. It stood about a quarter of a mile right of the public road, between the mountain and the village, surrounded by a few trees, and on a gentle rise some hundreds of yards from the valley stream . . . On the occasion of its opening they went in procession to a little wooded knoll, still used by their successors as a place of assemblage for recreation and out-of-door prayer, and recited the Litany of the Saints. The community was, also, with special invocation, placed under the patronage of the glorious patriarch St. Joseph.

Although a convert of barely two years' duration, Mother Seton evidenced a depth of interior life rarely found among Catholics of outstanding fervor. To have passed through the states of motherhood, widowhood, and religious profession in the brief space of fifteen years is in itself a barometer of the rapid growth in personal holiness that God demands of those He would use to further His work for souls. After her entrance into the religious life, this growth in the things of the spirit was one of degree rather than of kind. Elizabeth had long practiced the virtues of the nun before she assumed the obligations of one. Writing to Antonio Filicchi six months before her vows, she could testify:

> I have long since made vows which as a Religious I could only renew, and the thirst and longing of my soul is fixed on the Cross alone.

But these wells of holy love and abandonment had not been dug without pain, wounds, and darksome shadows. She gives us a glimpse of what these inner struggles must have been in a note written to a friend who had complained of her own trials:

> I have gone through more interior and internal trials since I began a religious life than you can conceive, but have always found and still find that they are very, very good for me—and so you must take them, dearest.

And again—

> Tribulation is the riches of his children whom he generally treats with outward severity, by giving them a share in his cup—and since I left New York every thing has been contrary to me—it seems as if Our Lord binds me to him by caresses and favors, everything has turned out far beyond my brightest expectations so far, but your friend, my dearest Rose, has many trials to go through as it has pleased Almighty God to appoint me a station full of cares and dangers, yet with him and supported by his all [sic] mighty arm, there is nothing to fear which he will not carry us thro'. . .

Nor were these merely passing trials attendant upon changing circumstances, but they constituted the very atmosphere of her entire life, as she herself testifies:

> Tribulation is my element; if it only carries me home at last, never mind the present. Year after year passes . . . the last must come.

In spite of the several torturing years of soul-searching that preceded her conversion, Elizabeth's spiritual life seems, on the whole, to have been quite simple. She had two great devotions: abandonment to the Will of God and an ardent love for the Blessed Sacrament. We know, too, that all her life her consuming desire was, like that of the great St. Paul, "to be dissolved and to be with Christ"—or as she so often expressed it "Death! Eternity!"

During her last illness, in speaking of her imminent death, she remarked:

> It all seems to me so simple, when I look up to the crucifix. Coffin, patches, grave; what a life indeed!
> "Eternity!" she writes to a friend, "oh, how near it often seems to me!" Think of it when you are hard pushed. How long will be that day without a night, or that night without a day!"

Her personal joy in the thought of leaving this world is evident in the comment:

> Thought of going *home*, called, and by His will! What a transport!

Mother Seton's description of a good vocation is "that in which we do not seek ourselves but do only the will of God," and in another place she expresses herself most emphatically on these two-fold devotions:

> ... the rest abandon
> abandon
> Communion
> Eternity
> Each of us dropping in a moment or only after the 20 or 30 or 40 years more! ! ! if so! ! !
> What if so?
> Abandon day after day—365 multiplied by . . .? What all this? A holy blissful adandon through immeasurable and inextricable grace of the Moment.

This so-called "grace of the moment" was another one of Mother Seton's spiritual attractions. Speaking of this urge in one of her notes, she says:

> I am truly silly, going as you know to meet everybody in the grace of the moment, which we never can know till we find the humor and temper of the one we are to meet with—

the many mistakes all swallowed and confronted by intention, intention, intention—Our true peace and security with our beloved as you so often delighted to tell me. . . .

Elizabeth had good cause to be proficient in the virtues of holy abandonment and detachment. From her earliest years her affections, her will, and her personal desires had been wrested from her to be forged on the anvil of deprivation, loneliness, and contradiction. Her fingers never closed in a possessive grasp about the few joys life offered her. She had learned her lesson too well for that.

This detachment left her spirit malleable to the touches of Divine grace. It accounts for the docility she evinced toward her spiritual advisers, both before and after she became a religious. Perhaps the external impression of Mother Seton's life might be summed up in what were almost her last words:

> May the most just, the most high, and the most amiable will of God be accomplished forever!

She did not expect consolations in this life; and that she had a most matter-of-fact attitude toward them is clear from her observation:

> It is the remark of all directors of souls that spiritual consolations never last long, so that when the soul possesses them she must be ever prepared to relinquish them. Nothing shows more the purity of intention we should bring to the service of God than this uncertainty of finding our consolation in it, or rather the certainty that we will not always find it.

3

Mother Seton was valiant, strong, unwavering. Tender of others she certainly was; her letters abound in what seems to our twentieth century taste as effusiveness, and her burning desire always to do God's will may be misconstrued by the unthinking as a sort of excessive yielding to all and every voice. Those who characterize Elizabeth Seton in this way have failed to gauge her stature correctly. Hear what she says about softness:

> A Soul which loves its own ease and pleasure will find itself beset with attractions of sweetness and delight which the enemy presents in vain forms and images to draw it in his snares.

Speaking to a friend of the trials God had sent her she says:

> For that I bless Him most of all. Where would I be now if He had not scourged and bound me? And in His infinite goodness he may do the same for you. What matter by whose hands? If I get to his kingdom, what matter how?

It is in this same spirit of interior heroism that Mother Seton directed a warning to one of the Sisters who had an attraction for the cloistered life:

> The only fear I have is that you will let the old string pull too hard for solitude and silence; but look to the kingdom of SOULS—the few to work in the vineyard of the Lord. This is not a country for solitude and silence, but for warfare and crucifixion. You are not to stay in his silent agonies of the garden at night, but go from post to pillar, to the very fastening of the cross.

This is not the language of softness! Here speaks the intrepid daughter of dauntless ancestors who also sacrificed their life of ease and comfort to dwell in a new unsettled land that promised religious freedom. Elizabeth, the one-time "belle of New York," a cherished wife and devoted mother, now the guiding spirit of a religious family, had only one desire left: to see every member of her Community living close to God. She did not stop to reckon the cost—either for herself or for those who elected to follow her. If suffering was the price—then gladly would she suffer.

My children must fight, looking to Providence and the grave. Well, you say, but if they do not. Well, I hope they will be punished by disappointment and adversities until they do. What a hard-hearted mother!

Mother Seton meditated daily on the Passion of Christ and incessantly urged her daughters to show courage and determination in bearing their own passing trials. She reminds them:

How much we will then wish we had doubled our penances and sufferings while the moment lasted! How we will laugh when we look behind at the troubles we stopped at, which will then appear in their true light! And that bright and glorious cross which we now drag along through the mud and dirt—how beautiful and lovely will it appear when we shall find it opens the door of out eternal happiness for us.

In keeping with her love of the Cross were the zeal and generosity with which she assumed the Rule of her Community, adapted with but few modifications from the original, written by St. Vincent de Paul for his Daughters of Charity in France. Referring to these regulations, she declared that "the rule is so easy that it is scarcely more than any regular person would do with in the world."

It may be well here to take a long look at what Mother Seton's interpretation of "easy" meant. Let her tell us in her own words:

You must be in right earnest, or you will do little or nothing. First, it requires constant guard over your senses. What sort of interior life would you lead if, every time the door opens or if anyone passes you, you must look up? if you must hear what is said, though it does not concern you? or, if you remain silent and in your modest attention to your duty, what would be your interior life if you let your thoughts wander from God?

On the Will of God:

> The first end I propose in our daily work is to do the will of God; secondly to do it in the manner he wills it; and thirdly, to do it because it is his will.
>
> ... then do it in the manner he wills it—not sewing an old thing as if it was new, or a new thing as if it was old; not fretting because the oven is too hot, or in a fuss because it is too cold. You understand: not flying and driving because you are hurried, nor creeping like a snail because no one pushes you. Our dear Saviour was never in extremes.

(What echoes here of Dr. Bayley's training of his impetuous Bette: "Calm that glowing spirit. . . .")

> You know how apt your mind is to wander, and how easily you are led away by sensible objects. You will never receive any lively impressions of grace until you overcome this dissipation of mind.
>
> So, all the prayers, readings, and good talk you love so much will be to little purpose unless you place a sentinel at the door of your heart and mind.
>
> You often lose in ten minutes by your dissipation of mind more than you had gained in a whole day of mortification. Not one grace is given but might by your fidelity to it become for you an eternal treasure.

One of the notes she made for herself on her obligations as Mother and Superior reveals the earnestness with which she herself assumed her own duties:

> To do violence to self on a thousand occasions. Renounce all satisfactions in particular. Endure the weakness of some, the murmurings of others, the delicacy of a third, yet forgetting no one! But graces will be proportioned to wants and duties, and the recompense proportioned also.

Regarding self-love, which Mother Seton must have found very difficult to understand in others, she herself being by nature and grace so very selfless, she observes:

> Our love of God is always opposed by self-love; our love of one another by the miserable pride and pretensions which create jealousy, rash judgment, and the pitiful dis-

likes and impatience which so often trouble us and wound charity.

You know how unwilling we are to deny ourselves, how unwilling to be reproved or contradicted, how trifling a thing will make us sad, how we delight to be commended, while, with a sort of natural cruelty, we see blame and fault in others which we are scarcely willing to excuse.

Petty faults of uncharitableness were completely alien to Mother Seton's character. In all her voluminous correspondence, particularly before her entrance into the religious life, when worldly views and attitudes might well have been expected of one in her position, there is not the slightest slur on another's reputation, no critical gossip of any kind, no recriminations against those who openly maligned and persecuted her. She advised her youngest daughter Catherine regarding prudence of speech:

You can never be bound, my love, to speak on any occasion or on any subject, unless you are sure of doing good by speaking.

Even when Elizabeth was the object of rancor and vilification, she did not retaliate, but sought to excuse the offense and ignore the hurt. It must be borne in mind that she wrote most frequently to her close and trusted friends to whom she might be pardoned for unburdening herself. She was not writing for publication, yet few, if any, lines need to be deleted, and those only because they are of a personal nature.

Elizabeth loved people—all people—with genuine affection. What in her father constituted a noble type of philanthropy, she carried into the realm of Christian love of neighbor. Black and white, rich and poor, young and old—all came within the ever-widening periphery of her kindly interest and sympathy. Writing to Father Bruté, her spiritual director, she has this good news for him:

... so many of your mountain children and poor blacks came today for the first Communion instructions—they were told from the pulpit all to repair to the Sisterhood—so they came as to a novelty, but we will try our best to fix them —poor dear souls so unconscious!!!

And again—

... and I have all the blacks, *all the blacks* for my share to instruct—Excellentissimo!

In the face of the interracial agitation rampant in our country at this time, it is a point of justifiable pride among the Sisters of Charity that Mother Seton made the instruction and welfare of the Emmitsburg Negro population one of the first of the social activities undertaken by her new Community. How deeply grieved she would be to witness their abuse at the hands of their fellow-citizens; how appalled would her staunchly ecumenical spirit have been by the idea of "segregation." This was not what she had learned from her maternal grandfather, the Rev. Richard Charlton, of St. Andrew Church, Staten Island, who organized the first society in New York for the Negro people. This Christlike tradition was carried on by Mother Seton's younger son Richard. After he had left his work with the Filicchi brothers, he went to Liberia as assistant United States agent at Monrovia, the capital of the Black Republic. The American Colonization Society, founded by Charles Carroll and other Maryland Catholics, to help free Negroes, a pressing social issue of the time, sent the first colony to Liberia in February, 1820, and it was through the influence of the Carrolls and Harpers, friends of his mother, that Richard Seton obtained this position. He died June 26, 1823, on board ship voyaging from Cape Mesurado to St. Jago. The United States agent wrote of him to his aunt:

His open, undisguised character, the simplicity of his manners and the native kindness of his heart, had won perhaps further on the affections of our black people than any other

agent had ever done in so short a time. I have heard from
them no other objection to Mr. Seton but that he was a
white man; the only fault which with some of them unfortunately is held unpardonable.

It is easy to speak lovingly to a loved one; it was
easy for Elizabeth to speak lovingly to everyone. The over-
flowing tenderness of her heart manifested itself in a spon-
taneous warmth of expression, perfectly natural, as it was
also perfectly supernatural. Many of the saints have evinced
this warmth of personal feeling toward those with whom
they were engaged in doing important work for God. St.
Teresa of Avila had a natural affection for certain friends
and did not hesitate to express herself tenderly. In a letter
to M. Maria de San José, she wrote:

> I assure you that, if you love me dearly, I for my part re-
> turn your love and like you to tell me of yours. How un-
> mistakable a trait of our nature is this wish for our love to
> be returned! Yet it cannot be wrong, for Our Lord wishes
> it too.

This human love is, of course, divinized in holy souls and
Teresa explains how this takes place:

> If they love anyone they immediately look right beyond the
> body, fix their eyes on the soul and see what there is to
> be loved in that. If there is nothing, but they see any sug-
> gestion or inclination which shows them that, if they dig
> deep, they will find good within this mine, they think
> nothing of the labor of digging, since they have love.

And the anxiety of these devout souls for the spiritual well-
being of all whom they meet fills them with longing—
> so that they cannot be happy unless they see that the be-
> loved one is making progress. If that soul seems to have
> advanced, and is then seen to fall some way back, the friend
> seems to have no more pleasure in life: she neither eats nor
> sleeps, is never free from this fear and is always afraid that

the soul whom she loves so much may be lost, and that the two may be parted forever.

How truly these passages describe Mother Seton's relations with everyone she knew! She longed to share with each one whatever graces God had bestowed on her and to set the steps of each in the pathway of salvation. How tactfully, how earnestly, she hinted at, urged, and desired the spiritual good of her father, of her husband, her several sisters-in-law, her friends Mrs. Scott and Mrs. Sadler, of her own children, especially her two sons whose peccadilloes never ceased to worry her. To obtain her father's recognition of God's influence in his life, she lifted her infant daughter from her cradle and offered the child in return for her father's soul. In her letters to Julia Scott she never omitted some reference, however veiled, to the importance of preparing for Eternity.

Her youngest daughter, Rebecca, had fallen while skating and had broken her hip. Having taken her first to Philadelphia and then to Baltimore in an effort to procure some alleviation of the child's pain, Mother Seton was obliged to leave the little girl in Baltimore. But serious complications set in and the child became a cripple. In a little note sent to the sufferer, Rebecca's mother, though agonized at heart, reveals where her real concern for her daughter lay:

With the little pen I answer my dear every day dearer, little darling, how much I desire she should go and unite still closer to our only Beloved. Go either Thursday or Sunday as the rest do, and make your careful preparation of the purest heart you can bring Him, that it may appear to Him like a bright little star at the bottom of a fountain. O my Rebecca! Child of Eternity! Let peace and love stay with you in your pains, and they will lighten and sweeten them all.

Oh, the joy to that mother's soul! The delight of her good angel presenting every moment of the suffering darling to her Crucified Saviour, Who counts her pains with His!

Trust all indeed to Him, my dear one; put all in His hands, and we shall see by and by, when we meet in our Jerusalem, how good and tender He had been in giving you the thorny crown.

In a birthday greeting sent to her eldest son William, Mother Seton reminds him delicately of his duties:

My own dearest child. Your birthday! You know your mother's heart. It has a dear Communion for you for eternity. Be blessed a thousand, thousand times. Take a few little minutes in the Church today, in union with your mother's heart to place yourself again and again in the hands of God. Do, dearest one.

When, contrary to her wishes, and only with her reluctant consent, he joined the Navy, William received the following earnest appeal from his mother:

Guard well, my dear one, that pure heart which will be the charm of our reunion. Oh, if our God should be forgotten in that heart and it should become . . .! No, no, no; never; let me die and be gone before that insupportable sorrow comes. I pray for you incessantly.

With what motherly solicitude Elizabeth cultivated the interior growth of the pupils in her schools and with what interest she followed their progress after they had left her supervision! How she hovered over the souls of her own spiritual daughters, her religious motherhood yearning for their advancement in prayer and virtue with the same depth of devotion that a tender mother of the world bestows on her natural children.

The ardor of St. Teresa and other great souls like Mother Seton for the improvement of everyone near and around them erupted in a burning zeal for the conversion of the whole world. Teresa would have gone to the ends of the earth to win souls. In this same spirit Mother Seton wrote to a priest who seemed to be wavering in an opportunity to do a greater good:

If I were a man, all the world would not stop me; I would go straight in Xavier's footsteps; the waters of the abyss and the expanded sky should be well explored. But I must wait until I get higher than seas or skies.

Gentle though she was, Mother Seton expected a high degree of sanctity—or at least the earnest striving for it—from her spiritual daughters. She asks:

How walk valiantly with our Saviour, dragging our foolish attachments after us, and ready to faint if the least weight of his cross presses on us?

Can you expect to go to heaven for nothing? Did not our dear Saviour track the whole way to it with his tears and blood? and yet you start at every little pain!

How is it that many of us keep the rule as to the letter of it, and also look pious enough? There is no want of good will nor idleness indulged; and in a house where it would seem so easy to become saints, you would say "What is the matter? Why are we not saints?"

One immortified passion, a single bad habit not corrected, a natural attachment, though innocent as to appearance, will stand like a big stone at the door of our hearts, and prevent us for whole years from advancing in the kingdom of the Lord.

In the presence of such sublime exhortations one loses sight of the fact that the speaker was but a few years in the Catholic Church, and fewer still in religious life. Although it may be said that Mother Seton, like St. Aloysius, accomplished a great deal in a short space, her grasp of the most profound religious principles, her wide knowledge of the works of leading spiritual writers, and her apparent "at-homeness" indicate that she had long been a Catholic at heart before she actually joined the fold. These instructions to her Sisters were the fruit of her own holy, mortified and prayerful life.

Elizabeth turned her French background and facility in the language to good advantage for her Community by translating many of the leading French authorities in the spiritual life. She gave her Sisters their first English version of the conferences of St. Vincent de Paul, as well as the words of another foundress, Mme. Le Gras, venerable Mother of the Daughters of Charity in France. St. Ambrose, St. Ignatius Loyola, and St. Teresa were among the favorite works she put into the hands of her religious family.

Mother Seton was a strict observer of every regulation, never idle, yet always cheerful, self-possessed, and tranquil. This woman who, in former years had, by right of kinship, entrée into the homes of the wealthy, the powerful, the distinguished, now cherished the sting of poverty for Christ's sake. The furnishings of her room, the articles she used were of the poorest, often castaways from the classroom. She employed the coarsest and cheapest writing paper. Her pens were stubs from the scrap basket. On one occasion, a Sister remonstrated with her for using a stump of a pen. Mother Seton replied, amiably but pointedly, "Well, my dear one, that is to atone for your waste of pens."

Writing to thank a friend for a gift of handkerchiefs, she said:

> Your handsome handkerchiefs were far too handsome for me, my friend. I have long ago offered them to God in the service of the altar in your name which was the greatest pleasure I could have in using them.

At table she refused to accept anything specially prepared for her although she suffered from a weak stomach and extremely poor health. One of the older Sisters who sat next to Mother Seton at the table related that "Mother frequently ate my crumbs." She rose at four o'clock with the community; when in the chapel, she knelt erect, never sitting or leaning on anything during the time of prayer and meditation—one hour. During her last illness, which was prolonged and painful, she was always pleasant and contented, giving a beautiful example to her Sisters of the most loving abandonment to God's will. In this regard her interior dispositions are manifested in the comment:

Why care for anything personal? If it is or is not, so or not so? The little remaining moment all too little indeed for penance, much less for reparation of love.

Obedience to the Rules, which she had so often preached, was practiced even on her deathbed, whence she followed as nearly as she could the spiritual exercises prescribed. Her own continued suffering over a period of two years she accepted in the heroic spirit one would expect of her. She writes to a friend:

Of course you are a prisoner . . . but a "Prisoner of the Lord." Blessed be His name. You could not be one without His permission, nor I, with a burning fever day and night, unless He willed it.

Compelled to take palliating remedies for many illnesses, Mother Seton felt that she was thereby giving bad example to the Sisters and apologized to them for her "weakness." A more comfortable mattress was provided for her, but she lamented her relief in using it. It was by her own shining example of fortitude and generous love that Mother Seton led her daughters, who had only to imitate their saintly Foundress to arrive at a high perfection.

Although Elizabeth would never consciously hurt the feelings of another, there were occasions when she felt it her duty either to rebuke or remonstrate, and this she did in crisp, direct words that left no doubt in the mind of the hearer as to just what was intended! One such incident occurred when Mother Seton gave kindly counsel to a young priest who had preached poorly and admitted that he had not troubled to prepare his sermon. Mother said:

Sir, that awakens my anger. Do you remember a priest holds the honor of God on his lips? Do you not trouble yourself to spread his fire he wishes so much enkindled? If you will not study and prepare while young, what when you are old? There is a mother's lesson.

Perhaps a more humanly amusing incident is the half-playful remonstrance made to Father Bruté for his uneven-ness of disposition which sorely tried his friends.

> . . . all is a true mystery to me in your disposition—much greater mystery than any of Faith. A man of your particular principle *on paper*, who has evidently the most dear and special graces, not given drop by drop as to other souls but poured over your head in torrents . . . yet I seldom see you but in such wild enthusiasm of your own particular impression of the moment that you can see nothing, hear nothing, but that one object, or else *reserved, hurt*, and *anxious* because you have not been consulted in things which spoke *for themselves*, or others which we would not dare take your advice about without knowing the Superior's will. . . .

Besides the reproof contained in this letter, Mother Seton shows herself a keen judge of character and an alert psychologist. Referring to Father Bruté's desire to urge Bishop Dubois, the ecclesiastical superior of the little community at the time, to visit his spiritual family, she says half-humor-ously, half-ironically:

> You ought to know our Rev'd Superior by this time, and see that he is not to be *pushed* anywhere and your urging him cannot but keep him away—when anything essential hap-pens I always inform him of it, and if the thing is not es-sential his absence hinders a fuss about nothing, and suffers pets and little passions to drop in silence.

A sharp reprimand was once given to a young Sister who had refrained from going to Holy Communion. Meeting her after Mass, Mother asked, "Why, my dear child, did you not come to our Lord for your recompense this morning?"

"Mother," replied the Sister, "I felt a little weak, and took a cup of coffee before Mass."

"Ah, my dear child," reproved Mother Seton, "how could you sell your God for a miserable cup of coffee?"

4

In addition to the usual difficulties attendant upon the establishment of a religious order in a setting of poverty and uncertainty, there were numerous other trials borne by Mother Seton, some passing, some of longer duration, such as her health which brought her to the brink of the grave several times and remained a constant threat to her well-being. Misunderstandings and personal ambitions among several of her followers caused her no small pain. Oblique mention is made of this trying situation in a letter to Father Bruté:

> You speak as if your Mother's confidence is deficient but it is surely not at this time I am to open your eyes on my situation in this Community. As to private concerns, I have none unless it be my trials occasionally at the conduct of different sisters, and that you have forbid me speaking of and since you think proper and I am acquitted before God, I am too happy it is so.

Vexing decisions regarding the functioning of the Community, made and carried out by her ecclesiastical superiors, were among the passing crosses Mother Seton had to bear. This last-mentioned difficulty was aggravated, no doubt, by the repeated changes in Directors and Superiors to which the young Community was subjected. Strangely enough, many of these clergymen were Frenchmen with whom Elizabeth should have been able to establish a quick rapport. Unfortunately, the French prelates seem to have been the most difficult for her to deal with.

In reference to the predominance of this national background, there occurs a provocative remark in a letter of Mr. Ogden to his wife's sister, Harriet Seton, remonstrating with her for her entrance into the Catholic Church. He says in part:

> Besides, let me remark that the establishments at Baltimore and Saint Joseph's are novel things in the United States,

and would not have been permitted by the populace in any other place than in the democratic, Frenchified State of Maryland. The religion they propose is uncongenial to the habits, manners, and nature of Americans, and I predict ere long, from many causes, the demolition of every building in that State in any wise resembling a convent or Catholic hospital.

Without being at all aware of it, Mr. Ogden had put his finger on the main reason for much of Mother Seton's mental suffering during the early stages of her religious ruling: the incompatibility of the "Frenchified" methods and points of view of these well-meaning gentlemen with the primitive needs and altogether American outlook and purpose of the new foundation. Mother Seton had inherited no small business acumen from both sides of her family, and one cannot help feeling that much of the confusion related to the progress of her Community and the maintenance of her schools could have been avoided if Elizabeth had been allowed to follow more readily her own good sense and clear judgment on secular matters.

She personally conducted the official business of the school and convent, keeping the account books, sending out tuition bills, and acknowledging the payments of them; she communicated with parents about their children, with her religious superiors about new building projects, and wrote out class schedules for her teaching staff. This class schedule for Sister Fanny is written in Mother Seton's own hand:

AFTERNOON

2nd class of geography	— during which French will be read alternately to Sr. Eliza
3rd class of geography	— Gartland
2nd class of reading	— Monday and Thursday (Sr. George)
3rd class of reading	— Gartland

Monday and Thursday — 1st class parsing
Tuesday and Friday   — 2nd and 3rd class parsing
while 2nd class parses — 3rd class reads French

Since she also taught French and catechism, Mother Seton must have been very busy indeed. In her own handwriting may be seen detailed records of expenditures for classroom supplies and food. How quaint the bill for Dec. 1, 1810, reads now—nearly 150 years later:

1	Ream paper—letter	$4.25
10	quires	1.62½
8	small slates	1.50
1	doz. Comley's grammars	6.00
2	orators	1.50
33	spelling books	6.00
6	practical reflections	5.25
½	doz. ink powder	1.68

This bill contains a notation:

May-June 1810 furnished to Veronica
  ½ doz. pen knives, ink powder
  1 doz. slates
  2 doz. catechisms
  12½ doz. codfish

Purchases at this time also included barrels of flour, tea and coffee.

In spite of her ill health and increasing burdens, Mother Seton could testify to her inward tranquillity. This letter to Antonio gives us an idea of what these burdens were:

I am in peace! Peace is found in the midst of fifty children, the whole day long, save early in the morning and late in the evening. One cannot get away from order and regularity here. . . . This, my manner of living, you understand, is to watch over twenty persons who are joined in a bond of common love and interest, and sharing in all that concerns them. I am as a mother surrounded by numerous offspring; their dispositions are different; they are not all

equally lovable, nor conform to that which pleases me, but
the mother is bound to love them all, to furnish an example
of cheerfulness and peace and resignation. . . .

The improvement and expansion of her establishments
were of serious concern to Mother Seton. Although there
was never a time in those first days when the financial status
of the new Community and its educational work was sufficient to bear the burden of operation, the undaunted foundress never ceased to plan for the future. One of her most
cherished desires, the one to which she had really hoped to
devote her life, was the erection of a building for the instruction of poor children of the neighborhood, Negro and
white. However, because of the extreme need for immediate income, only pay pupils were at first registered at St.
Joseph's, so that the aforementioned project did not mate-
rialize until 1810.

Previous to this date, however, Mother Seton had made
several foundations for orphans outside of Maryland. In
1814 Sister Rose White, with two others, opened an or-
phanage in Philadelphia. Three years later, in 1817, Elizabeth had the personal pleasure of sending her daughters,
again under Sister Rose White, to establish St. Patrick's
Orphan Asylum in New York City.

In the spring of 1820, only eight months before her
death, Mother Seton was engaged in correspondence with
Bishop Dubourg concerning a new brick building for the
free school. In June a contract for one story was given. In
the summer of that same year she also planned the erection
of a chapel that would adequately accommodate her growing Community, which now embraced more than fifty members, and the children of the school. With her Sisters she
walked over the grounds and personally selected the spot
where she wished it situated. The construction, however,
was deferred until after her death, but the site was retained.

Elizabeth's insistence on a suitable chapel sprang from
her burning love for the Blessed Sacrament in Whose Pres-

ence she appeared rapt, her whole attitude exhibiting humble love. This spirit of humility and ardent faith glows in every line she wrote on Holy Communion or the Eucharist. Her profound respect before the tabernacle is the subject of several reflections:

> Five thousand Bethsamites were struck dead for looking with disrespect at the Ark. Ah, then, who shall disrespect the Altar!
> I see nothing in this world but the blue sky and the altars: all the rest is so plainly not to be looked at, but to be left to Him, with tears only for sin.

Her ardent aspirations of love, adoration, and desire could not be restrained as the time for receiving Holy Communion drew near:

> Oh, Food of Heaven, how my soul longs for you with desire! Seed of Heaven, pledge of its immortality, of that eternity it pants for. Come, come my Jesus, bury yourself within my heart. It shall do its best to preserve that warmth which will bring forth the fruits of eternity.

The most touching example of her tremendous desire for the Bread of Life occurred during her last few hours on earth. Mother Seton had been anointed on December 30, and had been given Holy Viaticum. She was able to receive Holy Communion on the following Sunday. Sometime after midnight preceding January 1, the Sisters urged her to take a refreshing drink they had prepared to assuage her excessive fever. She whose heart was set on the morrow's Communion, brushed it aside, answering: "Never mind the drink. One Communion more and then Eternity." The witness of this scene adds, "and she waited until the morning." Well did this admirable woman deserve the brief but eloquent accolade of Father Bruté: "O Mother, Excellent Mother!"

In her last months on earth Elizabeth appears to have reaped a rich reward for the generosity with which she had responded to the numerous trials of her life. Her soul was closely united in an almost tangible union with God. What seem to have been mystic graces may well have been hers, if we can judge by her own account of her inner life given in her *Journal*:

> I never experienced so keenly the presence of this beloved Lord as I have since I have been ill. It is as if I were seeing the good Jesus, Him and His holy Mother, here, continually seated at my side, under a visible form, to console me, cheer me, and to encourage me through all the hours of my long and painful suffering. . . .
> This union of my soul with God is my wealth in poverty and joy in deepest afflictions.

Mother Seton passed to her "dear and unchanging Eternity" early in the morning of January 4, 1821, at the age of 46. A few hours before, she had uttered her spiritual bequest to the grief-stricken Community gathered around her bed:

> Love one another as Sisters of Charity, love the Church, love your rules.

One of the Sisters, knowing Mother's predilection for prayers in French, recited over and over in that language the *Gloria in Excelsis* and passages from the *Magnificat*. And thus it was that Mother Elizabeth Bayley Seton went home with the language of her Le Conte forebears lingering in her ears.

So may have died some saintly ancestor in his Norman monastery, surrounded by his brethren, with their lighted tapers, their strong voices hushed in the rhythmic chant of prayer—

> Je vous salue, Marie . . . priez pour nous, maintenant, et à l'heure de notre mort. Ainsi soit-il.

Epilogue

Elizabeth had betrayed her French heritage; she had taken sides with Rome against Protestantly Reformed England. She was indeed an enemy to her people. Yet this daughter of rebels was but reverting to type when she rebelled against the faiths of her ancestors—to types, that is, against which they themselves had rebelled barely two centuries before.

There had once been English Bayleys, loyal sons of Holy Mother Church, paying their liege homage to a Catholic king, pledging life and property in the defense of the Pope, hardy squires fighting under Our Lady's banner and swearing their oaths "by St. Mary"; or riding sedately with their wives and children to high Mass in one of the noble cathedrals of Exeter, Westminster, Canterbury, or—Hertfordshire!

And there had been proud and sensitive knights in the centuries-old family of the Le Contes, tossing their lofty plumes in bloody battles against Saracens, riding off to the Crusades with the blessing of Holy Mother Church, the bepearled sleeves of ladies on their spears; or sitting humbly at the feet of the great teachers in the Sorbonne; or joining with genuine French fervor in the pilgrimages to her many holy shrines.

It will be to the undying glory of this rebel daughter of rebel ancestors that once-Catholic England, "Mary's Dowrie," and France, the "eldest daughter of the Church," live again on new soil in the flame of Faith lighted in the soul of their own Elizabeth Bayley Seton!

Notes

I The Romance of a Road

1. The Shore Road, or the Pelham Road as it is likewise called, was originally an Indian trail extending from one Indian village to another along the Sound between Pelham and Davenport Neck.

Historical Landmarks of New Rochelle. Seacord and Hadaway. 1938. p. 36.

2. The opening of the Old Post Road resulted from an order issued on February 24, 1669, by Governor Lovelace that "a Cart way be cleared between this Towne and Harlem." In 1672 he issued an order for a "Post to go mostly from this city to Boston and back again." The first official post rider took his trip January 23, 1673. This roadway lay through New Rochelle—28 miles from the Battery in New York City to New Rochelle. It eventually was recognized as the King's Highway. Ibid.

3. The settlers laid out their plots across the old Indian trail, or Shore Road, from the Sound inland to the Old Post Road. "These lots were mostly taken up by those interested in commercial enterprise, many in foreign trade, and not a few private docks were built along the shore beside the old trail." Public landings were added at the end of certain roads that led to the water's edge. Ibid.

4. The names of the 23 Freeholders of New Rochelle in 1708 were predominantly French—Isaac Mercier, Guilleaume Le Counte [sic] Francois Le Counte, and others.

History of the Several Towns, Manors and Patents of the County of Westchester . . . Rev. Robert Bolton. Vol. I.

5. The general stage coach office in New York was at Fraunces Tavern, 49 Cortlandt Street. Three days' journey was required for the trip from New York City to Albany traveling from 5 a.m.-10 p.m. daily.

6. The British laid siege to New York in August 1776, and took it in September 1776.

7. The salt belonged to the Province of New York. This storage took place in the fall of 1776. Seacord and Hadaway. op. cit. p. 60.

8. Israel Bissel was a veteran postrider of the Boston-New York run. In this remarkable incident he covered the ground from Watertown in Massachusetts to Philadelphia in five days! It would have taken the fastest stagecoach six days to get as far only as New York. The entire incident is related in *From Lexington to Liberty.* Bruce Lancaster. pp. 115-116.

9. The German mercenaries to the number of 4,000 landed in New Rochelle on Davenport Neck under the leadership of General

Baron Wilhelm von Knuphauser. Ibid., p. 228.

10. For an account of the Coutant Cemetery see *Historical Land-marks*, pp. 105-106.

11. James Pugsley was a member of an old Westchester family, a widower at the time of the incident, and a Quaker. His unmarried daughter kept house for him. According to tradition the Pugsley house was occupied by Howe for ten days as his Headquarters. James died in 1790—his daughter in 1831. Ibid., pp. 108, 111.

12. The popularity of Thomas Paine with New Rochelleans may be measured by the doggerel sung about him at the time of his death:

> Poor Tom Paine! here he lies
> Nobody laughs and nobody cries;
> Where he's gone and how he fares
> Nobody knows and nobody cares.
> Bolton's *History of Westchester County*, Vol. I.

While Paine was in Paris he received word that the Provincial Government of New York had allotted him a large piece of land in New Rochelle which had been confiscated from the estate of one Frederick DeVeau, a Loyalist. Later he was notified that "avengers" for DeVau had burned the property. His own body was debased by local residents who hated the fast-living, coarse, but ardent patriot.

13. Regarding famous taverns in New Rochelle see the chapter on "Taverns" in Seacord and Hadaway, op. cit.

14. Names of the French War Leaders were obtained from Lancaster, op. cit. Chap. XXXI.

15. The account of Washington's farewell has been taken from the same source. Chap. XXXII.

16. Raising of the flag and poem is from *The Old Boston Post Road*, Jenkins, p. 35.

II From La Rochelle to New Rochelle

1. For date of Huguenot arrival see *History of the Huguenot Emigration to America*. Charles W. Baird. Vol. II. "The LeConte Family."

2. The name of the vessel is given in a "Memorandum" recorded for Wm. Lecounte [sic] in the claims he made against the estate of Lasty . . . "the Brigantine named La Pointe du Sable." *Abstracts of Wills*, Surrogate's Court, New York County Courts. Vol. I . . . (1665-1707). It is quite likely that Lasty and Le Conte had named their vessel after the much-disputed point of land on the northern tip of St. Christopher Island, called at that time Pointe du Sable, now known

as Sands Point. This area was hotly contested by both British and French governments.

It may be of interest to the reader to know that one of the earliest Negro heroes of this country was named Jean Point du Sable.

3. Isaac Mercier came to New York with the thirty families who fled St. Christopher's. He was naturalized in that city on Sept. 27, 1687, and is mentioned as one of the Founding Fathers of New Rochelle. (See picture of Monument, p. 6.) A resident of that city for many years, he was one of the most prominent and highly respected of the citizens. Isaac married Susannah Coutant, daughter of another distinguished Huguenot family. He lived to a good old age, his will being dated 1747. His wife survived him. It is through her will that the strands of many leading families were united and reunited in such a way as to create the complex pattern that gave Elizabeth Bayley kinship to so many of the prominent New Rochelle families. (For the text of Susannah Mercier's will see the Appendix, No. 1.) Ibid. Vol. II. Also *Old Wills of New Rochelle. Copies of Wills by Citizens of New Rochelle*, 1784-1833. New Rochelle Chapter of D. A. R. 1951.

4. Huguenot exiles may be divided chiefly into two groups. The first were those sent out by the governments with deliberate intent to colonize. Settlements were made between 1572-1664 in Brazil, Florida, Arcadia, West Indies, Hackensack in New Jersey, New Paltz and Fort Orange (Albany) in New York. The second group consisted of desperate, hurried establishments by ruined exiles. Such foundations were made at Boston, Oxford in Massachusetts, New Rochelle in New York; throughout Pennsylvania, Delaware, Virginia and South Carolina. *The Encyclopedia Americana*. Vol. 14.

5. In 1623 the vessel "New Netherlands" comprising about 30 Huguenot families sailed from Holland to New Amsterdam.

In 1636 a vessel stranded at the entrance of New York harbor, unable to reach the port of New Amsterdam, made a settlement on Staten Island, then a Dutch holding, which thus became the home for future Huguenot refugees. These people were Waldensian emigrees from Vaudois.

6. For the full account of this "Memorandum" see the Appendix No. 2.

7. Anne Martha's marriage to Guillaume Le Conte in the West Indies is listed in the Land Records, Westchester Co., N. Y., Register's Office, Court House, Surrogate's Records, White Plains, N. Y. (Lorenzo Knapp gives the same source in his *Notes on the Le Conte Families of New Rochelle, N. Y.* in the *Quarterly Bulletin* of the Westchester Historical Society, Vol. 19.)

8. Baird is the source of the information given by Archbishop Seton and others to the effect that Guillaume Le Conte married a

Marguerite de Valleau. There are no real grounds for this statement, nor any apparent ones that a thorough investigation has been able to uncover. The only solution seems to this writer to be the confusion in the oral transmission of this statement from one generation to the next. The real facts are these: Pierre Le Conte, companion and probable relative of Guillaume and Francois Le Conte, married Marguerite de Valleau, and lived on Staten Island. Mahault and Valleau are phonetically so similar that they might be misunderstood, especially when coupled with a Le Conte surname. The actual historical dates of Guillaume Le Conte's two marriages preclude any possibility of marriage to the aforementioned Valleau.

9. For Lasty's background consult: *History of Westchester County* . . . Bolton. Vol. 1: *History of the Huguenot Emigration to America* . . . Baird. Vols. 1-2: *Notes on the Le Conte Family of New Rochelle* . . . Knapp; *Historical Landmarks of New Rochelle* . . . Seacord and Hadaway.

10. Governor Dongan's Charter of Franchises was granted on April 27, 1686. It extended religious liberty, right to meet, to build . . . On May 20, 1686, the Charter was revoked by the English King James II "but all duties and taxes imposed by it" were continued.

On May 9, 1687, the French Protestants of New York petitioned Dongan for privileges: "they swear allegiance to the King and receive free trading privileges."

Iconography of Manhattan Island, 1498-1907, compiled by Philip Stokes. Vol. 4.

11. For inventory of Lasty's property made by Le Conte see Appendix. No. 4.

III   A Huguenot Becomes an American

1. Shortly after the Dutch obtained possession of the island of Manhattan they laid out farms or "bouweries." The Delanceys eventually obtained the largest parcel of these farms, thereby providing home lots for the exiled Huguenots. Jenkins, *op. cit.*, p. 69.

2. "Letters of administration" were granted to Le Conte as Lasty's executor. New York County Courts. *Abstracts of Wills*, Surrogate's Court. Vol. I (1665-1707). Liber 3-4. p. 299. (see Appendix No. 3.)

3. All references to public offices and deeds are contained in the collection and translation made by Jeanne Forbes in *Records of the Town of New Rochelle* 1699-1828.

4. "Francis LeConte . . . Victualler—April 18, 1694," listed with *Freemen made in the Mayorality of Charles Lodwik. Esq.* (Coll. of New York Hist. Soc. for the year 1885). In 1701—"an indenture of

the boy Andrew Maham aged 14years to Francis Leconte [sic] Baker, for seven years to date." Ibid.

5. For complete "Memorandum" see Appendix No. 2.

6. Jacob Leisler was a demagogue who for a brief time usurped authority in the Provincial Government of New York State. He was subsequently tried, and the jury being all of his enemies, he was convicted and hanged.

7. LeContes still resident in France in the 17th and 18th centuries are prominent. *Cardinal Louis Daniel LeCompte* (1655-1728) published in 1697 "memoirs and observations of a recent trip to China. It appears that the Cardinal was a Jesuit.
Francois Le Conte (1620-1689) wrote a description of his travels through Tongking and Laos in Indo-China.
Pierre Lecomte (1745-?) presented an opinion to the national Convention in Paris on Sept. 24, 1793, urging the annulling of two judgments rendered by that tribunal.

8. The houses in New York were built of Dutch brick, the City "encompassed by a wall of good thickness to the landward and fortified at the entrance to the River by a fort called James Fort." *Iconography of Manhattan Island* 1498-1907, *op. cit.*, Vol. 4.

9. The testimonial is contained in O'Callaghan's *Documentary History of New York*, 1693-1706. (London Documents) Vol. 4, p. 1007.

10. A letter of Thomas Standard, minister to the Secretary of the "Venerable Propagation Society" in Nov. 5, 1729, relative to the occupations of Westchester contains the statement about farmers. Bolton's *History of Westchester*.

11. For facts relating to early Huguenot houses see *Historic New Rochelle*. Herbert Nichols.

12. The three Jesuits were Thomas Harvey who had accompanied Gov. Dongan from England; Henry Harrison of Ireland; Charles Gage of Norwich. Leisler also added to the letter quoted on p. 30 this bit of asperity:
These sones went twice daily to the Collidge to be instructed by that hellish brude of Jesuits.
O'Callaghan, op. cit., Vol. 11, p. 147.

13. For the celebrations of Guy Fawkes Day see *The Catholic Church in Colonial Times*. Gilmary Shea. Vol. 11.

14. For Francois Le Conte's abjuration see Appendix No. 5.

15. Letter of Elizabeth Seton to Julia Scott:
Julia Sitgreaves Scott: a close, life-long friend of Mother Seton. Mrs. Lewis A. Scott was at this time a widow living in Philadelphia with her sister Mrs. James Cox.

16. Le Conte's marriage to Margaret Mahault may be found recorded in *Vital Records of the French Huguenot Church, New Rochelle, N. Y.*, kept by the Rev. Daniel Bondet (1695-1722), also in

O'Callaghan's *Documentary History*. Vol. 3. p. 141. Three variations occur for the spelling of Mahault: Maho and Manhomay. The introduction to *Vital Records* warns:

> Names are just as they appear and in some instances vary somewhat from the present day forms.

17. Census list. O'Callaghan, *op. cit.*, p. 571.

18. For the text of Le Conte's will see Appendix No. 6

19. Stapleton's *Memoir to the Huguenots*, p. 141, gives this tribute to the Le Conte family. (For further verification see Appendix No. 8.)

IV   Intricate Traceries

1. Katherine's marriage and departure from St. Kitts. See Baird's *History of the Huguenots*. Vol. II, *op. cit.*

2. Date of Bartholomew's death. *Ibid.*

3. Seacord and Hadaway in *Historical Landmarks*, p. 8 give this account of Bouteillier:

> Bouteillier was a merchant of the Island of Martinique as early as 1678, and upon his removal to New York, he became actively interested in assisting other refugees from the islands . . . Lasty, also a merchant, came to New York from St. Christopher, where he engaged in business, but eventually returned to St. Christopher, together with Bouteillier, both of whom died there.

4. In February, 1687, Bouteillier petitioned the Governor of New York that all the Huguenots arriving in this country be received as settlers. Bouteillier, Leisler, and several others purchased Davenport Neck (Bonnefoy Neck) which they subdivided into small lots of from six to forty acres apiece. It is thought that Bouteillier or one of the others represented the interests of Lasty and other purchasers. *Ibid.*, p. 9.

> David Bonnefoy, aged 40, appears in the census of 1706 with his wife Katherine, and children David and Catherine. He is listed as the head of the family in Staten Island.

5. On September 20, 1689, John Pell and his wife Rachael Pinckney conveyed six thousand acres of the Pelham Patent to Jacob Leisler as representative of the Huguenots in New York City. This purchase constituted the area covered by the present township of New Rochelle. See Bolton's *History of Westchester County*. Vol. 1, p. 583.

6. Mme. Bonnefoy's daughter, Katherine, married Isaac Coutant, a Huguenot. The story of her death has been told in Chapter II.

7. Katherine Bonnefoy's will was probated October 25, 1714. (For partial text of this will see Appendix No. 7.)

8. The exploits of Captain Mercier are outlined by one of his descendants. *Tales of Our Kinsmen*. Butler.

9. Henry Mercier, Katherine's eldest child, son of Bartholomew Mercier, was born about 1690. He died before January 1719. His wife was Christiana Hendricks. It was their son William Mercier (1717-1797) who became the famous Captain Mercier of Revolutionary War fame. Ibid.

10. Madame Bonnefoy's birthdate has been given as "about 1661." Ibid.

11. We do not know much about Hester's later life. Her name appears on a deed of property together with her brother's; she was sponsor at several baptisms and she signed a petition for the erection of a new French Church. With Isaac Mercier, she was godmother to her niece Anne Le Conte. In 1723 she was "Ester Bonyot."

V William Le Conte

1. Hester Le Conte married Ezechiel Bonyot 1715/1716. Their daughter Ester, born August 1717, has had as her godparents Isaac Le [sic] Mercier and Marianne Le Conte. *Records of Rev. Daniel Bonnet for the Church of New Rochelle.*

2. Pierre Le Conte (Margaret Mahault's son) was brought up on Staten Island by his baptismal sponsor, his maternal aunt, Marie Mahault Vergeraud. Later he moved to Monmouth, New Jersey, where he became a physician of note. He was godfather to his niece Susanna Le Conte (1726/27) who married William Bayley. Pierre died in Matawan, New Jersey (now New York), 1768. (For a full account of this branch of the family see the Appendix No. 8.)

3. For descriptions of Indian villages on Davenport Neck see *Historical Landmarks of New Rochelle.*

4. Transaction taken from Forbes' translation of *Records of the Town of New Rochelle.*

5. Letter of Elizabeth to Mrs. Sadler: August 11, 1796. *Memoirs and Letters* ed. by Msgr. Seton.

6. For Taverns in New Rochelle see *Historical Landmarks.* Guillaume Le Conte acquired the property from Louis Carre in 1694 or shortly before. In the same year he sold it to Francois Le Conte. However, it happened, we find this same tavern conducted by William Le Conte in 1733.

7. Incident cited in *Historical Landmarks*, p. 85.

8. William married Marianne Mercier, daughter of Susanne and Isaac Mercier. Knapp. *Quarterly Bulletin of Westchester Hist. Soc.*, Vol. 19. 1952.

9. James Flandreau, a native of France, in 1664; he appears as a resident of New Rochelle in 1710, together with his wife Catherine and their three children: James Jr., Peter and Betty. They settled in the southern part of the town where the Guions, Le Contes, and

Rhinelanders also lived. The name of James Flandreau is attached to the list of Church members in 1743. This is probably James Jr. since the father's name appears on a tombstone inscription for 1726:

Here lies the body of
James Flandreau
Died Feb. 19, 1726

10. Peter married Anne Le Conte, July 1, 1763. Record M. B. Vol. VII, p. 253. *Collections of New York Historical Society.*

11. Original record of Susanna's baptism:

Baptesme ... Aujourd'uy mecredy 8me de fevrier 1726/27 aprest la Pierre due matin monsr. louis Rou a batise Susanna Le Conte ne le 5me de ce mois presente au St. Batesme parle Sr. Guillaume Le Conte Pere du dit.
Enfan en la place de Pierre de Conte Parrain et susanne mercier Marriane la mere du dit. Enfan se nomme Marianne.

G. Le Conte
S. Mercier

Records of the Le Conte family taken from *Collections of the Huguenot Society of America.* Vol. I, ed. by Rev. Alfred Wittemeyer.

12. No date is given in any of the records for the marriage of William Bayley to Susanna Le Conte. It was probably 1742/43.

13. Four John Boyds are listed as inhabitants of Rye in 1683. Bolton's *History of Westchester,* Vol. 2, p. 139. Marianne Le Conte probably married one of them but investigation has yielded no real evidence.

14. For the complete text of William Le Conte's will see the Appendix No. 9.

VI   A Chapter on Bayleys

1. "14 yrs.—At uncle B's in New Rochelle, again." *Dear Remembrances.* E.A.S.

2. Baptismal record obtained from Trinity Episcopal Church, New Rochelle, through the courtesy of Mrs. Belle Egan, Parish clerk.

3. Pell's history . . . see Bolton's *History of Westchester County.* Vol. 1.

4. Sarah Pell. daughter of Joseph and Phoebe Pell, married William Bayley June 10, 1771. *Names of Persons for Whom Licenses were issued* . . ., Record M.B., Vol. XVII, page 107.

5. For the account of Anne Hutchinson see *History of Westchester.* Bolton. Vol. 1.

6. The description of the Bayley coat of arms as given by Archbishop Seton was as follows:

John Bayly of Hoddesdon . . . their crest, out of a ducal

coronet or. a nag's head ar." and the arms "1634 argent, 3
torteaux and two and one-a chief gules.

The writer contacted the British Museum for further information
to verify what has been given above. The following answer was received:

The Bayley pedigree you are interested in is printed in *The
Visitation of Hertfordshire*, edited W. C. Metcalfe, Harleian Society, London, 1886, p. 27, from the original MSS in the College
of Arms (G. 17 and D. 28).

There are copies of the pedigree among the collections of this
Department in Harleian MSS. 1546, f. 134; 1547, f. 66a, identical
with the printed text. The pedigree given is as follows:—

John Bayly of Hodson co. Hertf.

—Susan, da. of William Shambrooke.

John Bayly of Hodson,

eldest son—Lettice, da. of Sir William Skevington of
Fisherwick co. Staff.

| John Bayly | Richard Bayly | Elizabeth | Lettice |

The descriptions you give of the Bayly arms and crest are apparently alternative rather than conflicting. I think, however, the
description should be, of the crest, "Out of a coronet flory Or, a
nag's head Argent maned of the first", and of the arms, "Argent
three torteaux, or roundels), two and one, a chief gules."

Yours faithfully,
J. P. Hudson
Assistant Keeper

The British Museum of London, W. C.
Department of Manuscripts

28th July, 1955.

7. Archbishop Bayley says: "My father's (family) came from
Norfolkshire in England about 1690 and settled in Westchester Co.
N. Y."

8. To further substantiate this line of descent for the Westchester
Bayley's, a second source, *The Refugees of 1778 from Long Island to
Connecticut*, states that the first Bayley on Long Island was one John
who came there from the West Indies, having been born in England in
1617. These dates and facts fit well enough the description of the
John Bayley referred to in Chapter 6, p. 51.

9. *The Original Lists of Persons of Quality: Emigrants, Religious
and Political Rebels . . . 1600-1700* contains the following entry:

Jo(John) Baylie . . . 18 yrs. X Junig 1635 . . . to the Ber-
moodas or Somer Islands imbarqued in *Truelove* de London . . .

The record of the above-mentioned person continues:

This John Bailey [sic] appeared in Southhold, Long Island, the usual landing place for British immigrants. Some time later he went to New Haven, turning up in Westchester in 1654.

A study of the records seems to indicate that John moved from Southhold as early as 1646. Twenty years later, after he had been settled in Westchester for over ten years, his son Joseph received a gift of land from the Town of Huntington, Long Island, where in 1667, he built his home on a hill overlooking Huntington Mill Pond. He was a surveyor and one of the ten Patentees named in the Dongan Patent to the Town in 1688. He served as a captain of the "Train Bands", local military units who were exercised and drilled on the village common.

(It is of interest to note that Southhold was the first town on Long Island, founded in 1640 chiefly by English emigrants from Norfolkshire, who had spent a short time in the New Haven colony.)

10. The local church at Hertfordshire has two monuments to John Baily (spelled also Bayly in the same inscription) and his wife Lettice. The first of these reads:

In Memory of Lettice Twyne, a sister of Sir R. Skevington, Kt. and wife of John Baily, Gent. by whom he had issue, John, Richard, Elizabeth, Lettice and Susan.

The other inscription records the death of this same John Baily, and adds, what is for us, significant, the place of his birth:

Near to this Place lies buried the bodies of John Bayly of Hodesdon, Esq. and Lettice his wife, and daughter of Sir William Skevington . . . who (Bayly) was a Man of primitive Piety, and severe only to himself, he changed this Life for a better, the 6th of April, 1659, Aged 63.

See *The Historical Antiquities of Hertfordshire* . . . Chauncey, Vols. 1, 2. See also *Pedigrees of Hertfordshire Families* . . . Barry

A slight discrepancy is to be noted in giving "Lettice" as the daughter of Sir William Skevington (in diagram), as sister (above). No doubt the record in the British Museum is correct.

11. See *Old Wills of New Rochelle* . . . Pelletreau.

VII The Doctor

1. Inscription on Town Hall, Fairfield—*Old Boston Post Road*—Jenkins, *op. cit.* p. 196.

2. For William Bayley's arrival in this country see *Record of the Bayley Family*. Seton. See also Note 7, Chapter 6.

3. William married Suzanne Le Conte in her sixteenth or seventeenth year according to her baptismal record here translated from the original French:

Today, Wednesday Feb. 8, 1726/7, after the Morning Prayer,
M. Louis Rou baptized Susanne Le Conte, born on the fifth
of this month, presented to Holy Baptism by Sir William Le
Conte, father of the said child in place of Peter Le Conte,
Godfather and Susanna Mercier Godmother, Mother of the
said-child is named Marianne.

G. Le Conte
S. Mercier

Collections of the Huguenot Society of America. Vol. 1, edited
by A. Wittemeyer.

Note: 1726 is also the year given by Archbishop Seton for the
arrival of William Bayley in this country!

4. Pierre Stouppe, rector of Trinity Episcopal Church (1724-
1760), also kept "a private boarding school where instruction was
given in both English and French."

Seacord and Hadaway, op. cit., p. 94 (Schools)

5. "First, I give and bequeath unto my mother Susannah Garrineau [sic] now the wife of John Garrineau, for and during the time
of her natural life, all that my farm or plantation, lying and being at
Milo Square in the County of Westchester . . ."

Surrogate's Court, New York City, Liber 43, page 490. (For complete
text of Dr. Bayley's will see Appendix No. 14.)

Since Bayley left New Rochelle at an early age, it is to be presumed that, as the elder son, he had inherited this property from
his father. There is no evidence that he ever lived on it, or even
attended to its cultivation.

6. "Suzanne Besley [sic] and John Guerineau" married September 14, 1762. *Names of Persons for Whom Marriage Licenses were
Issued by the Secretary of the Province of New York, Previous to 1784.*

7. Dr. John Charlton from *Memoirs of Eminent Physicians Who
Flourished in America.* James Thacher. 1829.

also *Memorial History of Staten Island* . . . Morris

also *History of Medicine in New York.* Vol. 1, James J. Walsh.

8. Dr. Bayley married Catherine Charlton on January 9, 1769 in
Elizabethtown, New Jersey. See Appendix No. 20.

9. "Rev. Mr. Charlton preached in the English Church (Trinity)
on Thanksgiving Day, Nov. 21 1733." *Collections of the New York
Historical Society for the Year* 1870. This occasion was one of his
first appearances before the New York congregation.

10. Letter to Julia Scott, July 26, 1800, from Staten Island.

11. Thacher says that Bayley went to England in 1769.

12. The family estate of the Dongans on Staten Island has given
its name to the entire section, now known as Dongan Hills. (See
Appendix No. 12.

13. For character of Dr. Bayley see *History of Medicine in New York* and *Memoirs* . . . Thacher.

14. Bayley returned in the spring of 1776 "in the capacity of surgeon to Lord Howe." (Thacher). It would seem that Dr. Bayley returned with Lord Richard's fleet. The latter's brother Gen. William Howe, had been in command of the British land forces in this country for over a year and had fought the Battle of Bunker Hill in June of that year. Suffering heavy losses, Gen. Howe had moved his army down to Staten Island, British Headquarters at that period. Here he was joined by Admiral Lord Howe with a strong fleet and 150 transports on July 12, 1776. While the Admiral took his fleet up to Newport to prevent a sea attack by the French, Gen. Howe laid siege to New York. in August. The city fell to the British in September. Apparently Dr. Bayley went to Newport with Admiral Howe and remained there at the army base Hospital "as Hospital Surgeon for the Fleet and five or six thousand troops at Newport, R. I. in the Fall of 1776." (Thacher) Although serving in this capacity with the navy, Dr. Bayley had probably enlisted with the land forces; hence his appointments to higher ranks were issued from the headquarters of the Commander-in-chief, General William Howe.

15. Bayley's appointments are taken from "The Kemble Papers" of the *New York Historical Society*. Vol. 1.
The third appointment reads:

> Headquarters, White Plains. Camp, 31st Oct. 1776. 23rd Regiment—Sergeant-Major Robinson, 38th Regiment to be Quarter Master. vice Baily promoted. 31st Oct. 1776.

16. Thacher gives a rather detailed account of Bayley's relations with the Hessian Michaelis.

17. In 1795-96 Bayley was appointed Health Officer to the Port of New York.

In 1797, he published his work on yellow fever, "wherein he is at great pains to give distinctiveness to the terms 'contagion' and 'infection.'"

". . . as early as 1787, he delivered lectures in what later became the New York Hospital."

18. *Minutes of the Medical Society of the State of New York, from November 14, 1794-July 8, 1806.*

19. Ibid. Sept. 4, 1795.

20. Ibid. Feb. 29, 1796.

21. Ibid. January 12, 1796.

22. Description of Dr. Wright Post, from *History of Medicine in New York*. Vol. 4.

23. Dr. Wright Post's tombstone inscription in the churchyard of St. Peter's Church. Westchester (between Pelham and Eastchester) reads in part:

Here lies
the mortal remains of
Wright Post,
during many years eminent as
physician and surgeon
in the city of New York,
he was distinguished for sound judgment,
practical skill and unwearied diligence in
his profession, and for modest, dignified and
mild deportment in all the walks of life;

*   *   *

He retired from the city to his country seat
in this neighborhood . . .
He died June 14, 1828,
aged 62 years, 3 months
and 26 days.

Others buried near him are Oliver De Lancey, Captain Stephen Bayard, Philip Livingston, Philip Honewell. Bolton's *History of Westchester*.

24. *The Daily Advertiser* for September 27, 1786, speaks of "Wright Post and Richard Bayley (Doctors) who will give a Lecture on Anatomy."

25. We think our medical and surgical fees are exorbitant. There follow the fees established at a meeting of all practitioners on July 1, 1798. Considering the value of the dollar at that time, they seem as bad as those of our own time.

Visual advice, $5.00, A letter of advice, $10.00, An ordinary visit, $1.00, A visit with a single dose of medicine $1.25 (first time).

One might have his tonsil "extirpated" for $25, a limb amputated for $50, and a cataract removed for $125.

26: In the Archives of Mount Saint Vincent is a copy of a letter written to Mr. Thomas E. Cassidy regarding Dr. Bayley's service in Columbia:

Mr. Thomas E. Cassidy:

In reply to your inquiry of September 17, I beg to say that our records contain the name of Richard Bailey. not Bayley as you spell it. He was appointed Professor of Anatomy in 1792, Professor of Surgery, 1793.

> Frank D. Fackenthal
> Columbia University
> September 24, 1923

VIII   The Merchant

1. "At his store opposite the Coffee House Bridge . . . formerly

Parker's Printing Office . . ." *Rivington's Gazeteer*. New York, July 29, 1773.

2. ". . . has just imported in the Earl of Dunmore, Captain Lawrence, and the other ships from England, a vast and general assortment of all kinds of Japanese Ware of the newest fashion, now used in London, as also Hardware in general . . ." Ibid. (See also *Weekly Mercury*, June 13, 1774.)

3. "At his store in Beaver Street and at his store in the Fly Market . . . steel collars for young ladies . . ." *Rivington's Gazeteer*. July 29, 1773.

4. "James Barclay has for sale at his store on Hunter's Quay, opposite Messrs. Curson and Seaton, Jamaica spirits. West India Rum and Molasses . . ." (Ad for Jay and Barclay in *Rivington's Gazeteer*. op. cit.)

5. I have taken the arbitrary date of 1762 as a most likely one when juxtaposed with other events: Suzanne Bayley's second marriage to John Guerineau in September of that year; the fact that when Richard Bayley was married in 1769 to Catherine Charlton, he was already a promising young doctor; that by 1773 William Bayley was financially able to enlarge his business quarters and owned at least two stores.

6. McBride, hardware dealer of prominence. Collections of the New York Historical Society for 1870.

7. For the complete text of several of Bayley's ads see the Appendix, No. 11.

8. "Old Streets". In *Valentine's Manual of the City of New York for 1916-1917*.

9. Marriage License for William Bayley and Sarah Pell. *Names of Persons for whom Marriage Licenses were Issued*.

10. Theodosia Bartow who married Captain Aaron Burr was a cousin to Sarah Pell by the marriage of Bethsheba Pell, their common cousin, to Theophilus Bartow. The families were twice intermarried. The Burrs had one child, Theodosia, who was passionately devoted to her father. Long years after his famous duel with Hamilton, when feeling against him had somewhat died down, Burr returned to the United States from Europe. Theodosia, then Mrs. Ashton, wishing to be on hand to welcome her father, embarked in December 1812 from South Carolina in a pilot-boat distinguished for its speed, and bound for New York. The vessel was never heard of after leaving port. It probably foundered in a gale, and all aboard were lost. *Recollections of Persons and Events Chiefly in the City of New York. J. M. Mathews. D.D.* p. 96.

1. "Anne Margaret Barclay, daughter of Andrew Barclay, and Frederick Jay, merchant . . . November 18, 1773." *Names of Persons for whom Licenses were Issued*. 1763. Record M. B. Vol. VII, p. 253.

12. These titles were advertised in the columns of *Rivington's Gazeteer* during 1773.

13. *The Collections of the New York Historical Society for 1870* gives the interesting information about Major Andre and De Lancey.

14. "William Bayley at his store—Grate Warehouse, in Brown Street." (This ad occupied an entire column in *Rivington's Gazeteer* for 1773.)

15. "William Bayley has imported in the Ship Samson, Capt. Compar from London, and is now opening at his store—Grate Warehouse, in Beaver Street . . ." (*New York Gazette and Weekly Mercury.* June 13, 1774.)

16. The line-cut appeared in the *New York Gazette*.

17. Bruff's ad was carried in the *New York Gazette* for April 3, 1775 and subsequent issues.

18. This petition may be found in *New York in the Revolution.* Roberts.

19. The notice in the *New York Gazette* for November 28, 1774 reads:

> William Bayley
> Intends to remove from his store in Beaver Street, New
> York, to his store in Newport, Rhode Island, early next
> spring. This is therefore to inform the public that, at
> New York, consisting of a vast and general assortment
> of hardware, at prime cost . . .

20. For the account of the Marine Society of the City of New York, see the Appendix No. 13.

21. *Valentine's Manual for 1916*, op. cit. and *Collections of the N. Y. Hist. Soc. for 1870* contain detailed accounts of the great fire of 1776.

22. According to Stokes op. cit.: "Abraham Patten set fire to the city and acknowledged it." (1776 S 21)

23. Sign over Bayley's shed is from the same.

IX Dark Skeins

1. Incident about the death of Catherine is included in *Dear Remembrances*.

2. Elizabeth had lost in death her father, her husband, two daughters, and two dearly loved sisters-in-law. She was survived by her sister Mary (Mrs. Post), her son William, daughter Catherine Josephine who later became a Sister of Mercy, her son Richard who outlived his mother by a scant two years.

3. "Eight years of age—New Rochelle—Miss Molly B's . . ." from *Dear Remembrances*.

4. Elizabeth establishes the date of her birth beyond a doubt. In her *Journal* under the date of August 28th, she says:

> St. Augustine and my birthday, the first in the course of thirty-three years in which the soul has sincerely rejoiced that it exists for immortality.

Since her death occurred in 1821, at the age of forty-six, her birth year can be determined as 1774.

5. "Dr. Bayley-Charlotte Amelia Barclay. June 16, 1778." (The *Royal Gazette*, N. Y. Hist. Soc. Collections for 1870. Vol. 3.)

6. Charlotte Amelia's children were Amelia (known as Emma) m. William Craig; Richard (b. Aug. 7, 1781) m. Catherine White, granddaughter of Anna Van Cortlandt. He was killed in a horse-and-carriage accident on Yonkers Hill on May 29, 1815. Andrew, at one time engaged to Harriet Seton; William; Guy Carleton (b. 1786) m. Grace Roosevelt. Their son was James Roosevelt Bayley, Archbishop of Baltimore; Mary Fitch m. Sir Robert Henry Bunch of the Bahamas; Helen (b. 1790) m. Samuel Craig. (Known affectionately as "Aunt Craig").

7. Letter of Mary Post to Elizabeth, August 1, 1808, upon the occasion of revisiting New Rochelle.

8. Letter to Henry Seton, 1811.

9. Letter to Julia Scott regarding Emma's wedding:

> Emma is engaged to marry Craig, and they only wait the arrival of Mr. and Mrs. Sadler, who are hourly expected. It rejoices my heart that she is chosen by so good a man, for though he is far from those brilliant qualities which the world so much admires, he has those of a true upright heart with a very well-informed mind. (November 3, 1798)

The follow-up letter was written the next year: January 20, 1799.

10. For Dr. Bayley's will see Appendix No. 14.

11. "Sixteen years of age . . . Family disagreements . . ." *Dear Remembrances.*

12. Dr. Bayley at Albany: Letter to Mrs. Scott.

13. His interest in Julia:

14. Regarding her failure to write: Elizabeth to Julia, New York, November 19, 1800.

15. Dr. Bayley's comment on his life: MSV archives IX, 100 (no date).

16. On Emma's health: Letter no. 71 (MSV Archives), to her father.

17. Reference to Helen: Letter to father, February 26, 1799 from Bloomingdale. (Letter no. 81, MSV Archives) Elizabeth's letters have several mentions of Helen who was born only four years before her own marriage and for whom the young wife probably felt a motherly tenderness. There is evidence, also, that Dr. Bayley kept this last child

under his immediate care. He requested Elizabeth to send her a box of goodies when the little girl was in boarding school in New Jersey. Elizabeth herself writes to her father regarding a letter received from the school authorities asking permission for Helen to make a visit home.

18. A Memorandum of her father's death made by Elizabeth on September 5, 1801.

19. Letter to Julia Scott regarding Mrs. Bayley's death: August 28, 1805.

Bolton's *History of Westchester.* Vol. 2, p. 620 (Town of Yonkers) has this notation:

> On the Van Cortland Property is a vault . . . a small square edifice of stone, surmounted with a pointed roof, the whole enclosed by a solid stone wall. Within an adjoining vault, in the same yard, repose the remains of

Charlotte Amelia Bayley
relic of Doctor Richard Bayley
who died the 1st day of Sept. 1805

Mrs. Bayley's privilege of being buried in the family vault on this estate came from her sister Catherine's marriage to Augustus Van Cortlandt, in 1763.

X "At Uncle William's"

1. Elizabeth to Mrs. Sadler, August 1, 1797.

2. William Bayley's children were Joseph, William, Susanna (b. Mar. 4, 1775) and Anne (called Nancy). *Old Wills of New Rochelle,* pp. 69, 70, 71.

3. Susanna Bayley married Jeremiah Schureman II, son of Jeremiah Schureman and Margaret DeVeau, both members of pioneer families in New Rochelle. The Schuremans (or Scurmans) were the descendants of Frederick (b. 1630) and his wife Mary (b. 1640) of France. Their son Frederick was a freeholder in New Rochelle in 1708. "1796-Saturday, January 9th. Jeremiah Schureman of New Rochelle, and Susanna Bayley, eldest daughter of William Bayley, married Dec. 31, at Pelham." *Valentine's Manual,* p. 253.

4. William Bayley, Jr., "died young" according to the records, yet he is mentioned in his father's will made in 1805.

5. "Charlotte Coutant" (1770-1855), inscription on grave in Coutant Cemetery.

6. "1790-Saturday, June 12th. Dr. Wright Post and Miss Bailey,

daughter of Dr. Richard Bailey, of this city, married Thursday last."
Valentine's Manual, 1916-1917, p. 222.

   7. Thacher states:

   Beloved by his former officers and esteemed by his fellow-
   citizens, he seemed to be fast gaining reputation and comfort
   while the influence he possessed with several commanding officers was often exerted in saving lives and rescuing the property of absent friends and fellow-citizens from confiscation and
   destruction. *American Medical Biography.*

   In order to favor members of the leading families who had espoused the cause of Great Britain in the Revolution, the New York
State Government passed a law permitting close relatives to buy back
the formers' confiscated property from the Board of Forfeitures. *Disposition of Loyalists' Estates after the Revolution.* H. Yoshpe.

   8. The history of the house was given by the present incumbent,
Mr. Richard Kemble, direct descendant of one of the later owners,
to a reporter for the *Pelham Sun.*

   9. For an interesting incident connected with the later history
of the Bayley house see the Appendix No. 15.

   10. Bayley's career as a citizen may be gleaned from the *New
Rochelle Town Records.* Forbes.

   11. *Heads of Families at the First Census of the United States,
1790.*

   12. William Bayley's will. See Appendix No. 16. A scrap of paper
evidently torn from the end of a document bore this signature.

   13. *Life Notes or Fifty Years' Outlook.* Rev. William Hague, D.D.

   14. *Dear Remembrances.*

   15. Regarding the proposed visit: Letter June 11, 1801.

   16. Letter to Mrs. Sadler in Long Island, August, 1801.

   17. These passages all from *Dear Remembrances.*

   18. Incidents relative to Mr. Henderson are taken from Hague's
Life Notes.

   19. Dr. Mason was a Presbyterian minister, Provost of Columbia
College, Professor of Theology in the Seminary which he founded. He
died from "overwork" at an early age. *Recollections of Persons and
Events Chiefly in the City of New York.* J. M. Mathews, D.D. pp. 25-8.

   20. Regarding the effect of Episcopalian tenets Elizabeth later
remarked: "It was the knowledge of the Protestant doctrine with
regard to faith that made me a Catholic, for as soon as I found that
Episcopalians did not think everybody right, I was convinced that my
safe course was to unite with the church in which, at all events, they
admitted I could find salvation and where also I could be sure of the
apostolic succession." White, op. cit., p. 179.

   21. *Life Notes.* Hague.

XI A Daughter of the Huguenots

1. In 1750 Dr. John Bard was the most famous physician of his day. He and his son operated on George Washington without the use of an anaesthetic. Dr. Samuel Bard opened the Columbia Medical school in 1768. He opened New York Hospital in 1791, and with the help of Dr. Richard Bayley, the New York Dispensary in the previous year.

2. Eli Whitney was graduated from Yale Law School in 1792. He invented the cotton gin in 1793; it was patented in 1794.

3. The French Republic was proclaimed September 21, 1792.

4. Presidential electors cast their ballots on December 5, 1792. Washington received 132 votes for president; John Adams, 77 for vice-president. Both were re-elected.

5. Louis XVI was executed on January 21, 1793. Marie Antoinette died on the guillotine on October 16, 1793.

6. American Gilbert Stuart had studied under Benjamin West in London. Returning to the United States cir. 1793 after successful exhibits in England and Ireland, he set up a studio in New York City. In 1794, he opened one in Philadelphia where he executed the first and second traits portraits of Washington and his wife Martha. Eventually he painted his famous "gallery" of statesmen of the early Republic.

7. Philip Freneau, a Huguenot, edited the *National Gazette*, a pro-Jefferson, anti-Federalist paper. He was the major poet of the period from 1776-1788. His works reflect the idea of progress and hostility to tyranny which earned for him the title of "Poet of the Revolution." In 1781 he wrote "Eutaw Springs" or "To the Memory of Brave Americans." His sea poems include "The Memorable Victory of John Paul Jones" and "The Battle of Lake Erie." He died in 1832.

8. John Jay, another descendant of Huguenots, was a member of the 1st and 2nd Continental Congresses, Chief Justice of New York State, Secretary of Foreign Affairs and Governor of New York from 1795-1801. The founder of the family, Augustus Jay, came to America after the Revocation of the Edict of Nantes. His son John married Eva Van Cortlandt. Through her, John Jay Jr., came into possession of the Bedford estates, recently made into a national museum.

9. There is a family tradition that Nathaniel Hawthorne, after a visit to the Seton home, was so impressed by a miniature of young Seton painted in 1796 that he used it as the basis for his description of Clifford Pyncheon in the *House of the Seven Gables*.

10. The description of the dress is from an actual description of one advertised in the *New York Gazette*, May 15, 1789.

11. Reference to her eyes in letter to her father from Bloomingdale, September 10, 1799. (MSV archives IX-81-2).

12. A personal description of Elizabeth is given by Charles White in his basic work *Life of Mrs. Eliza Seton*, p. 20. Mr. White was in a position to give first-hand information on Mother Seton for excellent reasons: 1. Their families were connected by marriage. Elizabeth's half-brother Richard Bayley had married Catherine White. 2. The first edition of his work was published in 1853, only thirty years after Mother Seton's death when many who had known her personally were still living. White says:

> The information embodied in this volume relative to Mrs. Seton has been collected altogether from original and contemporary sources ... and from the manuscript of verbal statements respecting her and her family furnished by numerous individuals who were intimately connected with her. (Preface to First Edition)

13. Letter to William Seton from the home of her sister, Mrs. Wright Post, on John Street. (All of these letters to William Seton have been obtained from photostat copies of the originals at Emmitsburg.) (MSV Archives Letters IX. No. 66; IX, No. 68)

14. Marriage entry in the Seton family Bible; announcement in the *New York Weekly Museum*.

15. Dr. Bayley on French and music: White. op. cit. Chapter I, p. 15.

16. Letter to William Seton. (MSV Archives IX No. 67)

17. Letter written to Julia Scott while on a visit to a mutual friend, Mrs. Sadler (affectionately known as "Sad"), June 15, 1799.

18. Letter about Anna's French to Mrs. Scott, March 5, 1805; the follow-up letter to the same, December 20, 1799.

19. Reference to Rousseau is in a notebook manuscript kept by Catherine Seton herself. It contains admonitions and advice given her by her mother verbally or in letters.

20. *The Italian*. Advertised in *Greenleaf's New Daily Advertiser*, Tuesday, January 2, 1778.

21. *Evelina*. In the *Royal Gazette* for November 3, 1779.

22. *Juliet Greenville*. In *Rivington's Gazeteer*. August 1774.

23. *Charlotte Temple*. Ibid. ("At Number 24 on the Bowery, there stood after the Revolution, a small low frame house in which—according to tradition—Charlotte Temple lived out the last years of her blighted life." Jenkins, op. cit., p. 76)

24. Valentine Nutter was a printer and bookbinder of this period. One of his advertisements in *Rivington's Gazeteer* for February 23, 1775, gave a list of books for children and adults recently arrived by ship from England. Another such advertisement for children's literature was carried in the *Boston Gazette and Country Journal* for January 20, 1772, by the dealers Cox and Berry.

25. Letter to Julia Scott, March 8, 1808.

26. *Life Notes.* Rev. Wm. Hague gives the French background of New Rochelle culture.

27. Will of Guillaume Le Conte, see Appendix No. 6.

28. See Le Conte Genealogy table p. 130.

29. *Autobiography of Joseph Le Conte,* ed. by William Dallame Armes.

30. Teaching Emma her prayers. (*Dear Remembrances*)

31. On teaching the girls: to Julia Scott, November 25, 1798; March 10, 1801.

32. Elizabeth's children were Anna Maria (b. May 3, 1795); William (b. Nov. 25, 1796); Richard (b. July 20, 1798; Catherine (b. June 28, 1800); Rebecca (b. August 20, 1802. (MSV Archives obtained from the Office of the Corporation of Trinity Church, August 10, 1916.)

33. Letter to Julia Scott. January 7, 1802.

34. All quotes on school management are from Mother Seton's own *Notes* as cited in *Virgin Soil,* Sister Mary Regis Hoare. pp. 138-142.

35. American parents (MSV Archives XII 69-3.)

36. Letter to Mr. Elder. Ibid. III 92-I.

37. Letter of Jerome Bonaparte. Ibid. IV 100-1. Mother's reply. Ibid. IV 100-2.

38. Incident of General Harper's daughter. Hoare, op. cit. p. 113.

39. St. Peter's Church. *Diary.* March 1805.

40. Thomas Bayeux was made a freeman of New York City in May 10, 1705. He married Madeleine Boudinot by license obtained on July 14, 1703. His eight children were baptized in the French Church. Thomas m. Mary Lispenard; Jean died young; Madeleine m. Edward Holland; Anne m. John Groesbeck; Marie m. Rev. Richard Charlton; Jeanne, Elizabeth, Marianne have left no records. Susanne m. Jeremiah Schuyler.

Thomas Sr. died in 1742 leaving his home in King Street, N.Y.C. and all "his real and personal estate in the kingdom of France" to his son Thomas. Baird's *Huguenot Emigration to America.* Vol. 2.

41. On her disposition see White, op. cit. p. 19.

42. Dr. Bayley's advice. (MSV Archives IX, 105 n.d.)

43. Words of Mary Bayley Post to her cousin Anne Bayley Hague who repeated them to her son Rev. Wm. Hague. *Life Notes.*

XII Elizabeth Ann Bayley

1. Thacher says that Bayley went abroad in 1769, the year of his marriage. Dr. Bayley also spent the winter of 1775-1776 in London and Edinburgh. "The result of his conversations with Hunter (on this second trip) led to a request that Bayley's observations and dissections

might be placed before the public." *American Medical Biography*. Thacher.

2. Admiral Lord Richard Howe arrived with a strong fleet and 150 transports on July 12, 1776. On the 28th of the next month Elizabeth Bayley would be two years old. Her father had been in England since early 1775. Lord Howe's fleet, with whom Bayley probably arrived, moved up from their base on Staten Island to Newport, Rhode Island, where a decisive battle between them and the French Comte D'Estaing was broken off on August 10 by a storm that scattered both fleets.

3. Altogether, 100,000 Loyalists left the U. S. for Europe or Canada during the Revolutionary period and shortly after—to escape the "Test Acts"—a repudiation of loyalty to George III. *Encyclopedia of American Hist.*

4. Regarding the legacy of this uncle Elizabeth says: ". . . for interest, it is a fact that my mother's own Brother who had loved me more than anyone in the world made his will of an immense fortune and left me (the lawful heir) one thousand lbs., I believe—for I never heard of it since." (Letter XII 31-4 MSV Archives.)

Dr. Charlton actually left $2,500 to be divided between Elizabeth and her sister Mary. His will was probated July 31, 1806—after Elizabeth had become a Catholic. He may have altered the original bequest before he died, for according to his niece's testimony, "he was an old Church member," and may have been resentful of her conversion.

5. Evidence of Dr. Charlton's residence on Long Island is furnished adequately by the two following items. An advertisement in the *Royal Gazette* for February 7, 1778 read:

> Strayed or stolen from the pasture of Dr. Charlton, at Jamaica, on Monday, the 12th of January, a handsome black mare. . . .

In 1799 Dr. Charlton was one of several vestrymen of St. George Church, Hempstead, Long Island who formed a Committee delegated to bear to Rev. Henry Hobart the news of his election as assistant minister at Trinity Church in New York City. Rev. Hobart was at this times 25 yrs. old, tall and handsome. *St. George Church, Hempstead, L. Is.* Rev. W. Moore.

6. Catherine Charlton Bayley died in Newtown, Long Island, May 8, 1777. Surrogate's Records, New York City.

7. For Dr. Bayley's care in the education of his daughter see White. op. cit. Also the incident of Elizabeth's running out of the classroom to greet her father.

8. Melville in *Elizabeth Bayley Seton* gives "Mama Pompelion" as the school, p. 10.

9. Bloomingdale was a country residential section at the end of the Broadway Road at what is approximately now 78th-100th Streets. The Dutch called it "Bloemend Dol" which meant Flowery Valley.

10. *History of the Theater in America.* Dunlap.

11. Elizabeth tells about her "plans" in *Dear Remembrances*.

12. Letter of Mr. Ogden to Harriet Seton, his sister-in-law. Nov. 27, 1809.

13. See note 40—Chapter 11; note 6—Chapter 9 for collateral relations.

14. Letter to William. (MSV Archives, 1X, 69-2)

15. An account of Mr. Seton's accident was given by Elizabeth in a long letter to William's Aunt Cayley, the elder Seton's sister living in Ireland. July 6, 1798.

16. Letter to Julia Scott about Mr. Seton: June 3, 1798.

17. For an account of the Seton family see Appendix No. 17.

18. Regarding the pictures, letter to Julia: June 3, 1798.

19. Letter to Julia about the six children: July 5, 1798.

20. To explain the complete failure of William's business it should be known that the loss of one ship off the island of Texel carrying a large amount of specie to Amsterdam caused the failure of the English partnership with Maitland. This reverse reacted on the New York establishment which was already suffering from the French spoliations. It appears also from the accounts given by Elizabeth that Maitland, a brother-in-law, took care of his own future to clear out with whatever was due to him, leaving young Seton to foot all unpaid bills and to meet all creditors against the house of Maitland and Seton!

21. Letter to Julia Scott on reverses. March 18, 1800.

22. Letter to Rebecca Seton on William. March 20, 1800.

23. Richard's birth, July 20, 1798. Letter to Julia, August 31, 1798.

24. Letter about pantries. November 25, 1798. To Julia.

25. In reference to the illnesses of the children: to Julia, May 14, 1799 and April 2, 1799.

26. Letter to Julia, July 26, 1800.

27. About her difficulties regarding old habits. February 2, 1799; and her age, to Aunt Cayley, December, 1799.

28. Both accounts of her religious resolutions are taken from *Memoirs and Letters of Elizabeth Seton*, edited by Monsignor Seton.

29. The letters quoted in evidence of her sense of humor are from those written to Julia Scott as follows: January 20, 1799; January 12, 1802; February, 1802; October 27, 1801; June, 1801; March 18, 1800; November 28, 1804; February, 1799.

30. At this time the U. S. was at war with Morocco and the seas were overrun with pirates.

31. Provision was made for William, Richard, and Catherine Seton to stay with their mother's close friend, Mrs. Sadler, who had no children of her own; James Seton, William, Sr.'s brother, took his

sisters Cecilia and Rebecca. Harriet went to live with her married sister Mrs. Ogden.

32. On the Setons' decision to take Anna. Letter to Mrs. Sadler, September 28, 1803.

33. Remark to Rebecca Seton in a letter dated October 2, 1803, the day of their sailing for Italy.

34. Date of arrival taken from Mother Seton's *Journal* of the trip. This has also furnished all intimate details of this unhappy voyage.

35. The *Journal*, kept as a long letter to be sent eventually to Elizabeth's well-loved sister-in-law Rebecca furnishes these two pictures, dated February 18, 1804.

36. Account of Rebecca's death. *Journal*, June 4, 1804.

37. Her feelings at the homecoming. Ibid.

38. Elizabeth's letter to Antonio Filicchi regarding the reception of Bishop Carroll's letter was written August 30, 1804.

39. Bishop Cheverus' note to Mrs. Seton, June 8, 1807.

40. Letter to Amabilia was written in Jan., 1805. Seton, op. cit.

41. Just a few days before her official conversion. Ibid. March 14, 1805.

42. The day of her First Communion. Ibid. March 25, 1805.

43. Re: Mr. John Wilkes, an Englishman, whom the elder Seton received into the banking business thus giving the younger man a good start in a new country. The Setons and the Wilkes remained close friends.

44. Remark of her sister Mary Post. *Fifty Years' Notes.* Hague.

45. Elizabeth's comment on the coldness of past associates: November 20, 1804.

46. Antonio's letter to Elizabeth regarding her financial position: April 18, 1805.

XIII   Mother Elizabeth Seton

1. Comments regarding her unworthiness to be Mother from White. op. cit. p. 167.

2. Ibid.

3. Regarding her health: On March 12, 1800, she wrote to her father: ". . . my health has been worse and worse this winter, but is a little mended since the fine weather—the thought that I may so soon depart has brought with it many imaginations about my five darlings." (MSV. IX-86-4)

N.B. These and many of the quotations herein given have been read from photostats of the *Seton Papers and Related Documents* contained in the Archives of St. Joseph's Central House, Emmitsburg, Maryland. These photostat copies are in the possession of the Motherhouse of the Sisters of Charity of New York at Mount Saint Vincent.

4. Letters concerning her obligations to her children: to Archbishop Carroll, September 5, 1811; to Julia Scott, July 20, 1810; to Mrs. Duplex (Dué), February 4, 1811.

5. On the matter of her going to Montreal or Quebec consult Melville, op. cit. pp. 124-125.

6. The incident of the meeting between Mrs. Seton and Father Dubourg is given by White, op. cit.

7. Letter to Antonio Filicchi.

8. In a letter to Julia Scott, April 23, 1808, Elizabeth tells of the proposal made to give her the land for building.

9. Note about the Paca Street House: to Julia Scott, July 4, 1808. (MSV-VI-73)

10. Letter to Rose Stubbs. Balt., Feb. 20, 1809. (MSV Letter A)

11. Letter from Bishop Dubourg: September 13, 1809.

12. Description of the Community by Mother Seton: in a letter to Rose Stubbs, op. cit.

13. *Memoirs and Letters of Elizabeth Seton* ed. by Msgr. Seton.

14. Letter to Filicchi. January 21, 1809.

15. Letter to Rose Stubbs. (MSV Letter B)

16. Two letters on "tribulations". Ibid.

17. Death and Eternity. White, op. cit. p.

18. Description of a good vocation. (MSV-III-95, no. 8)

19. On Abandonment. (MSV-XII-28-2).

20. On her practice of the "grace of the moment": (MSV XII-50)

21. Mother Seton's last words and deathbed scene are given by White. op. cit.

22. Concerning spiritual consolations. (MSV-III-95-7)

23. Lovers of our own ease. (MSV-III-95-2)

24. Gratitude for suffering. White, op. cit.

25. On the Rules. (MSV—Letter to Rose Stubbs) op. cit.

26. Letter to the Sister on mission. White, op. cit. p. 383.

27. On the spirit of her children. Ibid.

28. All of these quotations are taken from White, op. cit. p. 322ff.

29. The account of Richard Seton's death and the tribute sent to Mrs. Post as the nearest surviving relative (in lieu of parent) was taken from an article that appeared in the *Catholic News* for August 6, 1938, on the occasion of the World's Fair. The brochure of which it formed a part comprised items of Catholic interest in and around New York. Reference to the Negro children in letter to Father Bruté. (*Soul of Elizabeth Seton*, pp. 82-83.)

30. St. Teresa's exposition of the love of spiritual friendship may be found in her *Way of Perfection*. tr. by Allison Peers. The extracts in their order are from 1: a letter to M. Maria de San José. Letter II, p. 878; Letter VI, p. 29; Letter VII, p. 30.

31. The letters to Rebecca and William are contained in *Letters*

and Memoirs of Elizabeth Seton and *The Soul of Elizabeth Seton*, pp. 78-80. (Written cir. 1815)

32. These several quotations have been taken from Code, *A Daily Thought from the Writings of Mother Seton.*

33. A note of thanks.

34. Letter to Father Brute. (MSV-XII-76)

35. Ibid.

36. Letter of Mr. Ogden to Harriet Seton. N.Y., Nov. 27, 1809

37. Class Schedule. (MSV Archives)

38. List of purchases. Ibid.

39. Extracts from Code's *Daily Thought.* Also—White, op. cit.

40. An interesting observation on Mother Seton's taste in head-dresses occurs in her *Dear Remembrances.* It may explain, in part, the simplicity of habit she later adopted for her religious community.

> When fourteen years of age the Methodist spinning girls . . . their continual hymn "and I am only born to die" made a deep impression, yet when I would be my own mistress I intended to be a Quaker because they wore such pretty plain hats— excellent reasons.

Appendix

1. *Susannah Mercier*

"Widow of Isaac Mercier—advanced in years." Leaves to grandson "James Besley, eldest son of my son-in-law Oliver Besley all the rent he hath had in my house in New Rochelle, for some years past." Mentions granddaughter Ann, wife of Peter Flandreau; Susanna, wife of John Gerrineau; "my niece Mary Ann Ferris, and granddaughter Mary Besley." The executors are to sell all real estate.

Further mention is made of "my granddaughter Susanna Goodwin; Mary, daughter of Oliver Besley, Mary Ann Boyd, Ann Flandreau, Susannah Garineau [sic] daughter of my son-in-law Wm. Le Conte deceased. My son-in-law Oliver Besley, and my friend Peter Flandreau, executors.

N.B. It can be seen by this will that William Le Conte, the younger, and Oliver Besley each married daughters of Isaac and Susannah Mercier. This explains the confusion that has arisen in the names Besley and Bayley. Both are intimately connected with the Le Contes. (See the genealogical tables for these families.)

* * * * *

2. *Abstract of Wills*

Recorded for Wm. Lecounte. [sic] "Memorandum of what is due

to me, Wm. Lecounte, by the late James Latys." 1,300 lbs. money lent. 16,000 pounds of sugar, in goods and merchandizes, at 5 lbs. the thousand, £80. For his half of the Brigantine named "La Pointe de Sable," which hath been 6 months at his service, at 200 pounds of sugar by day, makes my one half 18,000 pounds of sugar. For three years of my service upon his Plantation, with use of my Negroes, by virtue of Letters of Attorney to me directed at St. Christophers by the said deceased, bearing date March 19, 1688, by which it appears that I transported myself, purposely from St. Christophers, for the direction of the affairs and Plantations of the said deceased, as I have declared by a petition to the Governor bearing date as the Letters of administration granted to me by his Honour.

My requests for my salary for the said time of 3 years, with my Negro man, is 360 lbs. For interest of said 1,300 lbs. for 3 yrs. at 6 per cent, 234 lbs.

Due to M. Deschamps, 28 lbs. To Mr. De Bonrepose, 54 lbs. The debts of said deceased amount to the sum of 2,226 lbs. and 18,000 lbs. of sugar. (Wm. Leconte, liber 5-6; p. 236.)

3. *Letter of Administration*

"Whereas James Laty, late of New York, hath died intestate, Letters of administration are granted to Wm. Le Count of New Rochelle, husband of Anna Martha, the eldest daughter of said James Laty, November 9, 1691."

New York County Courts. Liber 3-4 p. 299.

* * * * *

4. *Inventory of Estate of "James Latey"*

Inventory of estate of James Latey, taken May 1, 1692, by Wm. Le Count, administrator. 810 acres of land, in several parcels and a small island, £109,10; 7 oxen ,£26,5; 8 cows, £16; 12 pigs, £1,4; a Turkey hen, 1 shilling; 20 common hens, 10 shillings; 14 geese and ganders, 14 shillings; 4 great Negro men, £120; a Negro boy, 12 years old, £22; a mulatto, 5 yrs. old, £15,1; a little Negro boy, 3 months old, £2; 4 Negro women, £96; Negro girl, 4 years old, £12; 2 pieces of gold, weighing 2 ounces, £10,6; 24 Spanish Pistoles (one light), £32; 29 light pieces of 8, £75; Total, £693.

The inventory shows extensive farming operations.
(*Abstracts of Wills* Liber 3-4 p. 379.)

* * * * *

5. *Abjuration of Francois Le Conte*

Auioudhuy Septieme de May 1963,
Francois le comte natif du pont Leveque en Normandie Royaume

de France ne et eleve dans la Religion Romaine ayant demande diverses fois Etre receu a faire abjuration du Papisme Dieu lui ayant fait le grace den connoitre. . . .

The English translation of this abjuration reads in part:

Francis Le Conte, native of Pon Leveque in Normandie, Kingdom of France, born and brought up in the Romish religion, having asked at different times to be allowed to abjure popery, God having given him the grace, by the reading of the Holy Scriptures and other books, to recognize its errors, and to embrace the Protestant religion, of which he has similarly recognized the truth after different examinations, has been finally received today in the presence of this church. . . .

* * * * *

6. *Guillaume Le Conte*

"In the name of God, Amen. Be it known and manifest unto all people that I, Guillaume Le Conte, of New Rochelle, being at this point very sick in body, in the city of New York, I leave to my beloved wife Margaret, the income of all estate for the education of my children until my son Guillaume, or my daughter Esther shall come of age or be married. I leave to my eldest son, Guillaume, £10, and as soon as he is come of age my estate is to be divided, one-half to my son Guillaume and my daughter Esther, and the other half to my wife Margaret and my youngest son Pierre. I appoint my wife and my friend Paul Droillet, and Mr. George Guion, executors.

Dated June 15, 1710/11.   (Proved March 2, 1711.)

* * * * *

7. *Katherine Bonnefoy*

"In the name of God, Amen, the 25 October, 1714. I, Katherine Bonnefoy of New York, widow. I leave to my son, Henry Mercey, £4. To my daughter Katherine all household goods. All the rest to my three children, Henry Mercey, David Bonnefoy, and Katherine Bonnefoy. I make my son Henry Mercey and my kinsman William Le Count, executors.

(Proved November 4, 1714.)   Abstracts of Wills. Liber 8. p. 361.

* * * * *

8. *Pierre Le Conte and New Jersey Descendants*

Pierre married first Margaret Pintard, March 18, 1733. After her death he married Valerie Eatton, of Eattonville, New Jersey.

1. Eldest son William, b. March 20, 1738, married Elizabeth Lawrence. He died in Georgia in 1788.

II. Second son John Eatton, b. September 2, 1739, was a famous patriot of the Revolution, a member of the guerrilla group known to the British as the "Malignant." His place in Liberty Co., Georgia, was burned by the English in 1778 because of his membership in this hated group. Eatton carried money and provisions, contributed by the patriots, to General Washington for the relief of the "Boston Sufferers" in 1775. In 1776, Eatton married Jane Sloan. He died in 1822.

III. Third child was a daughter Margaret, b. July 11, 1741.

John Eatton's son John Eatton II, born in Shrewsbury, New Jersey, 1784, was a noted entomologist and a Major of Engineers in the United States Army. He died in 1860.

A second son, Lewis Le Conte, born in Shrewsbury in 1782, was a well-known scientist, especially as an authority on botany. He was a Georgia planter on a very large scale. He was the father of Professors John and Joseph Le Conte of the University of California.

John Lawrence Le Conte of New York City, 1825, studied at St. Mary's College, Emmitsburg, Maryland. He entered the College of Physicians and Surgeons and graduated but never practiced. He was one of the greatest scientists of the century and president of the Entomological Society.

Prof. Joseph Le Conte, 1823, professor of geology and natural history, made a world-wide reputation as a naturalist.

Colonial Families of the United States of America. ed. by George Mackenzie. Vol. II. 1911.

* * * * *

9. *William Le Conte*

"In the name of God, Amen. I, William Le Conte, of New Rochelle, being of sound mind. My executors are to pay all just debts and funeral charges. I leave to my daughter Anne, £50. I leave to my 2 grandsons, William and Richard Bayley, £20 and all my clothing, and my gun, sword, and watch, and I also leave £20 to their mother, Susannah Bayley, my daughter. My executors are to sell all real estate. Of the money, one-third is to be put at interest for my daughter Susannah, wife of William Bayley, and the principal is to be paid to her after his decease and the rest of my 2 daughters, Mary and Anne, wife of John Boyd, and Anne Le Conte. I make my daughter Anne and my friend Samuel Gillett, executors.

Dated Oct. 9, 1758. Liber 21, p. 164.
Proved Dec. 13, 1758.

* * * * *

10. *Rev. Richard Charlton*

"In the name of God, Amen. I, Richard Charlton, Rector of St. Andrew's, in Richmond County. I leave my Body to the Earth to be interred with that decency and frugality as shall seem meet to my executors. I leave to the children of Thomas Bayeux, of New York, and Henry Bayeux, of Poughkeepsie, £300, 100 of which I leave to Thomas Bayeux, son of Thomas Bayeux who served his time to my son John Charlton. Of the rest of my estate I leave one-third to my grand-son, John Charlton Dongan, when he is of age, and one-third to the children of my daughter, Catherine Bayley, deceased. (There follows the disposal of six Negroes to the above-mentioned legatees.) I make my son John, executor."

Dated June 23, 1777. New York Historical Society Publications, *Collections for the Year 1900.* Vol. XXXIII. *Abstracts of Wills.* Vol. IX.

Proved Oct. 10, 1777.

11. *Re: William Bayley*

Notice in *New York Gazette and Weekly Mercury* for Nov. 28, 1774.

William Bayley

Intends to remove from his store in Beaver Street, New York, to his store in Newport, Rhode Island, early next spring. This is therefore to inform the public that he will sell off his stock now on hand, at New York, consisting of a neat and general assortment of hardware, at prime cost for cash. And all persons that are indebted to him are desired to make speedy payment, and all those that have any demands against him, are requested to bring in their accounts, and they shall be paid.

(This advertisement was repeated in three issues.)

*   *   *   *   *

Notice in *New York Gazette and Weekly Mercury* for April 3, 1775.

William Bayley

Is removed from his house in Beaver Street, into the house where Messers. Mercer and Schenck formerly lived in Hanover Square. where he has for sale, on the lowest terms, a neat and general assortment of Hardware, Japaned Ware, and Paper Hangings.

The house wherein Mrs. Colvell lately lived in Hanover Square, is to be let. Enquire of William Bayley.

*   *   *   *   *

Notice in the *New York Gazette and Weekly Mercury*, June 13, 1774.

William Bayley has imported . . .

a New and general assortment of hardware, toys, and trinkets; plated, japan'd and brown tea urns and coffee pots of the newest fashion; a large assortment of paper hangings of the newest patterns; a great variety of portable printing presses, from 10s. each to 51s. each; gentleman's tool chests of various prices, with a number of other articles too tedious to mention. . . . Ready money for bees-wax and old brass.

*   *   *   *   *

12. Re: Governor Thomas Dongan

Thomas Dongan was of an aristocratic Irish family. He was a bachelor of about fifty years of age when, after commanding a regiment in France, he became Governor of New York State. As nephew to Richard Talbot, Earl of Tyrconnel, a trained soldier and professed diplomat, Thomas earned for himself the accolade "among the best of our colonial governors."

Dongan was an extensive landowner here in America. One farm covered the present town of Castleton, Staten Island (named for another Castleton in Co. Kildare in Ireland). A larger tract on the Hudson, near Haverstraw, and some property in New York City, together with 400 acres near Hempstead, Long Island, gave him the "feel" of this new country over which he had been placed. The Governor was a staunch Roman Catholic as were also the Lieutenant-Governor Brockolls and the army chief Major Baxter. Dongan made the three Jesuits, Fathers Harvey, Harrison and Gage, residents at Fort James. When, however, King James II gave alarm to the Protestants of New York, they asked for the removal of Dongan, fearing that the state would be forced into Catholicism. Therefore, Dongan was relieved of his office and replaced by Sir Edmund Andros. Dongan retired to his estate at Hempstead, but in 1690, a warrant for his arrest caused him to flee to New Jersey, thence to Boston. He returned to England after which he was created Earl of Limerick in his native Ireland. He died in 1715, at the age of eighty-one, and is buried in St. Pancras Churchyard, London.

His heirs were his nephews John, Thomas, and Walter.

Dongan gives us a thumb-nail sketch of himself in a report he sent to the King dated May 20, 1687:

"I am a bold man, building chimneys from the ground, sodding the fort (Fort James at New York), mounting all the guns, and paving the batteries with freestone from Newark, which though expensive, will be made up by its lasting maybe forever."

Descendants in America

Walter—oldest nephew—(1692-1749) b. in Castleton, St. Is. m. Ruth Floyd and Sarah Harriman.

Thomas—son of Walter—(1717-1765) m. as a second wife *Mary Magdalen Charlton*, da. of Rev. Richard Charlton. *John Charlton Dongan*—one of the first members of the University of the State of New York when it was established in 1784.

Staten Island and Its People. Leng and Davis. Vols. I and II.

* * * * *

13. *Re: The Marine Society of the City of New York*

It was instituted in 1769.

Obligations: to distribute alms and visit the fatherless and widows. An example of their charity is the purchase of a cow to supply nourishment to two motherless children.

Activities: In 1799 the Society, with its flag draped, joined the throng that mourned George Washington.

It petitioned for lighthouses on the coast, buoys in the channels; it tested ship timbers.

It attended to the burial of victims of the fires of 1776 and 1778, and the plagues of 1795 and 1798.

It founded Sailors' Snug Harbor at the beginning of the 19th century.

In the first ten years about 650 persons were enrolled.

Some Members—Not Masters of Vessels

William Bayley	admitted 1770
Thomas Barclay	admitted 1772
James Barclay	admitted 1779
Aaron Burr	admitted 1788
Stephen De Lancey	admitted 1771
Oliver De Lancey	admitted 1772
James De Lancey	admitted 1772
Frederick Jay	admitted 1772
His Excellency John Jay	admitted 1788
Dr. Wright Post	admitted 1791

Admitted with vessels:

James Barclay	admitted 1801
William D. Seton	admitted 1798
(It would seem that the "D" is a mistake)	
William Mercier	admitted 1770

The Marine Society of the City of New York, in the State of New York. The Marine Society, N. Y., 1877.

* * * * *

14. *Dr. Richard Bayley*

In the Name of God, Amen. I, Richard Bayley, of the City of New York, Practitioner of Physick, being of sound and disposing mind, and understanding, do make this my last Will and Testament, in manner and form following:

First, I give and bequeath unto my mother Susannah Garrineau [sic] now the wife of John Garrineau, for and during the term of her natural life, all that my farm or plantation, lying and being at Mile Square in the County of Westchester, and all the rest and residue of my Estate, both real and personal, of what nature or kind soever (together with my said farm, after the decease of my said mother) I give, devise and bequeath to my beloved wife, Charlotte Amelia Bayley, to her heirs and assigns forever. And I do hereby nominate, constitute and appoint my said wife, Charlotte Amelia Bayley, sole executrix of this my last Will and Testament, hereby revoking all former or other Wills, Codicile, or Codiciles, by me heretofore made, and declaring this only to be and contain my last Will and Testament.

In Witness whereof I have hereunto subscribed my name and set my seal this 3rd day of December, 1788.

Richard Bayley (LS)

Signed, Sealed, and Published, and Declared by the Said Richard Bayley, as and for his last Will and Testament, in our presence, who subscribe our names as Witnesses thereto in his presence at his request, Rd. Morris, Mary Popham, W. Popham. December 3, 1788. (Liber 43.)

(This will was proved on the 26th of August, 1801. *Historical Records and Studies*, Vol. XXII, 1932. p. 97. MSV Archives.)

15. *Re: Bayley House*

In 1847, the great English Shakespearean actor, William Macready, engaged in a jealous rivalry with the American actor Edwin Forrest. Both were playing *Macbeth* in New York City. Toward the latter part of the drama Forrest spat out the words of the despairing Macbeth: "What rhubarb, senna, or what purgative drug would scour these English hence!"

The house rose and cheered; scenes of violence followed. Among the supporters of Macready were Washington Irving, John J. Astor, Herman Melville, and Chief Justice Robert Emmet. They rallied around Macready, and to prevent him from suffering physical harm from the mob who had roared their way up Broadway to the Drury Theatre where Macready was acting, they spirited him out a back door to Justice Emmet's city home.

At 4 a. m. the next morning Macready set out in a chaise driven by one of the Judge's sons to their home in New Rochelle whence he took a train to Boston and set sail for England, never to return.

* * * * *

16. *William Bayley*

Dated: October 17, 1805. Proved: April 24, 1811.

In the Name of God, Amen, I William Bayley of the Town of Pelham in the county of Westchester and State of New York considering the uncertainty of this mortal life and being of sound and perfect mind and memory, blessed be Almighty God for the same, do make and publish this my last Will and Testament in manner and form following (that is to say)

First I order that all my just debts and funeral expenses be paid first. I give to my beloved wife Sarah all my household furniture to be and remain at her disposal. I also give her the use and profits of the farm on which I now live so long as she remains my widow, but that during that time, no wood or timber shall be sold or carried off the farm. I also give and bequeath to my said wife the annual interest arising on the Monies secured to be paid to me by Mortgage, Bond or Note excepting the sum of twelve hundred and fifty dollars which I give and bequeath to my son Joseph to be paid to him as soon as conveniently may be after my decease out of monies due me on bond or note. My said wife to be entitled to the Interest on the residue of my monies as aforesaid during the term of she shall remain my widow and at her death or re-marriage whichever may happen I give and bequeath the principal sum due on such Mortgages, bonds, or notes to my two sons Joseph and William and my two daughters Susannah, the wife of Jeremiah Schureman and Nancy the wife of James Hague in equal parts. All my moveable property not already mentioned I order to be sold as soon as my Executors may think best, and the monies arising from the sale thereof to be equally divided among all my children before named.

Also further I do order and direct that at or upon the death or re-marriage of my said wife whichever shall first happen that all my Real Estate be sold at public or private sale as My Executors may think most beneficial to my Estate and the monies arising from such sale I do give and bequeath to my two sons and my two daughters before named in equal parts share and share alike. It is further my Will that my Negro woman Sarah shall be supported and maintained by my said wife during the natural life of the said Negro woman and in case she should survive my said wife that she be maintained in decent and comfortable manner out of my Estate further I give the use of my Negro boy Isaac otherwise called Ike to my said wife so long as she remains my widow and at her death or re-marraige whichever shall happen first the Value of him to be ascertained by an equitable apprisement and that he have his Election to live with whichever of my said children he may think proper such child paying the amount of such appraisal. All the residue of my Estate if any herein before bequeathed I give to all my said children in equal parts. And lastly I do appoint my beloved wife Executrix and Jeremiah Schureman and James Hague Executors of this my last Will and Testament hereby revoking all former Wills by me made. In Witness thereof I have thereunto set my hand and Seal the seventeenth day of October in the year of our Lord one thousand eight hundred and five.

William Bayley (L.S.)

Old Wills of New Rochelle [copies] by *Citizens of New Rochelle.* New Rochelle Chapter, National Society of the Daughters of the American Revolution. New Rochelle, 1951, pp. 69, 70, 71.

*   *   *   *   *

17. *Re: Seton Family*

William Seton, Sr. came from London to New York in 1763. He was a descendant of a long line of Scottish nobility, the last distinguished branch being the Earl of Winton whose property had been confiscated in reprisal for their support of Mary, Queen of Scots.

He carried with him letters of introduction to Richard Curzon, a wealthy merchant of Baltimore. Within two years, young Seton was settled in his own business in New York City where he became well known as an importing merchant of European and Italian goods and a member of the New York Chamber of Commerce in 1765.

In 1767 he married Rebecca Curzon, and after her death, her sister Anna Maria (1776). His house was open to the best society of New York. A Loyalist at first, he later became a citizen of the United States. Mr. Seton founded the firm of Seton, Maitland and Company of New York (1764). He died June 9, 1798, aged 52, from a fall suffered on his own doorstep.

By his first wife William Seton had four sons and three daughters: William Magee, James, John, Henry, Anna Maria, a celebrated beauty, Eliza, and Rebecca. By his second wife there were two boys and four girls: Edward-Augustus, Samuel, Charlotte, Mary, Harriet, and Cecilia. All the children were distinguished for their tallness and good looks.

William Magee Seton, eldest son of William Seton, Sr., was born at sea on April 20, 1768. He was very handsome, well-educated, and trained to succeed his father in the mercantile world. He was a skillful musician, especially a violinist, having brought back with him from Europe the only original Stradivarius to be owned in the United States at that time. He married Elizabeth Ann Bayley in 1795. He died in Italy in 1801.

William Seton, eldest son of William Magee Seton, was born in York City on November 25, 1796. His mother was Elizabeth Ann Bayley (later Mother Seton) and he was brought up in the Catholic faith. He was educated in part at St. Mary's College in Emmitsburg. At one time he was a lieutenant in the United States Navy. After his mother's death in 1821, he settled down in the States. On July 17, 1832, being 36 years old, he married Emily Prime of the famous old New England family and took up residence on property belonging to his wife at Cragdon, near Mount Vernon, Westchester County, New York. Their children were: William (III), Henry, Robert, later Monsignor Robert Seton, George, Emily, Elizabeth, Helen, and Isabella.

Monsignor Robert Seton became rector of St. Joseph Church in Jersey City. He was born August 28 (same date as his revered grandmother, Mother Seton), 1839. He was Dean of all the Monsignori in the United States, having been the first American to be raised to the Roman Prelatura. The University of Notre Dame, Indiana, conferred an honorary degree on him for his famous oration on the "Dignity of Labor" published in 1893. The archives of Notre Dame University was made a depositary of the Robert Seton letters and papers.

Of the other children, Emily and Elizabeth remained unmarried. Helen became a Sister of Mercy, following in the footsteps of her aunt Catherine, Mother Seton's youngest child.

Isabella married Thomas Jevons, Esq., a grandson of the historian Roscoe. They had three sons and one daughter. One of the sons is still living in Huntington, Long Island.

* * * * *

18. *Bayley, Guy Carleton*

Great-grandson of Dr. Richard Bayley, grandson of Dr. Guy Carleton Bayley, he was born at Eden Hill, Poughkeepsie, Oct. 16, 1850. He was a student of Dr. H. B. Sands and later a physician at St. Barnabas Hospital, New York City. In 1882 he was Surgeon-in-chief and Superintendent of Vassar Brothers' Hospital. He served in this dual capacity from this year of the institution's opening until 1906. His picture and an article by him on "The Medical Profession," a historical survey is contained in *The History of Dutchess County, New York*. Edited by Frank Hasbrouck. S.A. Matthieu Pub. Poughkeepsie, N. Y. 1909. pp. 528-596.

* * * * *

19. An interesting sidelight on the life of Dr. Bayley was the tradition of high professional skill and devotion to the care of the needy passed on by him to several of his descendants.

Among those of his family who carried on in the fields of medicine and nursing were the two doctors mentioned in Note 18. A scholarship granted by the Westchester Cancer Committee is called the H. Richard Charlton Award.

A great-granddaughter of Dr. Bayley, May Seton Bailey (later

Mrs. Walter Large) became one of the founders of the American Red Cross in Westchester County. She saw active service during the Spanish American War and filled the office of Secretary, Vice Chairman and Chairman of the Westchester Chapter until her death in 1927. The May Seton Bailey Large Memorial Award is a prize for a student nurse outstanding for her achievement during the year.

20. In a letter to Reverend Mother Mary of the New York Sisters of Charity, dated January 6, 1955, Mrs. Henry G. Steinmeyer, wife of a director of the Staten Island Historical Society, reported her finding of the marriage record of Dr. Richard Bayley, as follows:

Dr. Richard Bayley to Catherine Charlton. Both of Staten Island.
Jan. 9, 1769. Married by Rev. Dr. Thomas B. Chandler.

This record was found by Mrs. Steinmeyer while reading through the parish records of St. John's Episcopal Church in Elizabeth, New Jersey. The register is in the Library of the New Jersey Historical Society, Newark, New Jersey.

21. Dr. Bayley, Rev. Dr. Richard Charlton and his wife, Catherine, and their daughter, Catherine Bayley, are buried beneath the east wall of St. Andrew's Episcopal Church, Richmond, Staten Island.

The remains of Dr. Wright Post were transferred from St. Peter's Cemetery, Westchester, to this same place, next to Dr. Bayley, and beside those of his wife, Mary Magdalen Bayley Post, who died April 9, 1856, aged 88 years.

22. Huguenot Park, Staten Island, is one of the earliest settlements by the French exiles in this country, made shortly after the first colony was set up at Fresh Kill Road, in Richmond. In May 1924, the Church of the Huguenots was established as a national monument of the Huguenot-Walloon tercentenary. It is regarded as the central shrine of the Huguenot Tradition in America.

In the church there are eight alcoves dedicated to each of the eight Huguenot settlements in various parts of the nation. The New Rochelle Alcove was the first to be dedicated. Other historic parts of the building include: "Pillars of the Pioneers," "Windows of Family Memories," "Tablet Memorials to the Early Settlers."

The original name of Huguenot, Staten Island, was Bloomingview.

23. Peter Fanueil (Fannel) was born and reared in New Rochelle. A rich uncle in Boston offered to leave his fortune to the nephew who would join him in his business under the condition that the said young man would forego a marriage alliance for life. Peter accepted the challenge and inherited his uncle's huge fortune. He later built Fanueil Hall as a market place and public hall in 1740. It was so large that it took two years to build. This building has since been famous as The Cradle of Liberty.

Peter Fanueil, Senior, was one of the Huguenot Founding Fathers of New Rochelle whose name is honored on the Monument in Hudson Park.

24. Yonkers and the Mile Square constituted a township within the great manor of Philipsburgh, until the year 1779, when the manor was confiscated. The area is now included in the present Third Avenue of Mount Vernon, N. Y.

Bibliography

Abridged Compendium of American Genealogy of First Families of America. Pub. by F. A. Virkus and Co. 1926.

Abstract of Probate Records at Fairfield, County of Fairfield and State of Connecticut, 1648-1750 and 1704-1757. Compiled by Spencer P. Mead. New York, 1901.

Armes, William D., ed. *The Autobiography of Joseph Le Conte.* D. Appleton. New York, 1903.

Augur, C. H. *New Rochelle Through Seven Generations.* National City Bank. Privately Printed. 1908.

Baird, Charles W. *History of the Huguenot Emigration to America.* Vols. i and ii. Dodd, Mead, New York, 1885.

Ballard, Frank W. *Huguenot Settlers in New York City and Vicinity.* Manhattan Common Council. 1862.

Barr, Lockwood A. *A Brief but Most Complete and True Account of the Settlement of the Ancient Town of Pelham. . . .* Dietz Press. Richmond, Va., 1946.

Bayles, Richard M., ed. *History of Richmond County, Staten Island, New York, from its Discovery to the Present Time.* L. C. Preston and Co., New York, 1887.

Berry, Wm. *Pedigrees of Hertfordshire Families.* London. (County Genealogies.)

Bolton, Rev. Robert. *History of the Several Towns, Manors and Patents of the County of Westchester, from its First Settlement.* Cass Pub. New York, 1905. 3rd ed. Vols. i and ii.

Booth, Mary. *History of the City of New York,* New York, 1867.

Butler, Henry L. *Tales of Our Kinsfolk Past and Present.* Privately Printed. New York, 1919.

Chauncey, Sir Henry. *The Historical Antiquities of Hertfordshire.* London, 1826. Vols. i and ii.

Child, Samuel. *Fairfield Historical Society.* 1909.

Code, Joseph B., ed. *A Daily Thought from the Writings of Mother Seton.* Emmitsburg, 1929.

Colonial Families of the United States of America. Edited by George N. Mackenzie, LL.B. Seaforth Press, Baltimore. 1911. Vol. ii.

Cooke, William H. *Collections toward the History and Antiquities of the County of Hereford*. Part I. Koheman and Carver, Hereford, 1909.

Davis, William T. and Charles W. Leng. *Church of St. Andrew, Richmond, Staten Island: Its History, Vital Records and Gravestone Inscriptions*. Royden W. Vosburgh, Staten Island Historical Society. Staten Island, New York, 1925.

Dunlap, William. *History of the American Theater*. New York, 1832. *History of New York for Schools*. New York, 1837.

Fairbairn. *Book of Crests of Families of Great Britain and Ireland*. Part I, Vol. 2. Edinburgh, 1892. (Plate 51—No. 7.)

General Index of the Land Records of the Town of Hartford from the Year 1639 to 1839. Vols. 1. . . . Wilet, Waterman and Eaton. 1873.

Hague, William, D.D. *Life Notes or Fifty Years' Outlook*. Lee and Shepard. Boston, 1888.

Harlow, Alvin F. *Old Bowery Days: The Chronicles of a Famous Street*. D. Appleton. New York, 1931.

Hasbrouck, Frank, ed. *The History of Dutchess County, New York*. Pub. by S. A. Matthieu. Paughkeepsie, N. Y., 1909.

Herefordshire Biographies: a record of such of natives of the County as have obtained to more than local celebrity. John Hutchinson. Koheman and Carver, Hereford, 1910.

Hoare, Sister Mary Regis. *Virgin Soil*. Christopher Publishing House. Boston, 1942.

Hotten, John C. *The Original Lists of Persons of Quality: Emigrants, Religious Exiles; Political Rebels; and others 1600-1700*. Baker Co. New York.

Iconography of Manhattan Island, 1498-1907. Compiled by Phelps Stokes. Dodd Pub., New York, 1922. Vol. iv.

Index of the Rolls of Honor in the Lineage Books of the National Society of the D.A.R. 1916.

Inscriptions from Beechwood Cemetery, New Rochelle.

Inscriptions from Graveyards of New Rochelle. Compiled by Francis Spies. Privately Printed. NYPL.

Jenkins, Stephen. *The Old Post Road*. Putnam, New York, 1913.

Knapp, Lorenzo H. *Notes on the Le Conte Families of New Rochelle, New York*, in the *Quarterly Bulletin* of the Westchester Historical Society. Vol. 19. (January, April, 1953.) White Plains, N. Y.

Lancaster, Bruce. *From Lexington to Victory*. Doubleday, Garden City, New York, 1955.

Leng, Charles W. and William T. Davis. *Staten Island and Its People: a History 1609-1929*. Lewis Historical Pub. Co. New York. 1930. Vols. i and ii.

Mathews, J. M., D.D. *Recollections of Persons and Events Chiefly in the City of New York: being selections from his Journal*. Sheldon and Co. New York, 1865.

Melville, Annabelle. *Elizabeth Bayley Seton*. Scribner's Sons. New York, 1951.

Mercantile Library Association of New York City. Files for the American Revolution.

Moore, Rev. William H. *St. George Church, Hempstead, Long Island*. Dutton Co. New York, 1881.

Names of Persons for Whom Marriage Licenses were Issued by the Secretary of the Province of New York, Previous to 1784. Printed by order of Gideon J. Tucker, Secretary of State. Albany, 1860.

New York Historical Society. *Kemble Papers*. Vols. i and ii.

New York in the Revolution as Colony and State. arr. and classified by James A. Roberts, Comptroller. Albany, 1897. Vols i and ii.

O'Callaghan, E. B. *Documentary History of New York*. Albany, 1849. Vols. ii, iii, ix.

Old Wills of New Rochelle. Copies of Wills by Citizens of New Rochelle, New York. 1784-1833. Pub. by the New Rochelle Chapter, National Society of the D. A. R. 1951.

Pelletreau, A. M. *Early Wills of Westchester County from 1664 to 1784 with Genealogies and Historical Notes*. Harper. New York, 1898.

Phillimore, W. P. W. *Hertfordshire Parish Registers*. London, 1907. Vols. i and ii.

Porter's Genealogy of Hartford, Connecticut, Settlers. Vol. iv.

Records of the Town of New Rochelle, 1699-1828. Tr. by Jeanne Forbes. Paragraph Press. New Rochelle, 1916.

The Refugees of 1776 from Long Island to Connecticut. Frederick G. Mather. Lyon Pub. Co., Albany, New York, 1913.

Sabine, Lorenzo. *Biographical Sketches of Loyalists of the American Revolution with an Historical Essay* . . . 2 vols. Little, Brown Co., Boston, 1864.

Scharf, Thomas. *History of Westchester County*. Philadelphia, 1886, Vols. i and ii.

Seacord, Morgan H. and William S. Hadaway. *Historical Landmarks of New Rochelle*. New Rochelle Trust Co. under the auspices of the Huguenot and Historical Association. New Rochelle, 1928.

Seton, Robert. *Record of the Bayley Family in America*. Typed manuscript in the Archives of the University of Notre Dame, Indiana. *An Old Family, the Setons of Scotland and America*, New York, 1899.
Memoirs, Letters and Journal of Elizabeth Seton. New York, 1869. 2 vols.

Shea, Gilmary. *The Catholic Church in Colonial Times*. Vol. ii.

Stapleton, Rev. A. *Memorials of the Huguenots in America, with Special Reference to their Emigration to Pennsylvania*. Huguenot Pub. Co. Carlisle, Pa., 1901.

Thacher, James. *American Medical Biography*. Boston, 1828. Vol. ii.
The Soul of Elizabeth Seton by a Daughter of Charity. Benziger Bros. New York, 1936.
Tombstone Inscriptions in New Rochelle compiled by the New Rochelle Chapter of the National Society of the D.A.R. 1940-1941.
Valentine's Manual of the City of New York for 1916-1917. New series. Edited by Henry Collins Brown. The Valentine Co., New York, 1916.
Vital Records of the French Huguenot Church, New Rochelle by its first minister Rev. Daniel Bondet, 1695-1722.
Waldron, Duncan, ed. *Hertfordshire Families*. London. 1907. Vol. ii.
Waldron, William W. *Huguenots of Westchester and Parish of Fordham, New York*. W. H. Kelley and Brother Pub. 1864.
Walsh, James J. *History of Medicine in New York*. New York, 1919. Vol. i.
Warrand, Duncan, ed. *Hertfordshire Families*. London, 1907. Vol. ii.
White, Charles I. *Life of Mrs. Eliza A. Seton*. Baltimore, 1853.
White, William. *History, Gazeteer and Directory of Norfolk, England*. London, 1883.
Williams, Stephen W. *American Medical Biographies*. 1845.
Wittemeyer, Alfred Rev., ed. *Collections of the Huguenot Society of America* pub. by the Society. New York, 1886. Voy. i.
Yeagher, Sister M. Hildegarde, C.S.C. *Life of James Roosevelt Bayley: First Bishop of Newark and English Archbishop of Baltimore, 1814-1877*. Washington, 1947.
Yoshpe, Harry. *Disposition of Loyalists' Estates after the Revolution*. Columbia University Press, 1909.

*   *   *   *   *

Greenleaf's New Daily Advertiser, 1798.
New York Gazette and Weekly Mercury.
Rivington's New York Gazeteer, 1773-1777. *(Royal Gazette)*
Newspaper Index—Historical References from American Newspapers relating mostly to the City of New York, 1704-1850. Thomas DeVoe.
Cushman, Elizabeth "As a Woman Thinks." . . . *Standard Star*. New Rochelle, New York, July 3, 1929.
Files of Title Guarantee and Trust Company. White Plains, New York. Dept. of Deeds and Titles.
Journal of American Genealogy published by the National Historical Society. Vol. i. 1922.
Historical Records and Studies of the United States Catholic Historical Society. xviii (1928); xxxii (1932).